Jewish Scholarship on the Resurrection of Jesus

Jewish Scholarship on the Resurrection of Jesus

DAVID MISHKIN

PICKWICK *Publications* · Eugene, Oregon

JEWISH SCHOLARSHIP ON THE RESURRECTION OF JESUS

Pickwick Publications
An Imprint of Wipf and Stock Publishers
199 W. 8th Ave., Suite 3
Eugene, OR 97401

www.wipfandstock.com

PAPERBACK ISBN: 978-1-5326-0135-4
HARDCOVER ISBN: 978-1-5326-0137-8
EBOOK ISBN: 978-1-5326-0136-1

Cataloguing-in-Publication data:

Names: Mishkin, David.

Title: Jewish scholarship on the resurrection of Jesus / by David Mishkin.

Description: Eugene, OR : Pickwick Publications, 2017 | Includes bibliographical references and index.

Identifiers: ISBN 978-1-5326-0135-4 (paperback) | ISBN 978-1-5326-0137-8 (hardcover) | ISBN 978-1-5326-0136-1 (ebook)

Subjects: LCSH: Jesus Christ—Jewish interpretations. | Jesus Christ—Resurrection. | Resurrection (Jewish theology)

Classification: LCC BM620 M4 2017 (print) | LCC BM620 (ebook)

Manufactured in the U.S.A.   09/01/17

In loving memory of my parents.

CONTENTS

ACKNOWLEDGMENTS

THERE ARE A NUMBER of people who helped make this book a reality. Ernest van Eck was my doctoral supervisor who provided wisdom and guidance. Others who helped in various ways include Elliot Klayman and Jewish Voice Ministries International, Joel Greenwood, Erez Soref and Seth Postell, Yaakov Ariel, Richard Harvey, Levi and Stephanie Hazen, Jim Sibley, and Anna Beth Havenar. As usual, my wife and daughter deserve the greatest amount of credit for their patience and encouragement along the way.

ABBREVIATIONS

AJOT	A Journal of Theology
AJS	Journal of the Association of Jewish Studies
AJT	American Journal of Theology
ATR	Anglican Theological Review
BAR	Biblical Archeology Review
BHR	Bulletin of Historical Research
BI	Biblical Interpretation
Bib Sac	Bibliotheca Sacra
BTB	Biblical Theology Bulletin
BW	The Biblical World
CBQ	Catholic Biblical Quarterly
CBR	Currents in Biblical Research
CCAR	The Reform Jewish Quarterly
CJ	Conservative Judaism Journal
CTM	Currents in Theology and Mission
CT	Christianity Today
CTJ	Calvin Theological Journal
CTR	Criswell Theological Review
Forward	The Jewish Daily Forward
HUCA	Hebrew Union College Annual
HTR	Harvard Theological Review
IBMR	International Bulletin of Missionary Research

EQ	Evangelical Quarterly
EJ	Encyclopedia Judaica
JAAR	Journal of the American Academy of Religion
JAJH	Journal of American Jewish History
JANT	Jewish Annotated New Testament
JAOS	Journal of American Oriental Society
JBQ	Jewish Biblical Quarterly
JBL	Journal of Biblical Literature
JBR	Journal of Bible and Religion
JES	Journal of Ecumenical Studies
JHC	Journal of Higher Criticism
JHI	Journal of the History of Ideas
JJMJS	Journal of the Jesus Movement in its Jewish Setting.
JJS	Journal of Jewish Studies
JJPHRP	Journal for the Study of Judaism in the Persian, Hellenistic and Roman Period
JJTP	Journal of Jewish Thought and Philosophy
JOR	Journal of Religion
JQR	Jewish Quarterly Review
JRB	Jewish Review of Books
JRJ	Journal of Reform Judaism
JRS	Journal of Religion and Society
JSHJ	Journal for the Study of the Historical Jesus
JSNT	Journal for the Study of the New Testament
JSS	Jewish Social Studies
JSP	Journal for the Study of the Pseudepigrapha
JTS	Journal of Theological Studies
MJ	Modern Judaism: A Journal of Jewish Ideas and Experience
MJS	Journal of Modern Jewish Studies
MT	Modern Theology
NTS	New Testament Studies

JETS	Journal of Evangelical Theological Society
PCJCL	Proceedings of the Center for Jewish Christian Learning
PTR	Princeton Theological Review
RBL	Review of Biblical Literature
R&E	Review and Expositor
RJ	Reform Judaism Magazine
RRJ	Review of Rabbinic Judaism
RSR	Religious Studies Review
Shofar	Shofar: An Interdisciplinary Journal of Jewish Studies
Sh'ma	Sh'ma, A Journal of Jewish Ideas
SJT	Scottish Journal of Theology
TB	Tyndale Bulletin
TJ	Trinity Journal
Tradition	Tradition: A Journal of Orthodox Jewish Thought
USQR	Union Seminary Quarterly Review
WTJ	Westminster Theological Journal

CHAPTER ONE
INTRODUCTION

THE JEWISH STUDY OF Jesus has been an evolving venture. Many aspects of the New Testament and the life of Jesus have been analyzed and discussed. But, there is one issue that has remained largely untouched in the conversation. Paradoxically, it is the very event that the New Testament proclaims as the most important of all, his resurrection from the dead. Paul could not have put the matter more clearly: *"And if Christ has not been raised, your faith is futile and you are still in your sins"* (1 Cor 15:17). This book will explore various aspects of the Jewish response to the resurrection of Jesus.

[1.1] HISTORICAL OVERVIEW

The first people to believe that Jesus rose from the dead were, of course, Jews. The remainder of the Jewish community perhaps had various ideas about what actually happened, although it is not clear from the earliest sources. The response of the non-believing Jewish community is documented by authors who either believed in the resurrection (whether Jews or Gentiles) or who were pagans. For this reason, the usefulness of these sources remains a matter of discussion.[1] The first reference appears in the *Gospel of Matthew* (28:12–15), and says that the Jewish leaders devised the story that the disciples stole the body. Brief allusions to this passage are found in the *Gospel of Peter* (8.29ff) and Justin Martyr's *Dialogue with Trypho* (*Dial.* 108).

The second-century pagan writer Celsus wrote against Christian claims and incorporated arguments stemming from a particular Jewish man. This is preserved in Origen's *Contra Celsum,* written about a century

---

1. Baumgarten, "Jews, Pagans and Christians on the Empty Grave of Jesus"; Setzer, *Jewish Responses to Early Christianity,* 40–41; Stanton, "Early Objections to the Resurrection of Jesus."

later. According to Celsus's Jew (as he is known), arguments against the resurrection include its similarity to pagan Greek myths, the unreliability of the witnesses which include a "hysterical female," and the fact that the resurrected Jesus appeared to a limited number of people.[2] This was the first source to not comment on the empty tomb. At around the same time, Tertullian responded to a theory that said a gardener removed the body of Jesus because he did not want visitors to the grave trampling on his lettuce.[3] Some have suggested this idea might have had Jewish origins,[4] and as will be seen immediately below, Tertullian's writing very likely influenced later Jewish literature.

One of the earliest comments from a specifically Jewish source appears in the Talmud. Because of censorship over the centuries, references to Jesus in the Talmud were deleted or disguised. Exactly which references were originally referring to him is not always clear. But, there are a few passages that are commonly accepted as referring to Jesus. One such passage appears in tractate *Gittin*. At the end of *Gittin* 56b, there is mention of Onkelos who wishes to convert to Judaism. In order to understand Judaism and the fate of those who speak or act against it, Onkelos raises three people from the dead and asks them questions. First, he raises Titus by "magic arts." Then, at the beginning of *Gittin* 57a, he raises Balaam "by incantation." He then raises "the sinners of Israel," also by incantation.[5] This term ("the sinners of Israel") is commonly understood to have been a reference to Jesus before being changed as a result of censorship. It is used by the Soncino Talmud, as cited here. The footnote in this edition simply says "Jesus."[6] The text of the Steinsaltz edition of the Talmud in modern Hebrew is more explicit. It says ישו הנוצרי (Yeshu ha Notzri, Jesus the one from Nazareth). In the notes it explains that this was the original reading of this verse and that "sinners of Israel" was added later because of censorship.[7] More recently, Burton L. Visotzky also acknowledged that this passage is one of the few definite references to Jesus in the Talmud.[8] It says that Jesus was raised by Onkelos for a specific time and purpose,[9] yet the point is to demonstrate that he did not

---

2. *Contra Celsum* 2.55.

3. Tertullian, *De Spectaculis* 30.6

4. Horbury, "Tertullian and the Jews in Light of *De Spectaculis*."

5. Simon, "Gittin: Translation into English with Notes, Glossary and Indices," 260–61.

6. Ibid., 261.

7. Steinsaltz, *Talmud Bavli, Gittin*, 244.

8. Visotzky, "Jesus in Rabbinic Tradition," 580.

9. The fact that he is described as being raised—albeit temporarily—could perhaps be an apologetic to argue that even if he was raised it was by magic and not by God.

ultimately rise from the dead as is the Christian claim. According to one contemporary commentator this was meant to send a strong message to his followers, telling them that "they better give up any hope for an afterlife for themselves: as with their hero, there is no afterlife reserved for them; they will be punished in Gehinnom forever."[10] Because this appears in the Talmud, this passage is arguably the most authoritative Jewish opinion on the resurrection of Jesus.

Another early and specifically Jewish source is the *Toledot Yeshu* (*the Generations of, or the Life of, Jesus*). It is a counter version of the story of Jesus and fragments of it appear in various forms throughout the middle ages. Perhaps the only point of scholarly agreement is on how mysterious the document is regarding its authorship and dating. The oldest extant copy is an Aramaic source from the tenth century, and some have argued that it originates as early as the third century.[11] The *Encyclopedia Judaica* suggests that the Talmud offers hints of this story (Sotah47a, Sanhedrin 43a, 67a, 107b), although later Jewish apologists would claim these passages refer to a Jesus that lived two hundred years earlier.[12]

The storyline takes various turns in the different versions, but there are some general points of agreement. The mother of "Yeshu" (Jesus) was Miriam, a woman of questionable character. The father was a bad man who left before the child was born. Jesus is credited with supernatural powers. His death is also a subject of consideration. According to Aramaic fragments from the Cairo Geniza, Jesus was brought before Rabbi Joshua ben Perachiah and then was crucified on a cabbage stalk. Jesus then remembered what is written in Deuteronomy 21:23, which says that bodies that are hanged should be buried and not remain on the tree. He then tells his followers that if they do not see him the next day it is because he ascended into heaven. He died on the cross and was taken to Rabbi Judah the gardener (rather than remaining on the cross which would have brought a curse upon the land, according to the Deuteronomy passage). His followers came the next day and assumed he had risen to heaven. In order to disprove this, Judah the gardener removed him from the grave where he was placed. The body was then presented to Pilate and the disciples.[13] Scholars[14] have recognized similarities between this and Tertullian's reference, and have assumed that his writings had some influence on later versions of the *Toledot*

---

10. Schafer, *Jesus in the Talmud*, 90.

11. Schafer, "Introduction," *Toledot Yeshu Revisited*, 3.

12. Roth, "Toledot Yeshua," 1207–8.

13. Newman, "The Death of Jesus in the Toldot Yeshu Literature," 63–64.

14. Ibid., 65; Deutsch, "The Second Life of the Life of Jesus," 286.

Yeshu. There are also some obvious differences. Tertullian's version spoke of lettuce and not cabbage, and this represented the place of burial rather than the means of execution. This spawned quite a bit of literature over the centuries in the Christian, Moslem and pagan worlds.[15] To whatever extent the *Toledot Yeshu* was influential,[16] it provided an alternative explanation for the empty tomb.

Polemical literature in the middle ages dealt almost exclusively with theological concerns, and the few examples which do address historical issues do not mention the resurrection.[17] On the whole, the Jewish response to the resurrection of Jesus in the middle ages was silence. This was noticed by Catholic scholar, Steven J. McMichael, in a 2009 article. The key areas of apologetic concern, he wrote, were the Trinity, the law, and the messiahship of Jesus. He continues, "But, they believed that once the former doctrines were disproved, especially the non-Messiahship of Jesus, the latter doctrines (such as the resurrection of Jesus) would become in a way non-issues."[18] The first Jewish scholar to specifically mention the resurrection after the Middle Ages was Baruch (Benedict) Spinoza in the seventeenth century. He was already excommunicated from the synagogue, so he did not approach the subject as a member of the Jewish community. His polemic against Christianity was that of a skeptic arguing against miracles, a stance he virtually created or at least popularized. He was in a unique position, and he had positive and negative things to say about both Judaism and Christianity. Regarding the resurrection he wrote:

> I therefore conclude, that the resurrection of Christ from the dead was in reality spiritual, and that to the faithful alone, according to their understanding, it was revealed that Christ was endowed with eternity, and had risen from the dead (using *dead* in the sense in which Christ said, "let the dead bury their dead"), giving by His life and death a matchless example of holiness. Moreover, He to this extent raises his disciples from

---

15. Ibid., 66–70

16. According to Berger, the *Toledot Yeshu* was "accepted as simple truth" by many Jews in the Middle Ages. Berger, "On the Uses of History in Medieval Jewish Polemic against Christianity: The Quest for the Historical Jesus," 26.

17. See Berger, *The Jewish-Christian Debate in the High Middle Ages: A Critical Edition of the Nizzahon Vetus*; Lasker and Strouma, *The Polemic of Nestor the Priest: Quissat muj adalat al-usquf and sefer Nestor ha Komer.*

18. McMichael, "The Resurrection of Jesus and Human Beings in Medieval Christian and Jewish Theology and Polemic," 17.

the dead, in so far as they follow the example of His own life and death.[19]

Spinoza greatly influenced the Enlightenment rationalism that emerged a century later. This brought new challenges for Biblical studies, both in the Old Testament and the New. The highly critical New Testament studies of Reimarus and others in the late eighteenth century would have a profound impact on Judaism and Christianity. The purely rational approach to the Scriptures which questioned or denied the supernatural, along with social factors of the day, would allow Jewish scholars to begin thinking about Jesus and the New Testament in a new way. Moses Mendelsohn was the first major Jewish figure to publicly interact with Christianity,[20] although he did not comment on the historicity of the resurrection. In the nineteenth century, Christian scholars were busy searching for the historical Jesus as Jewish scholars first began to seriously consider Christianity. The Jewish study usually focused on theological and social issues, and how Jews should think about Christianity in the modern world. Joseph Salvador wrote a book about Jesus in 1838, which has been called the first modern study of Jesus by a Jewish author. It begins by questioning whether Jesus really existed,[21] and does not comment on the resurrection. The works of three scholars who did approach the subject at this time (Isaac M. Wise, Heinrich Graetz, and Joseph Jacobs) will be discussed below in chapter 4.

Also in the nineteenth century, a new group emerged known as Hebrew Christians. These were Jews who came to believe in Jesus as the Messiah, and yet maintained their Jewish identity.[22] This had not happened for over a millennium. One notable Hebrew Christian was Oxford professor,

---

19. Letter XXIII to Oldenburg, in Spinoza, *On the Improvement of the Understanding / The Ethics / Correspondence*, 304. Spinoza's assumptions about the impossibility of miracles dictated both his conclusions and his approach to the texts. One contemporary Spinoza scholar observed the following: "Spinoza's resort to allegorical interpretation is quite astounding given his scathing critique of Maimonides' own allegorical interpretation of the Bible . . . Oddly enough, it seems that when Spinoza had to address the New Testament, he suddenly adopted a Maimonidean approach to the holy writ." Melamed, "'*Christus Secundum Spiritum*': Spinoza, Jesus and the Infinite Intellect," 151.

20. Mendelssohn, *Writings on Judaism, Christianity and the Bible.*

21. Salvador wrote: "But is it appropriate to believe that Jesus really existed? Or should it be concluded from the silence of contemporary Jewish writers that his memory is simply a pious effort of the imagination of an applied school to redress these doctrines with a living symbol? Such is one of the first questions that the spirit asks, and that is entirely resolved as I have announced it, in favor of the true existence." Salvador, *Jesus-Christ et Sa Doctrine*, 156; author's translation.

22. Darby, *The Emergence of the Hebrew Christian Movement in Nineteenth-Century Britain.*

Alfred Edersheim. His book, *The Life and Times of Jesus the Messiah*, was originally published in 1883 and it prefigured the trend to place Jesus in his Jewish context by a full century. He also wrote it in response to the highly critical theories of David Friedrich Strauss, Ernest Renan, and others who suggested rationalistic alternatives to the New Testament's claims. The resurrection was a key area of dispute. Edersheim evaluated their explanations and concluded the following: "The theories of deception, delusion, and vision being thus impossible, and the *a priori* objection to the fact as involving a Miracle, being a *petition principii,* the historical student is shut up to the simple acceptance of the narrative."[23] Here is an interesting twist. These "Christian" scholars did not believe in the resurrection of Jesus and this Jewish scholar did. Mainstream Jewish scholars would more fully join the quest for the historical Jesus in the twentieth century. In this context the resurrection would, slowly, become part of the discussion as well.

[1.2] THE RESURRECTION AND THE MODERN JEWISH STUDY OF JESUS

A century ago it was still all but taboo for Jewish scholars to talk openly about the life of Jesus, but a few pioneers attempted to break new ground. Even small admissions that fell short of christological claims were costly. Claude Montefiore wrote: "[F]or many centuries to say that Jesus was a good man and a fine teacher, but not divine, was exceedingly dangerous."[24] These scholars often proceeded with trepidation. Christians would not like a less than orthodox portrayal of their savior, and the Jewish community would also cast aspersions on these studies. Such attempts, Hyman Enelow wrote in 1920, were regarded by the Jewish community as a "sign of weakness, if not disloyalty" if they showed "symptoms of admiration" for Jesus.[25] The trickle in scholarship at the beginning of the century became a deluge by the end of the twentieth and beginning of the twenty-first centuries (see the discussion in the following chapter). Today, there are many Jewish scholars in the field of New Testament and related studies, and they are able to speak freely about Jesus the Jew with unprecedented candor. A number of social conditions, particularly in the United States, helped yield this new wave. Changes in both Jewish-Christian relations and biblical scholarship (specifically the

23. Edersheim, *The Life and Times of Jesus the Messiah,* 906. For more quotes by Edersheim about the resurrection of Jesus, see Mishkin, *The Wisdom of Alfred Edersheim,* 145–46.

24. Montefiore, *The Synoptic Gospels,* xviii.

25. Enelow, *A Jewish View of Jesus,* 1.

acknowledgment of the importance of the Jewish background for New Testament studies) have greatly helped the discussion.

The specific study of the resurrection of Jesus did not advance quite as rapidly. Montefiore was the only Jewish scholar who significantly interacted with the topic for about the first three quarters of the century. The first complete book on the subject was written by Pinchas Lapide in 1978.[26] He argued that the best explanation of the historical evidence is that Jesus rose from the dead, although he was not the Messiah for Jews. A number of Christian writers reviewed this book,[27] and more than a few commented on the novelty of an Orthodox Jew coming to this conclusion. But, one reviewer noticed something else. Not only were Lapide's conclusions unique, the fact that he addressed the question of the resurrection at all was noteworthy. J. P. Galvin wrote the following: "The resurrection of Jesus occupies a central place in contemporary theological discussion. It does not, however, figure prominently in Jewish treatments of Jesus, even in those works which assess Jesus positively as an important part of the history of Judaism."[28] Schalom Ben-Chorin noticed the same phenomenon a few years earlier and offered an explanation. He was a Jewish scholar who not only wrote about the life of Jesus, he also analyzed the Jewish study of Jesus. In one article he produced a list of topics that are part of most Jewish studies. These include the baptism by John, parables, healings, prayer, his Jewish identity, use of the term "Son of Man," and finally the passion. He then explains,

> The resurrection myth, the appearances of the resurrected in Emmaus, Galilee, and Jerusalem, as well as the ascension, are eliminated from the Jewish image of Jesus. The Jewish Jesus-image thus recognizes neither Christmas with the crib and the star of Bethlehem nor Easter with the open grave and the resurrection. The Jewish Jesus-image is the human, all too human, portrayal of a tragic genius, of a deeply Jewish human being.[29]

Ben-Chorin suggests a pattern; the resurrection is not of interest to Jewish scholars personally, therefore it has not been discussed academically. It is also assumed to be non-historical. This pattern will be seen in many of the works summarized below in Chapter 4. But, more recently, the resurrection has begun to emerge as a topic of serious discussion among Jewish authors. Almost twenty years after Lapide's book, Dan Cohn-Sherbok

---

26. Lapide, *Auferstehung: e. jud. Glaubenseriebnis.* (The English version, *The Resurrection of Jesus, A Jewish Perspective*, will be used in this study.)

27. Bauckham, Bode, Court, Horbury, Re'emi, Verhay, see the bibliography.

28. Galvin, "A Recent Jewish View of the Resurrection," 277.

29. Ben-Chorin, "The Image of Jesus in Modern Judaism," 430.

contributed an article in a symposium about the resurrection.[30] Then, in the first decade of the twenty-first century, several major works appeared. Alan F. Segal wrote extensively on resurrection in general and interacted considerably with issues pertaining to the resurrection of Jesus.[31] Two other scholars (Jon D. Levenson[32] and Claudia Setzer[33]) also wrote significant works on resurrection in general, although with varying degrees of interaction with the resurrection of Jesus. In the same decade, Geza Vermes wrote the second complete book on the resurrection of Jesus by a Jewish scholar.[34] The resurrection has also emerged as an issue in Jewish polemical literature.[35] The time has come to study Jewish views of the resurrection of Jesus.

[1.3] GOAL OF THIS STUDY

This book seeks to contribute to the overall scholarship on the Jewish study of Jesus. Chapter 2 will survey the previous literature in this general field. More specifically, this study will examine Jewish interaction with the historicity of the resurrection of Jesus. This is the first research of its kind, and it seeks to answer a straightforward question: *what have Jewish scholars said about the historicity of the resurrection of Jesus?* Based on the observations of Galvin and Ben-Chorin, the initial response to such a question might be: "not much." Because of this, it is important to first examine the issues that may be responsible for a lack of interest in, or the premature dismissal of, a discussion of the resurrection. This will be the focus of chapter 3. Following this, chapter 4 will survey the writings of Jewish authors who have touched on the topic in one way or another. They are divided by category. What is of interest here is how the resurrection is approached as well as how much of the canonical New Testament's narrative is acknowledged as historical. Chapter 5 will summarize these findings and conclude by addressing two questions: 1.What does Jewish scholarship tell us about the

---

30. Cohn-Sherbok, "The Resurrection of Jesus: a Jewish View."

31. Segal, *Life after Death*; Segal, "The Resurrection: Fact or History."

32. Madigan and Levenson, *The Resurrection: The Power of God for Christians and Jews*; see also Levenson, *The Death and Resurrection of the Beloved Son: The Transformation of Child Sacrifice in Judaism and Christianity*; and Levenson, *Resurrection and the Restoration of Israel*.

33. Setzer, *Resurrection of the Body in Early Judaism and Christianity*; Setzer, "Female Witnesses to the Resurrection."

34. Vermes, *The Resurrection: History and Myth*.

35. Cook, *Modern Jews Engage the New Testament: Enhancing Jewish well-being in a Christian Environment*, 149–62; Sigal, *The Resurrection Fantasy, Reinventing Jesus*; Alter, *The Resurrection: A Critical Inquiry*.

resurrection of Jesus? 2. What does the resurrection of Jesus tell us about Jewish scholarship?

The authors surveyed in chapter 4 are all Jewish, but represent an eclectic group. They were born in Europe, Israel, and the U.S., they span a timeline of about a century and a half, they wrote in English or were translated into English, they represent differing degrees of Jewish religious belief and practice, and they produced various levels of scholarship. This study does not include those identifying as Hebrew Christians or Messianic Jews, although they will be occasionally mentioned. This is not because of the belief that they are not Jews (disclosure: the author of this book is a Messianic Jew[36]), but because one of the main goals of this study is to examine the historical and theological presuppositions within the traditional Jewish community that may affect this area of research as well as the study of the historical Jesus in general.

36. This term is being used in the broad sense, meaning a Jewish person who believes Jesus is the Messiah and who believes—to be specific for this study—that Jesus was physically raised from the dead. This is mentioned as the reader might want to know the perspective of the author.

CHAPTER TWO
PREVIOUS STUDIES

THERE ARE NO PREVIOUS books on Jewish views of the resurrection of Jesus, and the only major articles on the subject are my own.[1] But, the topic is part of a wider field of study that has been analyzed from a number of perspectives. This chapter will survey the main works (by both Jewish and Gentile authors) that have documented the Jewish study of Jesus and New Testament themes. It will serve as a backdrop to the remainder of this book, revealing the theological, cultural and historical issues relevant to the overall discussion. It will also reveal the evolution of the Jewish approach to this subject. Each section will discuss the work of a single author who wrote a significant book or article. Most of these works document the general Jewish study of Jesus, while a few are specific to either a certain subgroup (Israelis, artists) or topic (the Apostle Paul, the trial). This chapter will also further demonstrate that the resurrection has not been an issue of interest among Jewish New Testament scholars.

[2.1] CLYDE W. VOTAW

The first article to document the Jewish study of Jesus appeared in *The Biblical World* in 1905. Clyde W. Votaw writes as a Christian who was encouraged by the new scholarly interest in Jesus within Reform Judaism. He was challenged to write this article because of the words of Claude Montefiore, who had recently said that, "Christian scholars are wholly neglectful of the new and transforming light which modern Jewish scholarship has thrown

---

1. Mishkin, "The Emerging Jewish Views of the Messiaship of Jesus and their Bearing on the Question of his Resurrection"; and Mishkin, "The Resurrection of Jesus in Contemporary Jewish Scholarship."

upon the history of Judaism in Jesus' day."[2] Votaw begins by explaining the Reform movement and its embrace of modernity. The article focuses on the *Jewish Encyclopedia,* which was published just four years earlier and was a monumental work of Jewish scholarship. It became the authoritative standard in the twentieth century, at least among non-Orthodox Jews. It is also noteworthy for the attention it gave to Jesus and other Christian themes. The Section on Jesus is subdivided into three parts: "Jesus in history," "Jesus in theology," and "Jesus in Jewish Legend," written by Joseph Jacobs, Kaufman Kohler and Samuel Krauss respectively. Votaw believed that "an honest, candid effort has been made to judge Christianity fairly and to appraise it correctly." He is also aware that both Jews and Christians have "inveterate prejudices to overcome" regarding their respective views of the New Testament, principally concerning its Jewish themes.[3]

The Jewish perspective represented in the *Encyclopedia,* Votaw writes, will be found to agree with "the most radical positions of present-day Christian scholars, like Pfleiderer, Schmiedel, and O. Hotzman." The gospels are said to be based on facts, but the earliest forms of the narrative of Jesus have been "misunderstood, modified and elaborated during fifty or more years of transmission and translation."[4] These include the infancy stories, the baptism, the temptation, the transfiguration, and the resurrection.[5] Jesus was an Essene and he did perform healings. However, "all originality in the content and point of view is denied to Jesus."[6] As for his death, it was confined to "a small number of priests" and "the Jewish nation was not responsible."[7] Jesus was a good Jew who observed the law, while "Christianity" was the invention of Paul. Votaw sees irony in the fact that the Reform movement chose to distance itself from a movement wherein the Law is radically reinterpreted.

> The position of the modern Jewish scholar seems peculiar. They have themselves arrived at just this freedom from their ancestral Law which Christians suppose Jesus taught. As may be seen above in the platform of Reform Judaism, they do not regard the statutes of the Law as binding upon themselves further than they approve for their own lives. They, too, assume a position

2. Votaw, "The Modern Jewish View of Jesus," 112.

3. Ibid., 104.

4. Ibid., 105.

5. Ibid., 106.

6. Ibid., 108.

7. Ibid., 111.

of superiority to their Law, judging what parts of it they should observe and which parts they need not observe.[8]

Votaw then spends some time responding to the *Encyclopedia's* critical comments. But, overall, he sees the new interest in Jesus among Jewish scholars as a very positive thing. He believed it to be an indication that the worst is past in the alienation of the Jews from Christianity, and that "Jesus' true greatness of person, character, work, and teaching will become increasingly apparent."[9] As he says in his final paragraph, "he was indeed a Jewish Christ."

[2.2] BENJAMIN W. BACON

The second pioneering work comes from Benjamin Bacon of the Yale School of Religion. In 1915 he wrote an article called, "Jewish Interpretations of the New Testament." He begins with comments from early Church Fathers who concede that the scriptures are best understood and expounded by someone with an understanding of the Jewish background. The same is true today. "Do his best," he says, "the outsider cannot enter into the spirit of Judaism, and understand its ideas in their continuous unfolding through the ages, as the genuine son of Abraham after both flesh and spirit."[10] There have been a number of Gentile scholars throughout Church history, sometimes called Christian Hebraists, who have attempted to interpret the scriptures through a Jewish lens. Beginning with Origen and Jerome, the more modern representatives included Lightfoot, Strack, Wunsche and Delitzsch. Bacon believed that this scholarship has been important, yet incomplete. He suggests that an understanding of modern Judaism, along with first century Jewish laws and customs, is equally important. They must learn to "appreciate sympathetically that branch of the elder stock which since the days of the New Testament has been in violent opposition to the Church."[11] He then turns his attention to the Jewish study of Christianity.

Bacon focuses on the works of Claude Montefiore and Moritz Friedlander. Both men represent liberal Judaism. Yet, their views of first-century Judaism (and by extension their views of Jesus), are quite different. For Montefiore, the "legalistic development of Judaism" as characterized by the synagogue, scribes, and Pharisees represents the "true line of growth." He was not interested in mysticism and had no qualms about the destruction of

---

8. Ibid., 114.

9. Ibid., 115.

10. Bacon, "Jewish Interpretations of the New Testament," 163.

11. Ibid., 167.

the Temple.[12] There is a chain linking the ancient prophets, the first-century sages Hillel and Akiva, the medieval rabbis, and the modern liberal synagogue. Unfortunately, cultural factors along the way lead to "narrow and mechanical modes of interpretation" that would cause rabbinic orthodoxy to go off course.[13] For Montefiore, Christianity has a unique "religious vitality" that is attractive. "Not unnaturally," Bacon writes, "he attributes this vitality to the ethical teachings of Jesus and the pathos of his martyrdom rather than to the symbol of the cross and the doctrine of the atonement." Jesus is to him "the last and the greatest of the prophets."[14] In the end, however, it is Montefiore's view of Paul (specifically on the issue of atonement) that prohibits him from embracing Christianity. Montefiore "does not find a doctrine of mediation in genuine Judaism."[15]

Bacon appreciated Montefiore's position, but believed a more comprehensive approach to the subject was needed. To understand the Judaism of Jesus' day, he says, one must go back to the Persian period and survey the developments up through the Hellenistic experience and into the first century. This is where Friedlander provides the greater contribution. Hellenistic Judaism, according to Friedlander, espoused a "broader interpretation of Mosaism," a "keener missionary spirit" and a "more universalistic ideal" than Montefiore's view of the scribes and Pharisees.[16] For this reason, it is the true heir of Israel's religious ideals. Both Jesus and Paul are planted firmly within this tradition. It is only with the second-century apologists and the Church Fathers that this tradition ceased, relinquishing the claim to be a "legitimate development of Judaism."[17] Despite his gift as a historian of religion, Friedlander's style was sometimes unnecessarily harsh, specifically on the Pharisees. As Bacon comments, "Friedlander lacks the sweet reasonableness of Montefiore's style."[18] Yet, the contributions of each of these men are extolled as a model to be emulated by Christians. He wrote: "As the two Jewish interpreters of Christianity to the synagogue in our time have set the example in a spirit of marvelous superiority to inherited predilection, so we may seek sympathetically to interpret Judaism."[19]

---

12. Ibid., 168.

13. Ibid., 169.

14. Ibid., 170.

15. Ibid., 172.

16. Ibid., 173.

17. Ibid., 174.

18. Ibid., 175.

19. Ibid., 176.

[2.3] HERBERT DANBY

Herbert Danby is most famous for his English translations of both the Mishnah and Joseph Klausner's groundbreaking book about Jesus. He was a Christian scholar with a great love and affection for the Jewish people. In 1927 he produced the first complete book to document the modern Jewish attitude toward Jesus, called *The Jew and Christianity*. Throughout the book he is concerned with the long and horrible history of "Christian" anti-Semitism and violence. In Danby's time, however, there was a new openness among Jews to discuss the issue. "The more Christians have conformed to the spirit of Christ," he says, "the more has Jewish respect been drawn to Christianity and to Christ."[20] For most of the book, Danby surveys the history of Jewish-Christian relations. Chapters focus on the first century, the Talmudic period and the Crusades before he arrives at the modern period. In the nineteenth century major social changes dramatically altered the Jewish attitude toward Jesus. He cites three specific factors: modernity, Emancipation (new rights for Jews in Europe), and Reform Judaism. All of these would allow Jews to take a fresh look at Jesus. This was because they "turned their faces away from Christians and gave their attention to the person of the Founder of Christianity."[21]

Danby realized that this trend was limited in scope (most Jews still did not turn their attention toward Jesus), but it was an important step in the right direction. Many were now able to see Christianity through glasses "no longer smeared by the mud and fog of former Christian treatment of them."[22] He then briefly surveys the writings of some of the Jewish scholars who dared to write about Jesus in the nineteenth and early twentieth centuries: Joseph Salvador, Abraham Geiger, Joseph Jacobs, Claude Montefiore and Ahad ha-Am. The final chapter of the book addresses his contemporary period. Not surprisingly, it deals almost exclusively with Joseph Klausner's book, *Jesus of Nazareth*. This book was immediately condemned by Orthodox Jews. Yet, Danby notes that to many Jews it was "accepted as a great and important addition to Hebrew literature and to Jewish history."[23] Danby ends on a note of sadness. He believed that Jesus is Israel's Messiah—good news for Jewish people—yet he had great empathy for those who could not see beyond the blood stained pages of history.

---

20. Danby, *The Jew and Christianity*, 3.
21. Ibid., 68.
22. Ibid., 4.
23. Ibid., 104.

[2. 4] THOMAS WALKER

The next book on the subject was written by Thomas Walker. In 1923 he wrote *The Teachings of Jesus and the Jewish teachings of his age*. Later, four years after Danby's book, he wrote *Jewish Views of Jesus*. He divides his study into three parts, using two scholars to represent each section. There is the orthodox view (Paul Goodman and Gerald Friedlander), the liberal view (Montefiore and Israel Abrahams), and then a section on "portraits," meaning biographies of the life of Jesus (represented by Klausner and Joseph Jacobs).

Walker ends his book with some reflections. He specifically wanted to see the diversity of opinions about Jesus from within the Jewish community. Some of the writers viewed Jesus as a prophet, while others did not. The question of originality in his teaching was also a point of contention. Jesus' view of God is alternatively explained as either "blasphemy" or in a unique way "very much part of Judaism." Most of the authors agree that Jesus put in a claim of Messiahship, but they are not agreed exactly on what idea of Messiahship he clearly entertained. Even the discrepancies found in the New Testament are not without difficulties. All of the authors point to "errors," but they "do not all point to the same things."[24] This diversity, Walker concludes, shows that Judaism is no more homogenous than Christianity. He applauds the Jewish scholars for their contribution to the study and believed that it would lead to more honesty in this field among both Jewish and Christian scholars.

[2. 5] JAKOB JOCZ

The first study of this literature by a Jewish believer in Jesus was done by Jakob Jocz, in his 1949 publication *The Jewish people and Jesus Christ*. It contains a historical overview of Jewish-Christian relations and includes topics such as the Jewishness of Jesus, the historic events leading to the split between the Jewish people and Jesus, traditional Jewish views of Jesus, the Church's attitude toward the Jewish people, and the usually neglected issue of Jews who believe in Jesus. Jocz's survey of Jewish attitudes toward Jesus begins in the Enlightenment, and more specifically the *Haskala*. This was the Jewish response to the Enlightenment, the time when the Ghetto walls of Europe finally came down and Jews entered the modern world. "What was achieved in Europe by a slow process of development covering several centuries," he wrote, "was appropriated by Jewry within the space of fifty

---

24. Walker, *Jewish Views of Jesus*, 114.

years."[25] Beginning with Moses Mendelsohn in the late eighteenth century, a new Judaism was developing. The Reform movement of the nineteenth century would clash with traditional Orthodox Judaism as they entered modernity, and each would have a unique stance regarding Christianity. He writes: "While for the Orthodox, Jesus is the Founder of Christianity and inseparable from the Church, the liberals differentiate between Jesus and historic Christianity, assigning its foundation chiefly to Paul."[26]

He then surveys the opinions in each camp. Orthodox Jews remained for the most part closed to the discussion; their main participation was criticizing the liberal camp for being too sympathetic toward Jesus. Any sign of a positive criticism was "decried as a betrayal of Judaism."[27] The discussion of liberal Jews begins with C. G. Montefiore. According to Jocz, he "contributed more than any other Jewish scholar towards a dispassionate and critical study of the person of Jesus Christ."[28] The next most important writer was Joseph Klausner. One of his contributions was his recognition that Paul (like Jesus) was undeniably Jewish. This, Jocz writes, marks a new departure in the study of Pauline theology "not only in respect to Jewish scholarship, but to scholarship in general."[29] The survey continues with Kaufman Kohler, Israel Abrahams, and others. Additional writers such as Robert Eisler, E. R. Trattner and Hyman Enelow are also considered. Jocz was aware that this field of study was still a new phenomenon, and he offers the following conclusion. "So far only individual Jews have spoken, but Judaism has not raised its voice. The effect of Jewish study resulted rather in the breaking down of prejudice than in the building up of positive conceptions. The last word concerning Jesus of Nazareth still belongs to a future age."[30]

Thirty-two years later, Jocz wrote a sequel to this book. His purpose was to "bring the convoluted story of Jewish—Christian relationships after World War II up-to-date."[31] This volume discusses the Holocaust, the Church's lack of response to the tragedy, the new attitude of the Church toward the Jews, new theologies that developed and, again, Jewish views of Jesus. Some of the scholars discussed here include Shalom Ben-Chorin, David Flusser, Samuel Sandmel, Hyam Maccoby and Ferdinand Zweig. But these new scholars, Jocz believed, added little to the discussion: "On the

25. Jocz, *The Jewish People and Jesus Christ*, 103.

26. Ibid., 111.

27. Ibid.

28. Ibid., 119.

29. Ibid., 133.

30. Ibid., 145.

31. Jocz, *The Jewish People and Jesus Christ after Auschwitz*, 7.

whole the Jewish study of Jesus has not progressed since Joseph Klausner's biography *Jesus of Nazareth* (English translation, 1925), though the background has been enlarged since the discovery of the Dead Sea Scrolls."[32]

[2.6] DAVID CATCHPOLE

The trial of Jesus before the Sanhedrin presents a number of challenges, specifically in regards to setting the culpability (or at least partial culpability) for the crucifixion. For this reason Jewish scholars have given it unique attention. Questions concern not only the legality and historicity of the trial itself, but subsequent Christian history as well. New Testament scholar David Catchpole has documented Jewish views of this event in a 1971 book that was based on his PhD-thesis from Cambridge. He is well aware that the trial of Jesus has been used to justify centuries of persecution. "For Jesus' own via dolorosa," he wrote, has tragically become "a blood-stained path for his fellow countrymen of later generations."[33]

Catchpole begins his survey with sections of the Talmud that speak of Jesus. While there is much debate about which passages are unmistakably referring to Jesus, one of the most famous passages comes from *b. Sanh.* 43a. Here, Jesus (called Yeshu) was hanged on the eve of Passover because he "practiced sorcery" and "led Israel astray." This happened after a period of forty days where "a herald went out" to find anyone who might plead on his behalf. It is clear from this account that the Jewish leadership was taking responsibility for his death. This would be the Jewish position for quite some time. "In a nutshell, the Jewish defense is found in a statement of the reasons *for* and the justice *of* their involvement, rather than, as has been the modern pattern, a denial of that involvement or reduction of it to the handing over of Jesus to Pilate."[34]

Jumping ahead to Moses Mendelsohn, a different approach begins to emerge. As an enlightened Jew, he was not as bound to the Talmud as his predecessors were. He was also more sympathetic toward Jesus and "allowed for the possibility of an unjust condemnation." He deviates from the traditional position of the Talmud by stating the "uncertainty" of the affair.[35] Later commentators will stray even further from the Talmud's position on the subject, and an apologetic of denial will emerge. In the nineteenth century, Heinrich Graetz's *History of the Jews* would have a major impact in

32. Ibid., 107.
33. Catchpole, *The Trial of Jesus*, xi.
34. Ibid., 5; emphasis in the original.
35. Ibid., 14.

the Jewish world. He wrote from an Orthodox Jewish perspective and was critical towards both Reform Judaism and Christianity. Catchpole notices that in the space of just a few years, a later edition of Graetz's book changed its position on the trial. Social factors made it difficult to maintain the view that augmented Jewish involvement. It was thought that this would "open himself to charges of giving opportunity to Christian opposition," especially in light of the fact that "liberal Jews of the standing of Geiger were producing the apologetic of non-involvement."[36]

By the mid-twentieth century, the pendulum would continue to swing away from claiming any involvement. In 1948, H. E. Goldin's book, *The Case of the Nazarene reopened*, completely rejected the historicity of the Sanhedrin trial. This was, in Catchpole's words, "an old-fashioned Troki-type approach, devoting considerable space to proving Jesus' falsity." He saw this as "growing pressure among Jews for a re-trial."[37] More than a decade later, Samuel Sandmel would re-cast the debate in another direction. "Perhaps we might be willing to say to ourselves that it is not at all impossible that some Jews, even leading Jews, recommended the death of Jesus to Pilate. We are averse to saying this to ourselves, for so total has been the charge against us that we have been constrained to make a total denial."[38] This issue has had enduring consequences. Virtually all Jewish scholars acknowledge that—whatever may have happened after the arrest—Jesus was taken to the cross where he died. Questions about the trials play a vital role in Jewish-Christian relations, but this does not interfere with the ultimate flow of the narrative and the question of the resurrection.

[2. 7] WALTER JACOB

In 1974, Rabbi Walter Jacob published *Christianity through Jewish eyes*. It focused on the individuals involved in the modern investigation of Jesus, and it remains one of the best sources to learn about the key players of this movement. At the start, he says of the nineteenth-century pioneers, objectivity was difficult. "The beginnings of this Jewish study of Christianity were rather angry, as if polemic were necessary to arouse interest in the problem and the air had to be cleared before a true discussion could begin."[39] By the time of his writing, Jews had begun to more seriously study the issues of Jesus and Christianity. After giving background information, he devotes

36. Ibid., 32.

37. Ibid., 69.

38. Sandmel, *We Jews and Jesus*, 141, cited in ibid., 69.

39. Jacob, *Christianity through Jewish Eyes*, 2.

a whole chapter to each figure. Moses Mendelssohn was "the first modern Jew," whose famous correspondence with Lavater was the beginning of the Jewish-Christian dialogue.[40] Mendelsohn believed that Paul ultimately created Christianity, but that the traditions of the Gospels can be considered reliable, "just as the Jewish oral tradition of that age seems reliable."[41]

Isaac Meyer Wise was one of the first in the United States to approach the subject. His interest in Christianity was mostly reactionary, in direct response to missionary activity. Jacob suggests that part of Wise's "harshness" was the result of a centuries-long silence, since "no such expression had been possible to a Jew for a long time."[42] In the realm of philosophy, Herman Cohen was "perhaps the first to emphasize Christianity's influence on Judaism."[43] Claude Montefiore was "the first Jew to view Christianity entirely sympathetically."[44] To round out the study, Jacob also surveys the life and writings of Geiger, Klausner, Rosenzweig, Baeck, Sandmel, Flusser and several others. Jacob's approach to the subject was largely sociological, as opposed to theological. His study encompassed authors within a period of approximately two hundred years. In that time, the Jewish approach to Jesus had softened and became more scholarly. But regarding the Jewish-Christian dialogue itself, "surprisingly little has happened." He believes that "in many ways we are not far removed from Mendelssohn and his first approaches to this complex matter."[45]

[2. 8] DONALD HAGNER

In 1984, Donald Hagner wrote *The Jewish Reclamation of Jesus*. By this time, others had already noted the phenomenon of the Jewish interest in Jesus. Hagner wanted to examine the theological positions of these writers in light of his own (evangelical) Christianity. He acknowledges his debt to German scholar, Gosta Lindeskog,[46] who analyzed and categorized some of this same information. He summarizes Lindeskog's position as follows.

> The first type, the most frequent, emphasizes the *common* elements. Jesus has taught nothing which does not have its exact

40. Ibid., 23.
41. Ibid., 26.
42. Ibid., 75.
43. Ibid., 89.
44. Ibid., 93.
45. Ibid., 228.
46. Lindeskog, *Die Jesusfrage im neuzeitlichen Judentum*.

parallel in the Jewish writings. The second type, which is characteristic of the Orthodox . . . admits that the teachings of Jesus
contains *un-Jewish* elements, which from the Jewish standpoint
must be rejected . . . The third type . . . stresses the positive, creative *originality* of Jesus.[47]

Regarding the authority of Jesus and his relationship to the Law, Hagner sees three main categories of Jewish writers. The first group, those who
believe Jesus made a "modest" break with the law, include Montefiore, Samuel Sandmel, and Joseph Jacobs. The next group—those who believe that
Jesus did not break the law—are represented by Israel Abrahams, Klausner,
Jules Isaac, and Kaufman Kohler. Finally, there are several scholars who
believe there is no essential difference between Jesus' view of the Law and
rabbinic Judaism. This group includes Shalom Ben-Chorin, David Flusser,
Pinchas Lapide, Geza Vermes, and E.R. Trattner.

Judaism and Christianity often share a similar language, although each
is invested with quite different meanings. Such is the case with the phrase
"kingdom of God." Most Jewish scholars admit the centrality of the kingdom for Jesus, Hagner says, "but argue that he taught only that the kingdom
was imminent, not that it was already present in and through his ministry."[48]
The question of Messiahship is also addressed, and Hagner states that "the
majority of modern Jewish scholars conclude that Jesus believed himself to
be the Messiah."[49] But, they also believe that he was "deluded" on this point.
Ultimately, he believes, many liberal Jewish scholars have embraced Jesus as
one of their own. But, this is achieved by discarding the elements that seem
foreign to Judaism. Hagner concludes by affirming both the Jewishness of
Jesus and the uniqueness of the Christian gospel. "Christianity rightly understood is not the cancellation of Judaism," he writes in the book's final
paragraph. "It is at the heart of all that Jews hold dear. Jesus the Jew is the
Christ of Christianity without being any less a Jew; Jesus the Christ is fully a
Jew without being any less the Christ of the church."

[2.9] PINCHAS LAPIDE

About a year after Pinchas Lapide wrote his book about the resurrection, he
studied Israeli views of Jesus in his book, *Israelis, Jews and Jesus*. It contains
three main sections. The first is a survey of modern literature in Hebrew. Of

47. Hagner, *The Jewish Reclamation of Jesus*, 307.
48. Ibid., 134.
49. Ibid., 243.

course, Joseph Klausner heads the list. In discussing the recent past, he sees four ways that the Holocaust has affected Jewish, and specifically Israeli, opinions about Jesus. The first way he calls a "sea of tears." Because of the immense emotional impact, "people sought refuge in a factual, scientific image of the Nazarene."[50] This may have helped secure the appropriate facts of the matter, but it has also kept Jesus the person—the fellow Jew—at a distance. The second result of the Holocaust was to make Jesus more approachable, a fellow sufferer. His humanity led many to see his Jewishness more clearly. He became "a human brother who lived an exemplary Jewish life in a world full of inhumanity." On the other hand, many Holocaust survivors could only see Jesus through the lens of the atrocity itself. This third way saw Jesus as anything but a brother. They could not separate Christ from the Christendom that committed or tolerated the murder of six million Jews. The final way—which Lapide sees as perhaps the majority opinion—is an attitude of acceptance. "But, on the whole," he wrote, "we are dealing with the Jewish recovery of Jesus, of bringing him home."[51]

After this summary, he provides a survey of modern Israeli writings. It is quite an extensive list, made up of various types of literature. He concludes: "The 187 Hebrew books, research articles, poems, plays, monographs, dissertations, and essays that have been written about Jesus in the last twenty-seven years since the foundation of the State of Israel, justify press reports of a 'Jesus wave' in the present-day literature of the Jewish State."[52] Lapide credits the "climate of independence" as the main reason for this Jesus wave amongst Israelis. It simply could not have happened in the diaspora. In a State of their own, he reasons, Jews can be free to explore the issue of Jesus—for good and for bad—with a degree of honesty and objectivity previously unknown.

The second main section is called "Jesus in Israeli schoolbooks." It focuses on how Jesus is portrayed as a historical figure. The books used by ultra-orthodox schools do not even mention him. But for most other curriculums, there is a clear delineation between Jesus the Jew and the Christology of the Church. Most of the books blame Pilate for his death and exonerate the Sanhedrin. Judas Iscariot is also said to be fictitious. In Lapide's opinion, the information in Israeli schoolbooks reveals three truths, each of them positive. First, the person of Jesus is not responsible for the centuries of Christian hatred. Second, Jesus himself was undeniably a Jew.

50. Lapide, *Israelis, Jews and Jesus*, 7.

51. Ibid., 7–8.

52. Ibid., 31.

Third, Jesus was not only Jewish (by birth), he was committed to carrying out and teaching the principles of Torah. In other words, he was a good Jew.[53]

The third and final main section is called "Rabbis speak of Jesus." This part strays from the book's focus on Israelis and includes rabbis from other parts of the world as well. One of the fascinating accounts is that of Italo Zolli, who was also known as Israel Zoller. In 1932, Zoller wrote a book called *The Nazarene*. A devout Italian Jew, he underwent baptism to escape persecution by Mussolini. He later became Chief Rabbi of Rome. After that, as a result of studying about Jesus for many years, he became a follower (by faith) in Jesus as the Messiah. Lapide acknowledges Zoller's history of helping fellow Jews, even after he embraced Christianity by faith. "In all fairness," Lapide writes, "it must be remarked that he reaped no worldly advantage from his conversion."[54]

Lapide's book provides a unique perspective on the Jewish study of Jesus. It was written over a generation ago, when Israeli attitudes and perspectives were still largely influenced by the European experience of the authors. For him, the whole issue of the Jewish study of Jesus was "a child of Jewish polemical writing about Jesus and nineteenth-century Protestant biblical scholarship."[55] But, since this work, a new generation has grown up in Israel, devoid of the influence of both Protestant scholarship and the need for polemical writings about Jesus.

[2.10] MATTHEW HOFFMAN

Jewish theologians and historians were not the only ones to take notice of Jesus. Matthew Hoffman's book, *From Rebel to Rabbi*, documents the work done by Jewish artists and writers in the early years of the twentieth century. He begins with a summary of Jewish views about Jesus from the late nineteenth and early twentieth centuries. These writings, Hoffman says, "tell us more about Jews than about Jesus."[56] The book's stated purpose is to "explore the pervasiveness and centrality of the figure of Jesus to modern Jewish movements as diverse as Reform Judaism and Yiddish modernism."[57] It surveys artists and writers who wrote in Yiddish, Hebrew, and English. This is an eclectic group comprised of Jewish voices that deviated, whether

---

53. Ibid., 65.

54. Ibid., 140.

55. Ibid., 130.

56. Hoffman, *From Rebel to Rabbi*, 2.

57. Ibid.

radically or in more subtle ways, from traditional Jewish expressions. Such artists "often formed an avant-garde or constituted an intelligentsia."[58]

One topic of interest was the cross. There was a fierce debate in a Yiddish newspaper about the appropriateness and the meaning of the works of two specific authors. Lamed Shapiro and Sholem Asch pioneered the use of Jesus, and specifically the cross, in Yiddish literature.[59] The debate concerned the fear that it might cause Jews to embrace Christianity, or at least make Christianity a viable option. A similar debate in the Hebrew press erupted in 1910. Zionist authors Ahad ha-Am and Yosef Chaim Brenner squared off on the issues of apostasy and the place of Jesus in the worldview of modern Jews. A new wave of Yiddish literature emerged after 1905. They distinguished themselves from earlier giants of the field like Sholem Aleichem. The new group sought to synthesize "the tension between secular universalism and cultural nationalism."[60] In doing so, they often incorporated Christian motifs to help explain Jewish life. Themes such as suffering, tragedy, war and redemption, Hoffman says, touched on many of the complex issues raised in the fierce debates raging in the Jewish press during the preceding years.[61]

The passion of Jesus—his trials, suffering and death—was another theme that emerged in Jewish art and literature. Since medieval times, the binding of Isaac (the *Akedah*) has been a traditional symbol to express Jewish suffering. In the twentieth century, a number of writers and artists focused on the crucifixion to dramatize Jewish suffering. Notable in this group are the painter Marc Chagall and the American poet Emma Lazarus. The key word in all of this was tension. "Throughout these works, Jesus is simultaneously idealized as a symbol of Jewish martyrdom and reviled as the emblem of the Christian persecutors of the Jews; again, this duality of Jesus as Jewish martyr and Christian god is a source of profound ambivalence and tension for the Jewish writers who engage him."[62] But, this duality would not last. The Holocaust once again "tainted the figure of Jesus with the stain of Jewish blood as in earlier times."[63] For this reason, many of the artists and writers in this subgroup would turn away from Christian themes. Marc Chagall and Sholem Asch are notable exceptions.

58. Ibid., 11.
59. Ibid., 61.
60. Ibid., 116.
61. Ibid., 119.
62. Ibid., 205.
63. Ibid., 252.

All of these writers, painters and poets knew the power of art to communicate a multitude of emotions and ambivalence. Jesus was discussed and debated in creative ways that made him accessible to the Jewish community. More recently, another artistic rendering—and reactions to it—have had the opposite effect. Mel Gibson's 2004 film, *The Passion of the Christ,* "places Jesus outside of the Jewish camp and casts the Jews as Christ's persecutors." This has been a setback. The Jewish intelligentsia of the early twentieth century sought to reclaim Jesus. As a result of this film, "the Jewish communal leadership of the twenty-first century wants him as far out of the public eye as possible."[64]

[2.11] DANIEL F. MOORE

The first Catholic scholar to offer a major contribution to the study is Daniel F. Moore, who teaches at the Catholic University of America. Writing at the end of the first decade of the twenty-first century, he sets out to review the Jewish scholarship on Jesus in recent decades. The word "emerging" in the book's title, he writes, is there to remind the readers that "what is now presumed was once not."[65] He focuses on seven authors, and these are subdivided into two groups. Those who provided a critical approach include Sandmel, Flusser and Vermes. The other category, the creative approach, includes Ben-Chorin, Lapide, Neusner and Eugene Borowitz. Lapide is specifically relevant for this present work. He wrote many books in German, although he is most famous for his book on the resurrection. Moore writes,

> Lapide is unique among Jewish scholars in embracing the resurrection of Jesus as a historical occurrence. In his dialogue with Jurgen Moltmann, Lapide states plainly: "I accept the resurrection of Easter Sunday not as an invention of the community of disciples, but as a historical event."[66]

Most of the book interacts with these seven scholars and their views of various New Testament topics. The conclusion synthesizes the information and addresses the relationship between beliefs and history. Neusner, for example, said that the study of the historical Jesus is largely "theology masquerading as history."[67] Moore acknowledges this critique and applauds the Jewish study for bringing new dimensions to the discussions. He wrote:

64. Hoffman, *From Rebel to Rabbi,* 256
65. Moore, *Jesus, an Emerging Jewish Mosaic,* 4.
66. Ibid., 181.
67. Ibid., 236.

"Our Jewish authors are not immune from such subjectivity or critique. Nonetheless, without their contribution, the Jesus we speak of today would be but a shadow of his authentic self."[68] He then lists the benefits of this trend, which include a new understanding of the Jewish Jesus of history and better relations between Jews and Catholics in the contemporary period.[69] His final comment is this: "Vermes and his Jewish colleagues have sounded the alarm, diminishing the halo but not the aura of the Galilean of Nazareth."[70]

[2.12] NETA STAHL

Neta Stahl is an Israeli scholar who teaches Hebrew literature at Johns Hopkins University. Her book *Other and Brother* is an expansion of a book she wrote in Hebrew.[71] It examines the figure of Jesus as portrayed by Israeli writers and to a lesser extent some Yiddish writers as well. It is similar to Hoffman's work, although more in depth regarding the Israeli sources. She focuses on the changing ambivalence between seeing Jesus as an outsider, and yet in many ways someone who rightfully, somehow, should be included in the fold. Zionism yielded new opportunities of expression.

The first chapter presents an overview of the modern Jewish study of Jesus, with an emphasis on the Israeli scene. Jesus was often used as a key to understanding the "new national identity" of the Jew returning to Israel.[72] He represented the "pre-exilic Jew."[73] Klausner was the first of these writers to become popular. His Jesus was a Jewish nationalist and would greatly influence the next generation of Israeli writers. This group was able to embrace the Jewish Jesus, "while rejecting the Jesus of Christianity, the threatening old Other."[74] One of the recurring themes, particularly among artists, was Jesus as a Jewish victim. This presents a paradox, as he also represents the very group responsible for persecuting the Jews. But, as Stahl says, the victimized, humanistic Jesus served a purpose and helped bridge a gap. This view helped to "assimilate both Jesus and humanism into Judaism."[75]

68. Ibid., 237.
69. Ibid., 242–43.
70. Ibid., 246.
71. ‏צלם יהודי : ייצוגיו של ישו בספרות העברית של המאה ה-‏, 20.
72. Stahl, *Other and Brother*, 10.
73. Ibid., 11.
74. Ibid., 13.
75. Ibid., 41.

Chapter two focuses on the poetry of Uri Zvi Greenberg. Born in Eastern Europe and later a survivor of the Holocaust, his personal biography greatly influenced his writings. His early works, in Yiddish, drew attention to the sufferings of Jesus. Greenberg, like the Jesus in his writings, looked toward the land of Israel. Jesus the man was not a problem for him, but the institutions of Christianity definitely were. This included theological claims. Greenberg was "bound" to Jesus by his humanity, but "repelled" by his divinity.[76] The next chapter surveys the figure of Jesus in general Israeli literature. After the creation of the modern state of Israel, a new breed of Israeli authors had a new sense of identification and empathy with Jesus. He became detached from the western Church that persecuted the Jewish people. These new writers did not make the connection "between the cross and the Church, the swastika, and Jesus."[77] Jesus became more of a brother and less of an "other."

The remainder of the book includes chapters on the works of Yoel Hoffman and Avot Yehurun. The epilogue is called "The Ironic Gaze at Brother Jesus." Stahl addresses the tension and conflict between what an author says and what is not stated blatantly. She begins with a discussion of the ancient text, the *Toledot Yeshu*. The use of irony or mockery about Jesus is used in place of explicit denial, a practice that may be used by modern Jewish writers as well. For example, H. Leyvik was one of the first modern Jewish poets to use such irony in regards to Jesus. In one of his works, Jesus is represented as a modern man undergoing psychoanalysis and revealing episodes based on the New Testament. Stahl concludes,

> In depicting the figure of Jesus as a neurotic man searching for a cure in psychoanalytical therapy, both Jesus and the rising trend are being ridiculed and being rejected as mere myth. Psychotherapy is presented not as a solution for man's problems but as yet another problem of modern times. By setting Jesus in a therapeutic context and depicting him as a hysterical patient, Leyvik stresses Jesus' humanity and even human weakness.[78]

There is one further point of irony that could be made about Stahl's book. It is most likely a simple mistake, and too much should not be made of it. But, it is nevertheless ironic. One of the poets (Wallach) envisions a scene that takes place in the Church of the Holy Sepulcher. Stahl refers to this as "the place where, according to Christian tradition, Jesus is buried."[79]

76. Ibid., 54.

77. Ibid., 84.

78. Ibid., 173.

79. Ibid., 110.

Of course, Christians, by definition, do not believe that Jesus "is" buried anywhere. Again, this is probably a simple error. But, given the vast amount written about the cross and the death of Jesus in Yiddish and Israeli literature, this may perhaps serve as a metaphor for the overemphasis on such themes, and the overwhelming silence on the issue of his resurrection.

[2.13] DANIEL LANGTON

The Jewishness of Jesus is accepted in virtually all circles of Jewish scholarship. Whatever type of Jew he was, however the true picture might be distorted, all are agreed that he was a Jew. But, as his reputation grew more positive in the Jewish community, it was the Apostle Paul who would become the villain. In the last century, however, Paul would also undergo a reclamation within the Jewish community, although by no means to the extent that Jesus has. The jury is still out on Paul. Daniel Langton has documented these changing attitudes in his book, *The Apostle Paul in the Jewish Imagination*.[80] Paul is nothing if not extreme, and Jewish opinions are quite varied. "He is both a bridge and a barrier to interfaith harmony; both the founder of Christianity and a convert to it; both an anti-Jewish apostate and a fellow traveler on the path to Jewish self-understanding; and both the chief architect of the Judeo-Christian foundations of Western thought and their destroyer."[81]

Jewish interest in Paul began during the Enlightenment, and at first he was universally seen in a negative light. Langton lists three reasons for this. The first was in response to the growing recognition of Jesus as a Jew. Christianity was still seen as the opposition, and there was a "need to find a replacement for Jesus as Jewish public enemy number one." Second, liberal Christian scholars of the day were busy debunking the New Testament and they were looking for parallels (to Paul) in pagan sources rather than Jewish ones. Third, Paul's view of the Law—at least as it was understood at the time—was a "misrepresentation of Judaism and the Law."[82] Langton sees other forces as well, even today, which have caused such a negative reaction to Paul. These go beyond the historical study of the New Testament and enter the realms of sociology and psychology. Paul's life and teachings raise issues of vital concern to the Jewish community, including "apostasy,

80. Langton, *The Apostle Paul in the Jewish Imagination*. See also Bird and Sprinkle, "Jewish Interpretations of Paul in the Last Thirty Years"; Hagner, "Paul in Modern Jewish Thought."

81. Langton, *The Apostle Paul in the Jewish Imagination*, 1.

82. Ibid., 40.

conversion, Jewish missionary work, those who abandon or subordinate the Torah, those who blur the boundary lines of Judaism and Christianity—and even the "threat of Jewish self-hatred."[83]

The classic (negative) Jewish view of Paul comes from writers in the nineteenth and early twentieth centuries such as Graetz, Benamozegh, Baeck, Kohler, and Buber. After summarizing their contributions, he moves on to different categories, including the "intra-Jewish" debate. These authors have been much more open to seeing Paul, like Jesus, as a Jew. This group includes Emil Hirsch, Montefiore, Klausner, Micah Berdichevsky, Hans Joachim Schoeps, David Flusser, Samuel Sandmel, Daniel Boyarin, Alan Segal and Mark Nanos. Langton further subdivides some of these newer voices by category. For example, he recognizes the role of Jewish scholars who write from a feminist perspective. These include Pamela Eisenbaum, Tal Ilan and Amy-Jill Levine. He even includes Hebrew Christian/Messianic Jewish scholars such as Paul Levertoff, Sanford Mills and Joseph Shulam. Their inclusion is a surprising addition in a book written by a Jewish scholar who is himself not a Messianic Jew. The book continues with Jewish authors, artists and psychologists who have also interacted with Paul in one way or another.

The Jewish acceptance of Paul as a fellow Jew is still in progress. There have been major advancements in recent years and overall there is a definite difference between now and a hundred years ago. But, as Langton concludes: "Doubtless, the classic, negative Jewish view of Paul is alive and well, and there is no reason to believe that Paul will not continue to function as a figure of abuse in public discourse, in Jewish-Christian religious polemic, and in intra-Jewish debate for a long time to come."[84]

[2.14] WALTER HOMOLKA

The most recent full volume to address our topic comes from Walter Homolka, rector of Abraham Geiger College, Germany's only rabbinical seminary. It is a translation from his original German work. In light of persecution and misunderstanding, this book seeks to "do justice to Jesus of Nazareth in his Jewish setting and to depict the Jewish perception of Jesus throughout the centuries."[85] The book consists of an introduction, three chapters and a conclusion. Its title, *Jesus reclaimed*, implies a certain level of acceptance previously unseen in Jewish scholarship. The introduction is broken down into six subjects, each one just a few paragraphs long. These represent the

83. Ibid., 45.
84. Ibid., 283.
85. Homolka, *Jesus Reclaimed*, xx.

issues that have been relevant in the Jewish discussion of Jesus: the sources, his early years, his public appearance, his message, his arrest and trial, and his death. Homolka cites both Christian and Jewish sources to briefly explain the relevance of each. The categories are reminiscent of Ben-Chorin's list (see above) which describe the relevant issues in the Jewish quest but do not include the resurrection.

The first chapter surveys Jewish-Christian relations in antiquity through the Middle Ages. The second chapter examines the modern period and reveals the origins and motive behind the Jewish quest in distinction from the Christian quest. One key difference is their respective starting points. Christians study the historical Jesus in relation to the role he is assigned as the "central figure" of faith, while Jewish scholars approach the issue "without the dogmatic veil."[86] At times, the Christian approach to Jesus included a devaluation of Judaism, and even the Old Testament. The Jewish reaction was to validate both, a process which reinstated the Jewish Jesus. This was the case in Leo Baeck's response to the writings of Adolph von Harnack. He writes: "The Harnack-Baeck debate marks the first encounter and controversy between a Christian and a Jewish theologian on the formative period of Christianity. It was a strong attempt on the Jewish side to point out the lasting relevance of Judaism in line with the beliefs of Jesus of Nazareth."[87]

The second chapter continues with a survey of the modern Jewish scholars, which includes Klausner, Buber, Sandmel, Fluisser, Ben-Chorin, Schoeps and Lapide. Regarding Lapide, he writes: "Lapide goes so far as to declare Easter a Jewish moment of faith that opens a path to God for the gentile world."[88] These authors took differing approaches to Jesus, but, according to Holmoka, they share a common goal, namely apologetics. "Jews wanted to remain Jews and yet be part of the wider Christian society. How fortunate, then, that Jesus himself was a Jew."[89] Chapter three interacts with the writings of Joseph Ratzinger, or as he is more commonly known, Pope Benedict XVI, who has written three books on the life of Jesus. The only Jewish scholar mentioned in these books is Jacob Neusner, which Homolka felt limited Ratzinger's understanding of both the Jewish Jesus and modern Jewish beliefs. In the end, the differences between the Jewish and Christian approaches are exposed. Ratzinger's approach begins from a point of faith. Jews, on the other hand, "have come to look upon Jesus as one of us who has come a long way as a human to bring closer God's will to all humankind."[90]

86. Ibid., 45.
87. Ibid., 66.
88. Ibid., 76.
89. Ibid., 80–81.
90. Ibid., 108.

The conclusion surveys the contemporary situation. Homolka does not necessarily say anything that different from the other authors discussed above. But, there is more of a sense of closure in Holmoka's approach, beginning with the title. If Jesus has been reclaimed, as the title states, what does this mean? The quest which began defensively, he explains, "has now become a largely self-confident affiliation with Jesus."[91] He is considered one of the many voices in the Jewish world of his time and is neither perfect nor supernatural. He is, however, "a phenomenon and integral part of western civilization, he cannot be overlooked, even by Jews."[92] The ultimate question is asked and answered in the book's final sentence: "Was he the Messiah or even the Son of God? According to the Jewish understanding: no."[93]

[2.15] SHAUL MAGID

In 2011, Zev Garber edited a collection of essays that addressed "historical, literary, liturgical, philosophical, religious, theological and contemporary issues."[94] Both Jewish and Christian scholars contributed. The final article, by Shaul Magid, deals with Jewish attitudes (in America) toward Jesus in the last few decades of the twentieth-century and the first decade of our current century. New attitudes exist, he writes, because the Jewish community is more confident about its place in society than ever before.

> Liberal Protestantism is no longer dominant, Jewish success, and acceptance, in America is more well-founded, the Holocaust created a new paradigm for Jewish identity and existence (as well as sympathy for Jews and Judaism more generally), Jewish theology has extended beyond acculturation and into the more creative, and precarious, realm of adaptation and experimentation, and Jewish tradition is less unstable due in part to the rise of Orthodoxy and Hasidic spirituality, in part refracted through postmodern and New Age lenses.[95]

Contemporary Jews, he believes, want to understand Jesus in something other than a negative light. The article focuses on four authors who have attempted to find a unique role for Jesus. The first two utilize the

---

91. Ibid., 111.
92. Ibid., 114.
93. Ibid., 114.
94. Garber, ed., *Jewish Jesus*, 8.
95. Magid, "The New Jewish Reclamation of Jesus," 375.

rabbinic concept of the "dual-messiah principle"[96] in a move that "seeks reconciliation with Christianity through a shared Jesus."[97] Irving "Yitz" Greenberg suggested that Jesus was a "failed" messiah rather than a false messiah. By this he means that Jesus brought a Jewish message and his original Jewish followers were right to acknowledge him as a messiah, or at least a potential messiah. But since Jesus did not bring about the expected results of the messiah, Jews "simply cannot accept Jesus as a successful messiah on historical grounds." He compares Jesus with the "Joseph messiah"[98] of rabbinic tradition. This figure dies also. One of the problems Magid sees is that the death of the Joseph messiah is not a failure. "In fact, his death may be the completion of his task, as it makes room for the Davidic kingdom."[99]

Magid next discusses an article by Byron Sherwin which builds on Greenberg's work. Whereas Greenberg excludes Jesus from the Jewish narrative, Sherwin offers Jesus a much more inclusive role. "For Sherwin, "failure" is better understood as incompleteness, that is, Jesus' messiahship was "true" but he did not live to see its completion. And, by extension such an incomplete messiah he could still remain a legitimate messiah inside Judaism."[100] In Byron's view, Jesus actually was the Joseph messiah, not just someone whose role was similar. He argues that the rabbinic concept of the Joseph messiah was created for the very purpose of giving Jesus a place within Judaism. In other words it was "a tool to attract Jewish Christians back into Judaism."[101] Citing Buber, Sherwin believes that Jesus somehow does fit in the overall scheme of redemption for the Jewish people. But, even this inclusive gesture has its limitations. He continues by saying that Jews will never recognize Jesus as the messiah who has come, because this "would contradict the deepest meaning of our Messianic passion."[102] Nevertheless, this view goes well beyond any previous attempts at reclamation and the consequences, Magid suggests, should be seriously studied in Jewish educational institutions.[103]

The next two scholars take the reclamation of Jesus to even more radical levels, based on Jewish mysticism. Zalman Schachter-Shalomi presents a view that combines the logos theology of Philo with his own

---

96. Ibid., 360.

97. Ibid., 361.

98. Ibid., 365.

99. Ibid.

100. Ibid., 367.

101. Ibid.

102. Ibid., 368.

103. Ibid., 369.

"Hasidic-kabbalistic" perspective.[104] Uniquely, Schacter-Shalomi seeks to erase the category of "messiah" (for Christians and Jews), yet retain the "doctrinal dimension of Jesus as the embodiment of the divine."[105] This is the polar opposite of the traditional Jewish view which has always concentrated on Jesus the man of history. As Magid states, "he has given us perhaps the first New Age American Jewish Jesus."[106] Daniel Matt's views are somewhat similar, and may be seen as an amalgamation of influences including the scholarship of E.P. Sanders (who questioned Jesus' relationship with the law) and the mysticism of Hassidism, specifically that of Martin Buber.[107] For Matt, Jesus is a Hasid who founded a new religion, unlike the Baal Shen Tov who founded a new approach to Torah. Schacter-Shalomi and Matt have each created "a Jewish Jesus who reflects the sensibilities of a religious America that is firmly planted in a new age."[108]

[2.16] CURRENT TRENDS

As the Jewish interest in Jesus has continued, so has the documentation of this field of study. Numerous articles have appeared about the general phenomenon, and Israeli scholars have also joined the discussion.[109] Articles and books have also focused on key players in the movement such as Abraham Geiger, Kaufman Kohler, Claude Montefiore, Joseph Klausner, Leo Baeck, Martin Buber, and David Flusser.[110] In approximately the last twenty years—roughly

---

104. Ibid., 370.

105. Ibid.

106. Ibid., 372.

107. Ibid.

108. Ibid., 375.

109. See Alexander, "Yeshu/Yeshua ben Yosef of Nazareth: Discerning the Jewish Face of Jesus"; Batnitsky, "Jesus in Modern Jewish Thought"; Cook, "Evolving Jewish Views of Jesus"; and Cook, "Jewish Reflections on Jesus"; Saperstein, "Jewish Images of Jesus Through the Ages"; Flusser, "A New Sensitivity in Judaism and the Christian Message"; Sperling, "Jewish Perspectives on Jesus"; Mittleman, "Modern Jewish Views of Jesus: A Search for Self"; Heschel, "Jesus in Modern Jewish Thought"; Kessler, "Jewish Scholarly Studies of Jesus"; and Kessler, "Jesus from a Jewish Perspective." Along with the work mentioned earlier by Stahl, see also Shinar, יהודים מספרים על ישו—אותו האיש.

110. Heschell, *Abraham Geiger and the Jewish Jesus*; Ariel, "Christianity through Reform Eyes: Kaufman Kohler's Scholarship on Christianity"; Langton, *Claude Montefiore, His Life and Thought*; Bowler, *Claude Montefiore and Christianity*; Kessler, *An English Jew*; Sandmel, "Joseph Klausner, Israel and Jesus"; Homolka, *Leo Baeck and Christianity*; Kohansky, *Martin Buber's Approach to Jesus*; Balthasar, *Martin Buber and Christianity*; Berry, *Buber's View of Jesus as Brother;* and Gager, "Scholarship as Moral Vision: David Flusser on Jesus, Paul, and the Birth of Christianity."

corresponding to our current century—there has been a profound new wave of Jewish scholars studying New Testament themes. Three trends are worthy of note. The first is the influx of those who are specifically trained as New Testament scholars. Some of these are world renowned leaders in their particular areas of study. This has raised new questions about the interface between scholarship and personal presuppositions. Joshua Brumberg-Krauss observed the following: "Some scholars, such as Paula Fredricksen and the earlier Sandmel, do not mention their Jewishness or allude to it only indirectly, or, like Vermes, claim that for the most part it is irrelevant. Others, like Sandmel in his later work *Anti-Semitism in the New Testament?*, admit dual loyalties: "one is objective scholarship, the other is to my Jewish background.""[111] This discussion has only grown as Jewish scholarship has gotten more sophisticated, and it has surfaced in the discussion of Paul as well.[112] Pamela Eisenbaum has argued that since there is not one single Jewish perspective on Paul, "religious identity does not determine one's scholarly judgment in any predictable way."[113] Daniel Langton responded, saying that "in light of the history of Jewish-Christian relations, it is a little naïve to think that an individual's Jewish identity could be dismissed as inconsequential when the focus of the debate is Paul."[114]

The second contemporary trend builds on the first. The Jewish study of Jesus has traditionally been almost exclusively for scholars. In 1958, Samuel Sandmel observed that most American Jews were quite ignorant of the New Testament. Their understanding usually came from "oblique and random contacts" that may include a chapter from a literature course, or a portion from a Christian wedding or funeral.[115] Over fifty years later, according to Alan Segal, the situation remained the same. "On the whole," he wrote, "most Christians would be surprised to learn that ordinary Jews have not read any of the New Testament."[116] The contemporary scholarly wave would have its effect on "ordinary Jews" as well, as demonstrated in the *Jewish Annotated New Testament* (*JANT*). This book includes the work of fifty Jewish scholars who wrote commentaries on each of the New Testament books as well as additional articles. It brings Jewish New Testament scholarship to a new level, as did the *Jewish Encyclopedia* a century earlier. The purpose of this volume, the editors write, was "not to convert, whether to convert Jews

---

111. Brumberg-Krauss, "A Jewish Ideological Perspective on the Study of Christian Scripture," 7.

112. See Langton, *The Apostle Paul in the Jewish Imagination*, 4–9.

113. Eisenbaum, "Following the Footsteps of the Apostle Paul," 93.

114. Langton, *The Apostle Paul in the Jewish Imagination*, 9.

115. Sandmel, *A Jewish Understanding of the New Testament*, xi.

116. Segal, "Paul's Religious Experience in the Eyes of one Jewish Scholar," 322.

to Christianity, or to convert Christians away from their own churches." Rather, it was educational, an opportunity for Jews to learn the New Testament in its "social, historical and religious" context. This will help them better understand their neighbors, and shed light on much of the music and art of the Western world.[117] A book with similar goals was written by Julie Galambush, a former Baptist minister who converted to Judaism.[118] There are also books by Jewish authors which explain the Jewishness of Jesus to Christians,[119] and Zev Garber has recently edited a collection of articles about how the historical Jesus may be taught by Jewish and Christian scholars in various contexts.[120]

The Jewish reclamation of Jesus has come a long way since Montefiore and Enelow a century ago. In their world it was dangerous to publically acknowledge that Jesus was a Jew. The progress has been steady, based on the climate of both Jewish-Christian relations and the latest New Testament scholarship. The most recent studies, as demonstrated by Magid, are able to explore avenues that would have been unthinkable just a few decades ago. The views of Jewish scholars have been documented on virtually every relevant New Testament issue. The one exception to this is the topic covered in this present book, the resurrection of Jesus. Chapter 4 will survey the (often quite brief) comments made by Jewish scholars, including many of those who were mentioned above. But first, Chapter 3 will interact with a number of preliminary historical and theological issues. This chapter will demonstrate the third contemporary trend, namely a new willingness to challenge some of the most entrenched Jewish presuppositions.

---

117. Levine and Brettler, *JANT*, xii.

118. Galambush, *The Reluctant Parting: How the New Testament's Jewish Writers Created a Christian Book.*

119. Levine, *The Misunderstood Jew;* Moffic, *What Every Christian Needs to Know about the Jewishness of Jesus.*

120. Garber, *Teaching the Historical Jesus.*

CHAPTER THREE

PRELIMINARY ISSUES

ONE OF THE DIFFICULTIES in studying the historical Jesus is that every scholar approaches the Gospels with a set of presuppositions. This was noticed by Geza Vermes. "Christians read them in light of their faith," he began, "Jews, primed with age old suspicion; agnostics, ready to be scandalized; and professional New Testament experts, wearing the blinkers of their trade."[1] The question of the resurrection brings specific challenges. For those who identify as evangelical Christians, for example, the resurrection is their defining conviction. It is certainly legitimate to raise the issue of objectivity among such scholars.[2] Jewish scholars do not have a specific view of the resurrection of Jesus. It has been at best a secondary issue, hidden behind more pressing topics in the historic Jewish-Christian interaction. Both historical and theological factors have contributed to this, and these need to be reviewed briefly here.

The message of the resurrection was first proclaimed by Jewish disciples of Jesus. A visible Jewish remnant continued to believe for at least three centuries, up until the time of Constantine. There is also evidence for Jewish believers in Jesus in the fifth century.[3] Gentiles came to believe in the resurrection soon after the first Jews believed, and quickly became the dominant group. The term "parting of the ways"[4] is often used to de-

1. Vermes, *Jesus the Jew*, 19.

2. One edition of the *Journal for the Study of the Historical Jesus* addressed this theme. Articles include but are not exclusive to: Bock, "Faith and the Historical Jesus: Does a Confessional Position and Respect for the Jesus Tradition Preclude Serious Historical Engagement?"; Levine, "Christian Faith and the Study of the Historical Jesus: A Response to Bock, Keener, Webb."

3. Pritz, *Nazarene Jewish Christianity*.

4. See Dunn, *Jews and Christians: The Parting of the Ways*; Becker and Reed, *The Ways That Never Parted*.

scribe the development of Judaism and Christianity. At a certain point in time, decisive boundaries were formed. For one thing, Christians—a label that became synonymous with Gentiles—believed that Jesus rose from the dead, something Jews no longer believed. The Gentile branch of the Jesus-believing community detached from its Jewish roots at an early stage. Christianity came to mean something completely non-Jewish, and specifically something hostile. The charge of *deicide* put the blame for Jesus' death, exclusively, on the Jewish people. The horrific history of "Christian" persecution of the Jews has been well documented.[5] This history is familiar to all Jews, but unfortunately all but unknown to most Christians. Jewish scholars have therefore paid much more attention to Jesus' trial and crucifixion than his resurrection.[6] This issue was raised again in 2004 with the Mel Gibson movie, *The Passion of the Christ*. Jewish scholars were quick to respond.[7] Because the death of Jesus has had such negative ramifications for the Jewish people throughout history, anything else that may have happened a few days after his death has been a moot point.

By the time the ways had fully parted, two mutually exclusive groups had formed. The Church forgot its Jewish roots with disastrous results. The synagogue was forced to define itself, along with key theological points, in response to the new situation. This was an important factor in the evolution of Judaism. Many of the most important Christian beliefs were not only considered wrong or foreign; they became completely antithetical, nothing less than an affront to the very foundations of Judaism. Israel Yuval of Hebrew University wrote: "(T)he polemics between Judaism and Christianity during the first centuries of the Common Era, in all their varieties and nuances, played a substantial role in the mutual formation of the two religions."[8] A combination of factors then, both cultural and theological, helped create barriers to the Jewish study of Jesus. This is especially true of the resurrection, which may yield a variety of objections that may dismiss the discussion before it even begins.

---

5. See Cohen, *Christkillers*; Flannery, *The Anguish of the Jews*; Almog, *Anti-Semitism through the Ages*; Cohn-Sherbok, *The Crucified Jew*; Carroll, *Constantine's Sword*; Brown, *Our Hands Are Stained with Blood*.

6. Hirsch, *My Religion and the Crucifixion Viewed from a Jewish Standpoint*; Hunterberg, *The Crucified Jew*; Zeitlin, *Who Crucified Jesus?*; Goldin, *The Case of the Nazarene Reopened*; Cohen, *The Trial and Death of Jesus*.

7. Greenberg, "Anti-Semitism in 'The Passion'"; Segal, "How I Stopped Worrying about Mel Gibson and Learned to Love the Historical Jesus"; Reinhartz, "Reflections on Gibson's 'The Passion of Christ'"; Fredriksen, *On the Passion of Christ*; Garber, *Mel Gibson's Passion*; Sandmel, "Jews, Christians and Gibson's *The Passion of the Christ*."

8. Yuval, *Two Nations in Your Womb*, xvii.

The goal of this chapter is twofold. First, it will identify some of the presuppositions which have led to the assumption that the resurrection has no relevance for Jews and / or that it did not happen. The literature on these issues is massive, but the discussion below will be confined to comments by Jewish scholars in the context of studying the resurrection of Jesus. Second, this chapter will provide alternative views to these issues from other mainstream Jewish scholars. By doing so, this chapter will argue that the historicity of the resurrection should not be prematurely dismissed in Jewish (or any other) discussions of the historical Jesus.[9]

[3.1] THE NEW TESTAMENT TEXTS

The search, or quest, for the historical Jesus in the nineteenth and most of the twentieth centuries was often marked by the assumption that very little, if anything, can be known for certain about the life of Jesus.[10] This view has been changing in recent decades and Jewish scholarship in particular has been taking the New Testament texts more seriously. Martin Goodman wrote: "The modern notion that the whole biography of Jesus to be found in the various Gospels was pure invention is deeply implausible—not least because a story of this type about the career of a Galilean peasant was neither characteristic of religious literature of the time nor obviously helpful in spreading to the wider world the central Christian message that Jesus was also Christ and Lord."[11] There has not yet been a Jewish reclamation of the New Testament,[12] but some of the textual reasons previously given for abandoning the quest for the historical Jesus (and particularly the resurrection) are being re-imagined. Three of these presuppositions will be addressed in this section.

9. As to what would need to be addressed to constitute a "mature" study of the resurrection, see below, 5.1

10. Bultmann virtually canonized this view when he said, "[W]e can now know almost nothing concerning the life and personality of Jesus since the early Christian sources show no interest in either, are moreover fragmentary and often legendary." Bultmann, *Jesus and the Word*, 8.

11. Goodman, *Rome and Jerusalem*, 515.

12. The *Jewish Annotated New Testament* recognizes Jewish aspects, but ultimately views the New Testament as foreign, non-Jewish, literature.

[3.1.1] Dating

Most New Testament scholars, whether conservative or critical, place the writing of the four canonical Gospels somewhere between the years 65 CE and 100 CE. The contributors to the *JANT* fall within this range. For the Gospel of Matthew, "80–90 CE seems reasonable."[13] Mark was "likely written between 64 and 72 CE."[14] No date was given in the introduction for Luke,[15] although the commentary on Acts says it was likely composed "after 70 CE."[16] Finally, the Gospel of John is "generally thought to have been completed ca. 85–95.[17] To modern ears, this may sound questionable from the start. The proximity of the events themselves to the final form of the documentation, some would argue, is too great to be trustworthy. Michael Cook wrote: "So extensive a hiatus raises doubts: how accurately could these writings preserve not only the realities of Jesus' ministry but also the particulars of what Jews had then thought about him?"[18] There are other ways to interpret this. There are two biographies of Alexander the Great, each written over 300 years after his life and they are considered generally reliable. Acknowledging this, Paula Fredriksen observed that "forty to seventy years" by comparison is "not bad at all."[19]

The dating of the Gospels refers to the time they appeared in their written form. What also needs to be discussed is the process or transmission of the material. The more critical view says that all or most of the material originated with the evangelists and therefore represents the views of the early Church rather than what actually happened in the life of Jesus. By the end of the twentieth century this understanding of the texts, at least in its extreme form, began to wane in light of the new interest in studying the Jewish background of the life of Jesus. The so-called "Third Quest" for the historical Jesus[20] brought the focus back to the Second Temple world of Jesus, with less emphasis on the creativity of the evangelists. Contemporary Jewish scholars, as with scholars in the wider field, have approached this issue from various angles. Michael Cook maintains the more extreme

13. Gale, "Matthew, Introduction and Annotations," 1.
14. Wills, "Mark, Introduction and Annotation," 55.
15. Levine, "Luke, Introduction and Annotations," 96–97.
16. Gilbert, "Acts of the Apostles, Introduction and Annotations," 197.
17. Reinhartz, "John, Introduction and Annotations," 153.
18. Cook, *Modern Jewish Engage the New Testament*,
19. Fredriksen, *Jesus of Nazareth, King of the Jews*, 19.
20. See Witherington III, *The Jesus Quest: The Third Search for the Jew of Nazareth*.

position, arguing that the evangelists fabricated virtually all of their Gospels.[21] But, other Jewish scholars have offered a more balanced approach. To assign "every bit of material to the compositional level," Claudia Setzer wrote, "seems overly skeptical about the process of transmission."[22] Doron Mendels of Hebrew University wrote the following: "As a historian of antiquity (not only of Jewish and early Christian history) I can say that many of the traditions found in the narrative parts of the New Testament go back to the 30s and 40s of the first century CE, while some reflect an awareness of what these years meant in the communities some years later."[23]

The resurrection of Jesus, in particular, has early attestation. Paul's first letter to the Corinthians is commonly accepted as being written within twenty-five years of the crucifixion. Chapter 15 includes the earliest proclamation of the resurrection and the appearances of the risen Jesus (verses 3–7). It is an early hymn of faith which was passed on to Paul from the original disciples within just a few years after the crucifixion. This view is accepted by at least three of the authors addressed in this study. For Alan Segal, this is the earliest Christian teaching. It is "part of the primitive *kerygma* or proclamation of the early church."[24] Jon Levenson and his co-author, Kevin Madigan, said it was a "well-established tradition," and that, "In all probability, this gospel was already proclaimed during the decade in which Jesus died, some twenty years or so before Paul sent his letter to the Corinthians around 55 C.E."[25] Pinchas Lapide offered eight reasons why he believed this section is an early hymn. They include the following: the wording is un-Pauline, the parallels of the wording are "biblically formulated," the threefold "and that" characterizes Aramaic/Mishnaic Hebrew, the passive phrase "being raised" is reminiscent of Jewish construction so as not to mention the name of God, the use of the Aramaic name Cephas, the double reference to "in accordance with the scriptures," the term "the twelve" refers to a closed group of the original witnesses, and the inclusion of the four events revealed for salvation which appear in all later reports: "died for our sins, buried, raised, appeared."[26] The section below on the supernatural will reveal the difference between the attestation of the miracles of Jesus

---

21. See the discussion below (3.2.1)

22. Setzer, *Jewish Responses to Early Christianity*, 27.

23. Mendels, *Identity, Religion and Historiography*, 440–41.

24. Segal, *Life After Death*, 424; emphasis in the original.

25. Madigan and Levenson, *Resurrection: The Power of God for Christians and Jews*, 25.

26. Lapide, *The Resurrection of Jesus*, 98–99.

compared with other miracle workers in antiquity. It is again the difference between decades and centuries.

[3.1.2] Discrepancies

The Gospels have long been criticized for being less than adequate sources for historical study. At the same time, most scholars recognize a generally accepted outline of events. The crucifixion and the fact that the disciples believed in the resurrection soon afterwards are readily accepted by virtually all of the authors discussed below in Chapter 4. The problem, for many, is the inconsistencies between the four evangelists regarding the details. The resurrection narratives have the greatest number of discrepancies. Dan Cohn-Sherbok wrote: "It is well known that there is no universality of agreement, and if scholars cannot concur about such historical matters what credence can we give to the gospel accounts of the miraculous reappearance of Jesus to his disciples?"[27] A more dogmatic version of this objection is common in contemporary "anti-missionary" literature (see below, 4.6.8 and 4.6.9). Orthodox Rabbi, Tovia Singer, writes, "The stories told in the New Testament, and the passion narratives in particular, are so inconsistent, that the resurrection story collapses under careful scrutiny. The conflicting testimonies of the evangelists are so unreliable, they would not stand up to critical cross-examination in any court of law. In fact, there is virtually not one detail of the crucifixion and resurrection narratives upon which all four Gospel authors agree."[28]

There are other ways to address this issue as well. One way is to argue that the discrepancies can be harmonized when understood in their proper context.[29] The other approach is to compare and contrast the Gospels with the literature in antiquity to determine the genre and boundaries of literary license.[30] Jewish scholars have also recognized the importance of evaluating the texts in their proper historical context. Joseph Klausner commented on this almost a hundred years ago. "If we had ancient sources like those in the Gospels for the history of Alexander the Great or Julius Caesar," he wrote, "we should not cast any doubt on them whatsoever."[31]

27. Cohn-Sherbok, "The Resurrection of Jesus: A Jewish View," 197.

28. Singer, *Let's Get Biblical*, 329.

29. See Wenham, *Easter Enigma: Are the Resurrection Accounts in Conflict?*

30. See Alexander, "Orality in Pharisaic-rabbinic Judaism at the Turn of the Era"; Girhardson, *Memory and Manuscript*; Burridge, *What Are the Gospels?*; Keener, *The Historical Jesus of the New Testament*.

31. Klausner, *Jesus of Nazareth*, 224.

The modern interest in ancient literature has caused a number of Jewish scholars[32] to examine this more closely as well. Martin Jaffee, for example, noticed that the very things that may seem perplexing to modern exegetes are, in fact, very much part of ancient norms. "The line between the authorial creator of a book, its scribal copyists, and its interpretive audience was a rather blurry one and was often crossed in ways no longer retrievable by literary criticism of the surviving texts."[33] The study of the resurrection of Jesus does not hinge upon whether the New Testament documents conform to modern standards, nor on whether all of the discrepancies can be adequately explained.[34] While some scholars cite the discrepancies as a reason to abort the study altogether, others are less concerned about such details. This is the case with two of the Jewish scholars who wrote entire books on the resurrection. Pinchas Lapide was well aware of textual variants in the Gospels. He understood the negative conclusions made by scholars, but he also saw beyond the traditional accusations.

> No wonder then that the evangelists' contradictory reports on the resurrection have not been able to convince the skeptics, that agnostics write off all narratives as fairy tales of the nursery, and that the purely historical result for sober scientists is extremely meager. However, legends can also be bearers of truths, which by no means deprive the kernel of the narrative of its historicity, as any scholar of religion will bear out.[35]

Specifically, he argued, the New Testament needs to be seen as Jewish literature. Lapide then compared the Gospels with the Tanakh, Midrashic literature and the Targums to illustrate his point. Whatever obstacles may be present, there exists a redeemable historical core. "Under all the multiple layers of narrative embellishments and the fiction of later generations," he wrote, "the Jewish New Testament scholar finds such traces of authentic Jewish experience."[36] The actual event of the resurrection is not in question for Lapide. In fact, he finds evidence of authenticity and spends the rest of his

---

32. Schiffman, *Text and Tradition*; Elman and Gershoni, *Transmitting Jewish Traditions*; Talmon, "Oral Traditions and Written Transmissions, or the Heard and Seen World in Judaism of the Second Temple Period."

33. Jaffee, *Torah in the Mouth*, 18–19.

34. Edersheim wrote: "For—to take the historical view of the question—even if every concession were made to negative criticism, sufficient would still be left in the Christian documents to establish a *consensus* of the earliest belief as to all the great facts of the Gospel-History, on which the preaching of the Apostles and the primitive Church have been historically based." Edersheim, *Life and Times*, xiv.

35. Lapide, *Resurrection of Jesus*, 93.

36. Ibid., 95.

book explaining why he believes it is the best explanation. Whatever parts may have been "embellished," the resurrection itself is, for him, not among them. For one thing, there was a casualness that belies tampering. Unlike apocryphal literature that accentuated the supernatural elements, the Gospels seem to go out of their way to make the resurrection a non-spectacular event: "Instead of an exciting Easter jubilation we here repeatedly of doubts, disbelief, hesitation, and such simple things as linen cloth and the napkins in the empty tomb . . . It sounds almost as if any jubilant outburst should be dampened, more covered than uncovered, and as if the truth of the event needed no emphasis."[37]

Geza Vermes also interacted with the textual issues in the Gospels. He too was well aware of the problems. At first, he offers the following statement.

> The uncertainties concern the sequence of events, the identity of the informants and witnesses, the number and location of the apparitions of Jesus, the presentation of prophecies relating to the resurrection and finally the date of Jesus' purported departure from earth. The discrepancies among the various accounts regarding both details and substance cannot have escaped the eyes of the attentive readers.[38]

One of Vermes' chief concerns is that each story "contains unique elements missing from the other Gospels."[39] This means that each author chose to incorporate specific material, some of which overlapped with the others and some did not. But, additional information does not in itself mean conflicting information. A more serious accusation is that there are "flat contradictions between the sources."[40] Here he includes the differing number of women who visited the tomb and the fact that the apostolic mission is conferred on the disciples in Jerusalem according to Mark, Luke and John. Matthew places this in the Galilee.[41] Vermes, however, ultimately acknowledges that quite a bit of the resurrection narratives are historical, in spite of questions about the details. In fact, some of the discrepancies themselves are used as evidence to this end. The differing number of witnesses at the tomb is one example. He writes: "Yet it is clearly an early tradition. If the empty tomb story had been manufactured by the primitive Church to demonstrate

---

37. Ibid., 100.

38. Vermes. *The Resurrection of Jesus*, 106.

39. Ibid., 107.

40. Ibid., 109.

41. Ibid., 111.

the reality of the resurrection of Jesus, one would have expected a uniform and foolproof account attributed to patently reliable witnesses."[42]

One of the most bizarre and difficult passages speaks of the tombs opening and the dead being raised (Matthew 27:52). This too might present an obstacle. But, Vermes sees this as symbolic, as "an anticipatory resurrection" which was meant to bring a "religious message" combining the individual resurrection of Jesus with the general resurrection of the dead.[43] What is important to see is that however one explains this scene, it does not affect the historicity of the resurrection of Jesus per se. In fact, it was not even mentioned in Lapide's study. Another controversial passage, also in Matthew, is the story of the guard at the tomb who was told to say that the Jews stole the body (Matt 27:62–66). This, too, has been called, "unlikely"[44] and "historically problematic"[45] at best. Legitimate questions may be raised about this passage, and cogent answers have been given.[46] In fact, some have used this as evidence in favor of the resurrection on the grounds that there would be no reason to invent such a story if the empty tomb was not commonly acknowledged.[47] Neither Vermes nor Lapide addressed this passage, presumably because neither thought it to be historically accurate. It raises questions relevant for Jewish-Christian relations, but it is a secondary issue in determining whether or not the tomb was empty in the first place.

The Book of Acts has also been the subject of overly critical analysis by both Jewish and Gentile scholars, yet it is nevertheless a valuable resource. One of the common accusations concerns the difference in the way Paul is described in Acts as compared with Paul's own letters. Samuel Sandmel said the two pictures are as different as "the Jew of the East European ghetto is to the American-born Jew."[48] Pamela Eisenbaum said that Acts' description of Paul "differs markedly" from the epistles. Specifically, she cites the frequently made accusation that Acts makes no mention of Paul's letters. But this, she continues, may be quite understandable for a few reasons. Namely, these works are written by two different authors, writing different genres, and for a different purpose.[49] Acts, she explains, conforms to ancient rather than modern standards of history. But, this does not mean it is irrel-

42. Ibid., 142.
43. Ibid., 92.
44. Gale, "Matthew, Introduction and Annotations," 54.
45. Setzer, *Jewish Responses to Early Christianity*, 40.
46. See Craig, "The Guard at the Tomb"; France, *The Gospel of Matthew*, 1091–95.
47. Wright, *The Resurrection of the Son of God*, 638.
48. Sandmel, *The Genius of Paul*, 16.
49. Eisenbaum, *Paul Was Not a Christian*, 12.

evant for study. "On the contrary," she writes, "Acts constitutes an undeniable part of the historical record that can be mined for information about the origins of Christianity generally, as well as some of its central figures like Paul, as long as it is used with awareness of its literary tendencies and particular bias. (This is true of ancient and modern accounts of events.)"[50] Paula Fredriksen also affirms the general historicity of the Book of Acts. She acknowledges that the new movement went quickly beyond Jerusalem and established congregations in Judea, Samaria and Galilee, Bethany in Judea, Lydda, Joppa, Caesarea, Damascus and Antioch. "Within just five years of Jesus' death," she writes, "evidence abounds of this new movement's wide and rapid dissemination."[51] She offers neither an explicit endorsement nor a critique of Acts, but her view of what happened corresponds with the canonical narrative.

Regarding discrepancies, most relevant for this study are the three accounts in Acts of Paul encountering the risen Jesus (Acts 9:3–8, 22:6–11, 26:12–18). They disagree on secondary details. Historians must decide what to do with this, and how relevant these details actually are. The event in question is a supernatural one, and specifically one with profound implications. Because of this, it is especially problematic to the modern exegete and raises some important questions. For a start, would these types of variations be considered as serious if they appeared in a different (non-supernatural) context? At least two of the scholars in this study commented on these passages. Segal is less concerned with the discrepancies, and he believes that Paul did have an experience which he (Paul) believed to be an encounter with the risen Jesus. Segal's interest in these passages was in the context of Paul's commissioning as an apostle (which appears only in the third account, Acts 26:15–18). Segal raises the following question: "Was the commissioning part of the vision itself . . . or did it come later, after Paul had learned more of the Christian message?"[52] His answer represents both an understanding of ancient historiography and the nuances needed in modern interpretations.

> Of course, Luke may be historically accurate on all three occasions, merely recounting what Paul actually said. But this imports to Luke a higher degree of accuracy than was expected of ancient historians. In fact, the conventions of ancient historiography called on historians to invent speeches appropriate to their characters. Possibly, having related the scene twice, Luke

50. Ibid., 15.

51. Fredriksen, *Jesus of Nazareth, King of the Jews*, 236.

52. Segal, *Paul the Convert*, 8.

intentionally shortens the third narration of the account. But, by relating it three times, Luke signals his interest in emphasizing and dramatizing Paul's conversion experience. It thus appears that Luke is trying to place Paul's mission as close to the conversion as possible.[53]

Michael Cook also briefly commented on these passages. He refers to the discrepancies as "inadvertent inconsistencies," which he explains is "exactly what often happens when stories are made up."[54] This should be compared with Vermes' comments (above) that such inconsistencies are better understood as evidence of authenticity rather than deliberate fraud. Cook completely discards the Book of Acts as a historical source, and he is less convinced that Paul had a profound mystical experience. He nevertheless affirms that Paul originally persecuted the followers of Jesus, that he was influenced by them in Damascus, and that for some reason he went on to promote the belief in the resurrection of Jesus. Even with the most skeptical reconstructions, then, the Book of Acts—like the Gospels—provides evidence for the resurrection that must be addressed.

[3.1.3] CORROBORATION

The historical-critical approach to the New Testament may yield challenges, but it also may provide corroboration. The criteria of verisimilitude, for example, may help to establish the authenticity of a given context. Archaeology has been particularly helpful in this regard. The book, *Jesus and Archaeology*,[55] includes both Jewish and Christian contributors who have shed light on the narrative through archaeology. Such evidence may not be able to prove the historicity of a specific event in the Gospels, but it is often helpful in dismissing the alternative theories. The criteria of embarrassment may also help authenticate aspects of the narrative. For example, those who claim that the early church fabricated the stories found in the Gospels need to explain why there are so many embarrassing details about their leaders (such as Peter's disbelief and denials). These two criteria will be addressed here in relation to the burial of Jesus and the empty tomb.

The story of Joseph of Arimathea appears in all four canonical Gospels, but has often been dismissed as a literary creation rather than an actual

53. Ibid., 8.
54. Cook, *Modern Jews Engage the New Testament*, 68.
55. Charlesworth, *Jesus and Archaeology*.

event.[56] Jodi Magness, professor of Archaeology at University of North Carolina, Chapel Hill, is an expert on burial traditions in Jerusalem in the late Second Temple Period. She concluded that despite popular cries to the contrary, the New Testament's presentation of Joseph of Arimathea and the burial of Jesus do not conflict with the archaeological evidence of the period. She explains that rock cut-tombs were owned by wealthier members of society, while the poor were buried in "simple individual trench graves dug into the ground." Ossuaries were used for the collected bones of earlier burials and belonged to families.[57] A point of debate has been whether victims of crucifixion would have been theoretically entitled to a proper burial in an ossuary. Some have categorically said no, since that type of death was considered a curse. This, of course, would create a challenge to the canonical picture presented in the Gospels. But, Magness argues that this was not the case. For one thing, Jesus was condemned for crimes against Rome, not Jewish law.[58] In the Tanakh, criminals could be hanged for the purpose of public display "only after they were already dead."[59] The Sanhedrin did exclude those who were executed for violating Jewish law from being buried in family tombs (*m. Sanh* 6:5). However, the Mishnah "attaches no stigma to crucifixion by the Roman authorities and does not prohibit victims of crucifixion from being buried with their families."[60]

Evidence for this was found in the discovery of the remains of a crucified man named Yochanon in an ossuary. But, this evidence has been used for both sides of the debate. Some scholars, notably Jon Dominic Crossan, thought the discovery of Yochanon's remains was an oddity. He argued that given the thousands of crucifixions that we know took place, finding evidence for only one who was buried in a family tomb was simply insufficient. Magness disagreed. In fact, she argued, "the exact opposite is the case."[61] The fact that there is any evidence at all is important, and she provides several reasons. First, there are no undisturbed tombs from that period that have been excavated by archaeologists. Second, those who did have rock cut tombs were the Jerusalem elite, those who sought to keep the status quo with the Romans. For this reason, relatively few of them would have undergone crucifixion. Most of the victims of crucifixion belonged to the lower

---

56. Cook wrote the most extensively about this among the authors in this study, see below 4.6.7

57. Magness, "Ossuaries and the Burial of Jesus and James," 121.

58. Ibid., 141.

59. Ibid., 142.

60. Ibid., 143.

61. Ibid., 144.

classes, those who would not have owned tombs. Third, after the Romans removed bodies from a cross, there was usually no evidence of the means of death. In the case of Yochanon, a nail in his heel bone demonstrated that he had been crucified. But, according to several scholars, there were factors that made this a fluke. The olive wood found on the tip of the nail had a knot that made it uniquely difficult to remove the nail. Normally, there would have been no such trace.[62]

Virtually all scholars agree that Jesus came from a family of modest means and could not afford a rock-cut tomb. If Joseph had not provided a tomb, Magness continues, Jesus likely would have been disposed of in the manner of the poorer classes: in an "individual trench grave dug into the ground."[63] Joseph, as described in the Gospels, would have had such a tomb. Also, the Gospel accounts include an accurate description of Jesus' body being wrapped in a linen shroud. She concludes: "This understanding of the Gospel accounts removes at least some of the grounds for arguments that Joseph of Arimathea was *not* a follower of Jesus, or that he was a completely fictional character (although, of course, it does not prove that Joseph existed or that this episode occurred)."[64]

Claudia Setzer is a professor of New Testament and also a contributor to the *JANT*.[65] In one article, she focused on the role of women—specifically Mary Magdalene—in the resurrection narratives. There are two overarching factors in her study: "Women's presence and testimony as witnesses to the empty tomb and Jesus' appearance after death seems an early and firmly entrenched piece of the tradition. Equally early and entrenched is the embarrassment around that fact."[66] The women's witness of the empty tomb is "indispensable" to the story.[67] Mary Magdalene was the first to discover the empty tomb, the first (in Matthew and John) to see the risen Jesus, and she also witnessed the death and burial. This is important for apologetics purposes, as it "provides a continuous witness to counter those who might argue that followers were confused about which tomb was Jesus.'"[68] The prominent role of the women could not be abandoned, even as the authors were attempting to "mute the women's role and discredit their witness."[69]

62. Ibid., 144–45
63. Ibid., 145.
64. Ibid., 148.
65. Setzer, "Jewish Responses to Believers in Jesus."
66. Setzer, "Excellent Women: Female Witnesses to the Resurrection," 259.
67. Ibid.
68. Ibid., 261.
69. Ibid., 264.

The "muting" was done in various ways. For example, Mark 15:41 specifically refers to the women as "habitual followers of Jesus." Matthew's account (Mt 27:55–56) changes the form of the verb, describing "the simple physical act of following at a certain point in time, thus diluting the sense of continuing discipleship."[70]

Even within each Gospel, Setzer sees a difference between the way the women are portrayed in the resurrection narratives and how they appear earlier in the same Gospel. Mark has a "relatively positive view of women's discipleship," although the women "do not shine" in the resurrection accounts. This is demonstrated in Mark 16:8, when they "flee in fear and astonishment." This is contrasted with the men, who forsake Jesus before his death, while the women do so after his death. Matthew, conversely, shows "indifference to the idea of women as disciples," however they "fare better" in his resurrection account than in Mark's.[71] Luke, Setzer writes, "is mixed in his depiction of women." They appear quite faithful throughout, yet "in spite of their faithfulness, Jesus does not appear to them as he does in Matthew."[72] John presents "the most dignified picture of women," although they are "never clearly identified as disciples."[73] These and other examples lead to her conclusion, that certain elements of the story were "deeply embedded at an early, even pre-Gospel stage, and later Gospel authors or the traditions they received were not entirely at ease with these elements, producing an uneven "fit.""[74]

The second part of the article addresses how the resurrection narratives were portrayed. Along with two passages from the New Testament, she includes sources from early Church history; the Gospel of Peter, Justin Martyr and Celsus. Over time, the role of the women was not only downplayed but in some cases specifically denied. In the Gospel of Peter, for example, the women refuse to look at the empty tomb, run away afraid, and only men are witnesses of the resurrection.[75] Justin does not mention the women (although he does not specifically deny their involvement). Celsus attributes to Jews an argument that denied the resurrection because the witness was "a hysterical female."[76] These later works provide more blatant examples of muting. However, they may be behind the "curious reserve about women's

70. Ibid.
71. Ibid., 266.
72. Ibid., 266–67.
73. Ibid., 268.
74. Ibid.
75. Ibid., 269.
76. Ibid., 270.

witness" in the New Testament as well.[77] The first example comes from Matthew 28:11–15, the rumor about the stolen body. While she believes the historicity of this event is "doubtful," it is "probable" that there would be a response to the claim of a resurrection. Setzer offers this commentary: "Matthew's response to the charge that the resurrection is fraudulent involves no stirring defense of the credibility of Mary Magdalene and the women, but simply puts the source of the rumor of fraud in the mouths of the Jewish leaders."[78] Matthew already described Mary Magdalene's important role earlier in the very same chapter (Matt 28:1–8). That it was not mentioned again in this pericope is not necessarily an example of muting the role of women. Setzer is not claiming that it definitely is, but is merely exploring the possibility based on the more overt examples in Church history.

Her second example comes from John 20:15 and raises the same question. Here, Mary mistakes Jesus for a gardener and learns that the tomb is empty (and that the gardener is Jesus). The disciples, she says, do not believe her report and only "rejoice to see him" when Jesus shows his hands and side.[79] This argument, however, ignores the fact that in the preceding verses Peter and "the other disciple" *did* believe Mary's claim and went to see the tomb. The fact that Thomas (and perhaps others) did not immediately come to faith based on Mary's testimony is also not necessarily a reflection on the gender of the messenger.[80]

But, whether or not these last two examples contain evidence of "muting" the role of women, Setzer's main point is that there was an element of embarrassment about their involvement in the early Church. Christian apologists have used this line of reasoning to argue that the empty tomb story is not likely a literary invention. It is sometimes stated that a woman's testimony was not permissible in court. Setzer questions the value of this specific argument, since the situation at hand was not a legal context. Also, citing Judith Romney Wegner, she states that "in later rabbinic law, women's witness was valid in some contexts."[81] The argument that a woman's testimony was not permissible in court seems to be a way of explaining that it was not highly regarded. Even if it was allowed in some cases (and it is difficult

---

77. Ibid., 271.

78. Ibid., 269.

79. Ibid., 270.

80. Levine writes, "[M]any commentators claim, incorrectly, that the men did not believe because they do not accept women's testimony; to the contrary, the Eleven do not believe because they do not expect Jesus to rise (see John 20.25)." Levine, "*Luke, Introduction and Annotations*," 149.

81. Ibid., 261.

to determine if this later rabbinic ruling existed in the time of Jesus), it was still an oddity and a source of embarrassment as Setzer demonstrated.

[3.2] JEWS AND JUDAISM IN THE NEW TESTAMENT

The New Testament documents, and specifically the Gospels, have often been labelled anti-Jewish. An important factor in this debate is determining the identity and worldview of the evangelists. Do they represent a Gentile Christianity that had completely separated from its Jewish origins, or were they still part of—or at least in the process of transitioning from –the Jewish roots of the movement? This, too, may have implications for the study of the resurrection of Jesus. An anti-Jewish reading of the texts usually corresponds with the belief that much of the narrative is fabricated. On the extreme end, some scholars have suggested that foundational New Testament beliefs such as Christology or the passion narratives were created based on the inherent anti-Jewish bias of the authors.[82] On the other hand, even if the basic narrative is not in question, an anti-Jewish tone would still be enough to dismiss the Gospels as having any "good news" for Jews (even if Jesus *did* rise from the dead). The views of Jewish scholars on this issue will be presented in this section, and they are divided into three groups.

[3.2.1] Intentionally anti-Jewish

The first full book on the subject from a Jewish perspective was written by Samuel Sandmel in 1958. He employed the latest scholarship of the day, and he should be applauded for his pioneering efforts. Overall, however, he saw the New Testament in a negative light. He offers little discussion about the possibility of alternative explanations that might read certain passages differently. For him, the New Testament is "a repository for hostility toward Jews and Judaism."[83] The question of anti-Semitism[84] in the Gospels, Sandmel says, depends largely on whether they are historically accurate. If the events really occurred, then the authors are merely passing along truth of an understandable inter-Jewish feud. It could then more easily be compared to similar strong language in the Tanakh.[85] But if the authors have fabricated

82. See Reuther, *Faith and Fratricide*; Crossan, *Who Killed Jesus? Exposing the Roots of Anti-Semitism*.

83. Sandmel, *Anti-Semitism in the New Testament?*, 160.

84. Technically, anti-Semitism is an anachronistic term, as it may be traced to nineteenth-century racial designations, but it is often used in this context.

85. Sandmel, *Anti-Semitism in the New Testament?*, xvii.

material to meet the needs of their present day circumstances, then there is a stronger case for anti-Semitism in the Gospels. Sandmel believes the latter. Much of his book is actually a summary of the New Testament books with an accompanying explanation of how each was assembled. Sandmel believed it is "not correct to exempt the New Testament from anti-Semitism and to allocate it to later periods of history," since "its expression is to be found in Christian Scripture for all to read."[86]

His discussion of the Gospels begins with Mark, the first one to be written. Not only does Mark show unbelieving Jews in a negative light, his treatment of the Jewish disciples is "scarcely less derogatory than that of Jews." For example, they are shown misunderstanding Jesus, falling asleep at important moments, and even denying him. The motive for this, Sandmel writes, is to affirm the Gentile communities to whom Mark was writing. If the Gospel message began with Jews, he asks, how could non-Jews "be assured of their authenticity?" This Gospel, then, was constructed for the very purpose of assuring Gentile members of the Church of their "full validity." He writes: "In normal controversies the assertion of one's own validity is followed by denigrating one's opponent."[87] Matthew's Gospel, he continues, "is a mixture of sublimity and astonishing animosity."[88] This is perhaps best exemplified by Matthew 27:25, where the crowd says, "His blood shall be on us and our children." This, he suggests, may be "the most glaring" example of New Testament anti-Jewish sentiment.[89] Luke's Gospel, along with Acts, is much more subtle. Luke's concern was to "win Jews and still portray recurrent malevolence."[90] The very actions of the Jewish people in Luke's Gospel are, according to Sandmel, "their own indictment."[91]

It is in the Gospel of John that the debate takes a radically different turn. The Synoptics focus on what Jesus did, whereas the question in John concerns who he is. Sandmel acknowledges that the term "the Jews" could refer to Judaeans, but it is mainly used to designate opponents of Jesus. In John, "the targets are the Jews of that later period when his Gospel was written (between A.D. 100–110) and of the unknown area in which he lived."[92] All the disciples are Jews as well. But, Sandmel explains that John's strategy helps minimize the reader's understanding of this. It is achieved by

86. Ibid., 143–44.
87. Ibid., 46–47.
88. Ibid., 68.
89. Ibid., 66.
90. Ibid., 73.
91. Ibid., 83.
92. Ibid., 101–2.

including two unique phenomena not found in the synoptics. First, John writes of Jews who were part of the Christian movement but have fallen away. Second, he also writes of Jews who wanted to enter but who were deterred because of expulsion from the synagogue. In the synoptics, he says, the disciples are clearly displayed as Jews. In John, "it is as if the new movement has few if any Jews within it, and therefore the Jews are outsiders and opponents."[93]

A student of Sandmel's, Rabbi Michael J. Cook, approached the subject about a quarter of a century later. He confronts the claim made by conservative Christian scholars that although later traditions definitely put an anti-Jewish spin on the events, the New Testament itself does not. Cook responds that the "pejorative description of Judaism in later Christian theology takes its cue directly from the New Testament itself."[94] He also evaluates each Gospel separately. Mark's Gospel is best understood in his portrayal of Jewish leaders. Since Jesus is "repeatedly" in controversy with chief priests, scribes, elders, Pharisees, Herodians and Sadducees, Mark gives the impression that Jesus "is over and against the Jewish leaders of his time." But, this is not all. The "masses" in the passion narratives call for the crucifixion. Therefore, "in Mark's view the Jews as a people (and not merely their leaders) reject and condemn Jesus."[95] According to Cook, Mark's view of Jewish leaders is actually a strategy to condemn Judaism itself. This is explained by noting that the scribes and Pharisees were the forerunners of the rabbis who, after 70 C.E., "fashioned the Judaism which emerged from the ashes of the Temple's destruction."[96] Mark was therefore writing in response to his own circumstances, promoting Christianity by denigrating the roots of its current rival.

Cook sees Matthew's attitude toward Jews likewise as "often one of denigration." Matthew, he believes, intended to "intensify" the words and tone of Mark's message.[97] This is seen, most notably, in the strong words against scribes and Pharisees in Matthew 23. Matthew is also the only one who records such events as Matthew 27:25 ("let his blood be on our children") and Matthew 28:12 (the chief priests bribing the guards). He then discusses Matthew 5:17. While many scholars see this passage as demonstrating a favorable disposition toward Judaism, Cook has a different understanding. This and other seemingly pro-Jewish passages are just as suspect as those that immediately seem to be negative (a theme he elaborates on in another

---

93. Ibid., 102.

94. Cook, "Anti-Judaism in the New Testament," 127.

95. Ibid., 130.

96. Ibid., 131.

97. Ibid.

article[98]). What appears to be Matthew's positive view of the Law of Moses is "but a function of his overall disparagement of Judaism." Matthew's entire purpose in the Sermon on the Mount is to "demonstrate the inadequacy of Mosaic law in comparison to the new law introduced by Jesus to supersede it."[99] The Gospel of Luke "preserves many of the anti-Jewish notices of the other evangelists."[100] For example, Cook identifies "denigration of the Jews" in the parable of the Samaritan (Luke 10:29–37), as well as the parables of the Great Supper (Luke 14:15–24) and that of the Publican and Pharisee (Luke 18:9–14). Yet, Luke's image of Judaism is "distinctly more favorable" than Mark or Matthew. This, however, is based on an ulterior motive. The seemingly positive factors are actually Luke's "overarching concern" to demonstrate that the early followers of Jesus were faithful to Judaism, and that therefore "Christianity is the true continuation of the heart of genuine Judaism." Accordingly, he continues, those Jews who have rejected Jesus are, by virtue of that rejection, "inauthentic Jews."[101]

John's Gospel is singled out as the most anti-Jewish of the four. This is due in large part to the term "the Jews" that appears frequently, and usually in a negative context. For Cook, this makes the presentation "all the more severe." The enemies of Jesus no longer seem to be only a segment of the Jewish people, he writes, "but rather the entire Jewish people."[102] Jesus and his followers are also described in a way that "makes the reader of John apt to forget that they are Jewish." As examples, Cook cites 13:33 and 8:17 (where Jesus speaks of "your law"). Finally, the situation in John is heightened by its bold theological claim. Jesus is "identified with God" in this Gospel (John 8:19 and 8:24 are cited), therefore, "John's indictment of the Jews suddenly becomes the very sentiment of God himself."[103] In a more recent work, Cook uses this same line of reasoning as the backdrop to several of his arguments against the resurrection of Jesus (see below, 4.6.7).

Other scholars at the end of the century shared this more extreme view.[104] But, since the advent of the "Third Quest" and the focus on the Jewish background of the New Testament and its world, scholars have been less likely to assume such an anti-Jewish bias on the part of the Gospel writers.

---

98. Cook, "Interpreting 'Pro-Jewish' Passages in Matthew."

99. Cook, "Anti-Judaism in the New Testament," 132.

100. Ibid.

101. Ibid., 133.

102. Ibid., 134.

103. Ibid.

104. Freudmann, *Anti-Semitism in the New Testament*.

By the turn of the century, most Jewish and Christian writers began to take a fresh look at the subject.

[3.2.2] A Neutral view

In a 1999 article, Amy-Jill Levine addressed the subject of anti-Judaism in the Gospel of Matthew. Her assessment is somewhat mixed, as she explains in her opening. She believes that "there is, on my reading, an anti-Jewish component to the First Gospel." On the other hand, she continues, "there is less anti-Judaism in Matthew's text than has sometimes been suggested."[105] She then surveys various approaches that scholars have taken when addressing this subject, in three main categories. These include: 1. *Prophetic anti-Judaism*, 2. *Jewish-Christian anti-Judaism* and 3. *Gentilizing anti-Judaism*. The first category equates Matthew's Gospel with the Jewish prophets of old and/or with the Qumranic literature. It is seen as an internal critique, which would imply a sort of in-house debate. But such comparisons, Levine says, are "compromised."[106] For one thing, "the quantity or popularity of a particular manner of discourse does not keep that discourse from being abusive."[107] In this category she states that a comparison between the Gospels and the Dead Sea Scrolls "falters" since the former "presupposes an audience outside of Judaism broadly defined."[108] Also, Jesus was sometimes condemned because of what he said. Since his audience "did not find the rhetoric tolerable," she continues, "why should those outside the Gospel?"[109]

The second category, *Jewish-Christian anti-Judaism*, is "one of sociology."[110] This argument says that the Jewish Christians of Matthew's community are promoting a different, better form of Judaism. The main problem with this, she says, is that there are too many unsettled issues. For example, "debate still exists as to whether Matthew is inside, outside, in between."[111] Matthew's community is also somewhat of a mystery regarding geography, demography and their relationship to the synagogue. "Arguments for evangelist's Jewishness," she writes, "are equally fuzzy."[112] She continues: "To proclaim that Matthew is "Jewish" thus produces an overly

---

105. Levine, "Anti-Judaism and the Gospel of Matthew," 9.

106. Ibid., 16.

107. Ibid.

108. Ibid., 17.

109. Ibid., 18.

110. Ibid., 18–19.

111. Ibid., 20.

112. Ibid., 21.

expansive definition of Judaism, since the descriptions would also fit Judaizers or the gentile heirs of an originally (ethnically) Jewish congregation. But
to proclaim Matthew as "non-Jewish" may produce an overly narrow one."[113]

The third category is *Gentile anti-Judaism*. This view says that "Jews
are rejected as a people and Judaism is rejected as a practice."[114] Here Levine
cites several passages from Matthew that have been used to make such a
case. As she demonstrates, these interpretations are not the only or the best
way to read these verses. Two prominent examples will be discussed here.
Matthew 23 contains some of the strongest and harshest language in the
New Testament. Levine makes a distinction between the Jewish leaders and
the Jewish people as a whole in Matthew 23. On one hand, she says, "scribes
and Pharisees" may indeed represent all Jews. But, "vilification of the leaders may not indicate vilification of the followers," since Matthew separates
the leaders from the people, Jerusalem from outside regions and "the center
from the periphery."[115] The other passage which has caused great difficulty is
Matthew 27:25, where "all the people" shout the words, "his blood be upon
us and our children." While she does not believe this account is historical,
she nevertheless argues against an anti-Jewish reading. She makes a distinction between "all the people" who speak before Pilate, and "the Jews" as
a community. Since Joseph of Arimathea, the women who followed Jesus,
and Peter "do not stop being Jewish," the phrase "all the people" must refer
to the people of Jerusalem.[116] In spite of this, Levine concludes ("with great
reluctance") by stating that the Gospel of Matthew is anti-Jewish. Even in
Matthew's own community, she writes, the Gospel would have "stirred up
hostility" toward any Jew who preferred traditional Judaism.[117]

Three years later, Levine wrote an article on the same subject and took
a much more agnostic stance. She concluded that "neither historical nor
literary nor any other critical method can resolve the question of whether
the synoptic Gospels and Acts were written with an anti-Jewish agenda and/
or whether they were read as anti-Jewish by their original audiences."[118] The
Gospels remain a mystery. They can be seen as anti-Jewish, and they can be
exonerated. But, the mixture of these documents with the later writers who
used them toward an undeniably anti-Semitic end is ever an issue: "The synoptic authors would, I believe, be appalled at what has been done to Jewish

113. Ibid., 22–23.
114. Ibid., 26.
115. Ibid., 32.
116. Ibid.
117. Ibid., 35–36.
118. Levine, "Matthew, Mark and Luke: Good News or Bad?," 97–98.

communities in Jesus' name for close to two millennia. Nevertheless, these texts do plant seeds that, with certain types of fertilizer, yield an anti-Jewish growth."[119]

Like Levine, Adele Reinhartz is a leading New Testament scholar perhaps best known as the editor of the *Journal of Biblical Literature*. She has written extensively about this topic. In one early article, she discussed the New Testament as a whole and her conclusion was somewhat mixed.[120] But, the focus of much of her studies has been the Gospel of John. We will focus here on the article she contributed to the book *Jesus, Judaism and Christian anti-Judaism*, which she also co-edited. It most succinctly and directly addresses the topic, and it includes the relevant information from her other works. She begins by acknowledging that harsh words and thoughts do exist in the Gospel of John. However, it is "not entirely negative about Jews and Judaism." In fact, "the Gospel of John is intimately tied to the Judaism of its time."[121]

Reinhartz views the Gospel of John on three narrative levels, or stories that are taking place simultaneously. These include the historical, the cosmological and the ecclesiological. The first category, the historical, refers to the actual events of the life of Jesus. She acknowledges that Jesus and most of the other characters are Jews who "participate fully in the Jewish world of early first-century Palestine." They live according to the Jewish calendar, particularly the Sabbath and the festivals, and their lives revolve around the synagogue and the Temple.[122] Even Jesus' "Christological identity," she writes, "is in large measure expressed in Jewish terms" as, for example, the disciples recognize him as the Messiah promised in scripture.[123] But, there are also limitations to this presentation: "The Jewish identities of Jesus and his followers are taken for granted. Yet, despite their obvious Jewishness, the label "Jew" is applied to Jesus only once (by the Samaritan woman, 4:9) and his followers and disciples never."[124]

---

119. Ibid., 97.

120. "While it is true that the main thrust of the Gospels in their explicit descriptions of Jesus and the relationship of Jewish groups to Jesus is negative, there is other information within the Gospel stories themselves that could be seen as an internal critique of that description." Reinhartz, "The New Testament and Anti-Judaism: A Literary-Critical Approach," 536.

121. Reinhartz, "The Gospel of John: How the "Jews" Became Part of the Plot," 99.

122. Ibid., 100.

123. Ibid., 102.

124. Ibid., 103.

There are passages where Jesus "explicitly dissociates himself from Judaism."[125] This is seen in statements such as 8:17 and 10:34 where he uses the expression "your law." Reinhartz documents the events that show the Jews as "opponents" to Jesus. These include persecuting Jesus for both healing on the Sabbath and for "calling God his own father." They also took up stones to throw at him in John 8:59 and 10:31.[126] The remainder of the examples she offers are actually individuals or specific groups within Judaism, rather than "the Jews" as a whole. She mentions the arrest that was called for by priests and Pharisees, the trials before Annas and Caiaphas, and the chief priests who shouted "crucify him." She concludes: "The Jews, or at least their authorities, are directly responsible for Jesus' death on the cross, despite the fact that it is Pilate who gave the final order for Jesus' crucifixion."[127]

The second narrative level, or tale, is the cosmological. This approach deals with theological issues such as the covenant and choseness. The Jewish people are in a covenant with God based on the Torah. In John 5:39 and 5:46 Jesus says that the Torah prophesied his coming and bears witness to his identity. Many did not believe this about him and this caused the debate. The essence of the controversy, Reinhartz writes, "concerns precisely the question of their different and mutually exclusive ways of understanding the covenantal relationship."[128] Regarding salvation, the cosmological story includes two groups. Those who believe in Jesus as the Messiah and receive salvation are said to be in the light. The other group, those who reject Jesus, are in darkness. These are universal categories, equally true of Jews or Gentiles. But, as Reinhartz notes, "the Gospel consistently and directly associates the negative pole with explicitly Jewish characters within the narrative."[129] This is seen most clearly in John 8:44, where the opponents ("the Jews") are called children of the devil. Reinhartz sees this problem at every level: "But the Gospel of John ascribes a villainous role to the Jews in its historical tale, associates them with the negative terms through the rhetoric of binary opposition in its Christological tale, and undermines Jewish covenantal identity in its cosmological tale."[130]

The third narrative level is the ecclesiological. This tale, she writes, is "not explicitly present in the Gospel narrative."[131] It needs to be recon-

125. Ibid., 101.
126. Ibid., 103.
127. Ibid., 104.
128. Ibid., 106.
129. Ibid., 105.
130. Ibid.
131. Ibid., 111.

structed by scholars. This refers to the relationship between the Johannine community and others at the time of the Gospel's writing—the late first century. The debates in the Gospel of John, many believe, are based more on that contemporary situation than in the life of Jesus. The puzzling usage of the term *ioudaioi* is discussed in this context. Reinhartz reiterates that the term is "almost never used to describe Jesus or his followers." The term may be used in a "neutral and descriptive" way, and can even be used positively (she cites John 4:22). But, in most cases it is used to "express a negative view of the Jews as a group, as the ones who reject Jesus, refuse to believe in him, and ultimately plot his death."[132] For Reinhartz, the negative examples outweigh and make void the neutral and positive usages.[133] Scholars continue to debate John's use of the word *ioudaioi*. Some have suggested it means "Jewish authorities" while others say it refers to a geographical identity. Reinhartz responds that both proposals "let the evangelist off a bit too easily." In the late first century, particularly in the diaspora (where John was probably written), "the term was used to denote both an ethnic-geographic identity and a religious identity that was not limited to Jews who lived in Judea or who were born of Judean parents."[134]

What, then, was the author's purpose in using the word *ioudaioi*? Reinhartz's answer is sympathetic, as she places "Johannine beliefs" within the Jewish world (although the Johannine community itself was in a process of transition). However later commentators misunderstood John's message, his own motives seem to represent an intra-Jewish debate (although she does not use this phrase). She writes: "Perhaps, given the proximity of Johannine belief to its Jewish roots, the evangelist needed to distinguish his own understanding of salvation and the covenant between humankind and the Divine very sharply from that of other forms of Judaism."[135]

Reinhartz and Levine have provided valuable insight into the question of Jews and Judaism in the New Testament. But, questions remain. A nuanced approach is needed and some issues may never quite be understood. This is relevant for biblical studies. The value for Jewish-Christian relations may or may not be as clear. For some, the very link between these texts and their later misuse is enough to quarantine them.[136]

---

132. Ibid., 112.

133. Ibid., 114.

134. Ibid., 113.

135. Ibid., 115.

136. Cohen wrote: "Nevertheless, no efforts to put John's negative portrayal of the Jews into its proper historical context can undo the intensity of the anti-Jewish message that it transmitted to posterity. Once he circulated his gospel, the evangelist surrendered control over its meaning to his readers, and they, interpreting the gospel as they

[3.2.3] In-house debate

Louis Feldman brings a unique perspective to the discussion. He was an orthodox Jew who taught Classics at Yeshiva University for over sixty years. In 1990, he published an article in *Moment* magazine called, "Is the New Testament Anti-Semitic?" It included the following observation:

> That the New Testament and quotations from it have been used by anti-Semites for anti-Semitic purposes cannot be doubted. But that is a different question from whether the New Testament is in fact and by intention anti-Semitic. That question requires us to look at the book—or rather, collection of books—itself, and not just as isolated quotations … My own examination of the New Testament has led me to the conclusion that, as a whole, it is not anti-Semitic.[137]

A few years later, the article appeared in a slightly modified form in a collection of his writings. Here, the New Testament is first compared with other ancient literature. The anti-Judaism that does exist in these documents, he says, is understandable. He sees it as both a defensive move responding to claims that Christianity was "no longer Jewish," and also an offensive strategy "in claiming that it, and not its parent, was the true Judaism." In fact, it was a "common phenomenon" for new movements "to show special hostility towards his or its parents and vice versa." Examples are then given from Tanakh, the Dead Sea Scrolls and even Josephus.[138]

Passages from the Gospels are cited to make his point. Matthew 27:25, where "all the people" take responsibility for the death of Jesus is not actually a condemnation of all Jews. Rather, it refers to the specific crowd that was present at the time.[139] The anti-Judaism in Mark is "hardly prominent."[140] Luke's presentation is slightly more mixed. On one hand, he replaces the word "crowd" with "the people" who demanded the crucifixion (Luke 23:13). In Acts 2:36 and 3:13 the people are seen to be responsible for his death.[141] However, Luke (through the words of Cleopas, Luke 24:20), singles out the chief priests and rulers as being responsible. Luke also "softens the impact" of the accusations since he reveals the Jewish multitude later felt

---

did over the course of many centuries, only sharpened its anti-Jewish implications." Cohen, *Christ Killers*, 35.

137. Feldman, "Is the New Testament Anti-Semitic?," 32.

138. Feldman, *Studies in Hellenistic Judaism*, 278–79.

139. Ibid., 279.

140. Ibid., 281.

141. Ibid.

remorse (Luke 23:27–31, 48). Likewise, Jesus asked for forgiveness for the crowd because they did not know what they were doing (Luke 23:34), and Stephen (Acts 7:60) also asks for mercy on behalf of the Jews as he was dying.[142] In Acts, Luke sometimes uses the term "Jews" negatively, although, he states, some Jews did respond favorably to Paul's message, and others were divided. There are also frequent references to the prophets who were persecuted by the Jews. But this, Feldman writes, "is a common motif in the Jewish pseudepigrapha and in the rabbinic literature."[143]

The Gospel of John has always been the most troublesome. Feldman quotes Kaufman Kohler, who called it "a Gospel of Christian love and Jew hatred."[144] Regarding John's frequent use of the term "the Jews," Feldman proposes a solution. Since John was presumably writing to Gentiles, the specific categories of Jews (mentioned in the Synoptics) would be "hard to follow" and a general term might have been more relevant. He also acknowledges the following about the Gospel of John: 1. The term ("the Jews") sometimes simply means Judaeans, 2. John 4:22 says that salvation is from the Jews (to which Feldman remarks, "Could there be any more pro-Jewish comment than this?"), 3. Jewish leaders gave Jesus an "appropriate" burial, 4. some of the harshest words are actually spoken to Jewish Christians, not those who "remain Jews" (John 8:30–31), 5. Jesus is clearly identified as a Jew (John 4:9), 6. the Jewish festivals play a more prominent role than in the Synoptics; 7. Roman involvement in his death is mentioned at the trial (John 11:48), 8. John uniquely mentions Roman guards who came to arrest Jesus (John 18:3); and 9. the Synoptics have the crowd against Jesus, whereas in John "only the chief priests and the officers are present in Pilate's proceedings."[145] Although his overall assessment is positive, he is nevertheless aware that there are problem passages. These must be "acknowledged and condemned," and they are a "distinct minority" within the entire New Testament.[146]

In a 2002 article, Paula Fredriksen documents the changes that occurred over the early centuries of Christianity. While certain ecclesiastical structures began after Constantine, the basic points of theology—including a high Christology—"seem already present in the Christian canon."[147] To

142. Ibid.

143. Ibid., 282.

144. Ibid.

145. Ibid., 283–85.

146. Ibid., 286.

147. Fredriksen, "The Birth of Christianity and the Origins of Christian Anti-Judaism," 9.

understand the dynamic of the New Testament, it is important to recognize contemporary Jewish views of both Gentiles and rival Jewish groups. For example, she writes, Gentiles were in a sense expected to worship foreign gods although it was hoped they would eventually turn to the one true god of the Jews. This hope is expressed in the *Alenu*. But, the way Jewish groups reacted to one another was something quite different. "Extremely tolerant of those outside the fold, Jews were rancorously, almost exuberantly, intolerant of variety within the fold. Battling with each other over the correct way to be Jewish was (one could say, is) a timeless Jewish activity, and at no time more so than in the late Second Temple period, precisely the lifetime of Jesus and of Paul."[148]

In this context, the harsh words against Pharisees and others expressed in the New Testament are "extremely normal."[149] The Gospels and the letters of Paul were written during the time when the movement "was still a type of Second Temple Judaism." Indeed, the strong polemical tone contained in the New Testament, Fredriksen writes, "is exactly the measure of their Jewishness."[150] As the movement spread, it soon arrived in places devoid of any Jewish understanding. Leaders such as Valentinus and Marcion in the second century began to read the New Testament documents through the lens of Greek philosophy. The likes of Justin Martyr, Tertullian, Irenaeus and Hippolytus furthered the understanding of the New Testament away from its Jewish context. "This was the Church," Fredriksen writes, "that, in 312 Constantine chose to patronize."[151] In the eyes of these Church Fathers, "Jesus had taught against Judaism. So had Paul."[152] This, and not the New Testament documents themselves, is the genesis of Christian anti-Judaism.[153]

Jewish New Testament scholars have been steadily uncovering, and to various degrees embracing, the Jewish Jesus. The debate over how the Gospels present Jews and Judaism will not end any time soon. More research is needed. But, in the last generation or two, the trend has been to see both the life of Jesus and the documentation of his life within a Jewish context. This

---

148. Ibid., 15.

149. Ibid., 16

150. Ibid., 18.

151. Ibid., 27.

152. Ibid., 27–28.

153. Segal agreed with this view: "The argument between Judaism and Christianity was at the beginning largely a family affair. After Christianity separated from Judaism, the polemical passages in the New Testament were read in an unhistorical way, as testimony of hatred between two separate religions, when they should have been read as strife between two sects of the same religion." Segal, *Rebecca's Children*, 144.

has also led to a new interest in examining the historicity of specific aspects of his life.

[3.3] MIRACLES

There have been various views about the supernatural throughout Jewish history. The Tanakh clearly affirms God's existence and His ability to inter-act with His creation.[154] The later rabbis developed a much more rational system of belief, but nevertheless continued to assume that God performed miracles.[155] The first challenge to this view came from Maimonides in the twelfth century. He wondered how God could create a fixed order and yet work within it. Scholars still debate what Maimonides actually believed on this topic.[156] Spinoza was the first to dogmatically deny the possibility of miracles, based on his pantheistic beliefs which stemmed from medieval kabbalah.[157] The dawn of modernity produced new avenues for skepticism and disbelief, a phenomenon which greatly increased in the shadow of the holocaust.[158] Contemporary Judaism includes a wide range of beliefs. Along with traditional views, there are discussions about the meaning and pos-sibility of miracles,[159] and even options to practice Judaism without a belief in God.[160]

The claim that Jesus was raised from the dead is both a supernatural claim and a historical one. For many scholars, both Jewish and Gentile, the worldview of naturalism is presumed from the start. This section will not attempt to prove the existence of God and/or miracles. Rather, it will focus

---

154. There were, however, some people who chose to live independently from God, which may be listed as a form of practical atheism. Psalm 14:1 says: "The fool says in his heart there is no God."

155. Guttman, "The Significance of Miracles for Talmudic Judaism"; Baumgarten, "Miracles and Halaka in Rabbinic Judaism."

156. Langerman, "Maimonides and Miracles: The Growth of (Dis)Belief;" Kasher, "Biblical Miracles and the Universality of Natural Laws: Maimonides' Three Modes of Interpretation."

157. Spinoza was more dogmatic than the skeptics he would influence a century later. One of his modern biographers said: "For Hume, a miracle is highly unlikely, to the point of incredibility, for Spinoza, 'a miracle, either contrary to nature or above nature, is mere absurdity." Nadler, *A Book Forged in Hell: Spinoza's Scandalous Treatise and the Bbirth of the Secular Age*, 91.

158. Rubenstein, *After Auschwitz: Radical Theology and Contemporary Judaism.*

159. See Cohn-Sherbok, *Divine Intervention and Miracles in Jewish Theology*; Ra-dowsky, "Miracles;" Zakovich, *The Concept of the Miracle in the Bible*; Isaacs, *Miracles: A Jewish Perspective.*

160. Wine, *Judaism beyond God;* Seid, *God-Optional Judaism.*

on some of the naturalistic arguments that have been used to dismiss the historical investigation of the resurrection of Jesus. There is nothing necessarily wrong with skeptical theories. In fact, they are often helpful to the discussion. But, such theories need to be held to the same level of scrutiny as the beliefs they are challenging.

[3.3.1] Evaluating Miracles

One of the assumptions of much critical scholarship is that there is a vast difference between the "historical Jesus" and the "Christ of faith." Because of this, the resurrection often falls outside the discussion of historical inquiry. It is seen solely as a matter for adherents of the faith, irrelevant for the historian. Alan F. Segal was adamant that the resurrection cannot be deduced from history. He says the event is "neither probable nor improbable; it is impossible to confirm historically." The reason for this is that it "is not part of the world of scientific verification." He continues: "Historians cannot, in fact, deal with miraculous appearances."[161] Segal is perhaps half right. Historians cannot provide the same type of evidence as a chemist examining DNA evidence. But, history does not work this way, whether examining a supernatural event or anything else (how many non-supernatural events in the ancient world are affirmed by science?).

Segal's assertion is dogmatic, but his reasoning is not necessarily compelling. First, he tries an analogy. "I am suggesting that trying to prove the resurrection historically is the same as trying to prove the Trinity historically or trying to prove Adam and Eve scientifically—a category mistake."[162] He is correct that the trinity cannot be approached historically. There is, however, historical evidence for the resurrection. Segal was not only aware of this evidence, he spent more time interacting with it than anyone else in this study. Second, he says that if the supernatural claims about Jesus are accepted, miracles in other traditions should be accepted as well. His quote and a fuller discussion of this objection will be given below (3.3.3). For now, the short answer is that not all claims are equal. Third, he argues that the resurrection cannot be approached objectively because it is based on a faith commitment. He says that it is "absolutely crucial that every one of those who believe in the physical resurrection of Jesus as historical fact is also a

---

161. Segal, "The Resurrection: Faith or History," 137. Ehrman used a similar line of reasoning (Ehrman, *The New Testament: A Historical Introduction to the Early Christian Writings*, 241). For a review and response to Ehrman's arguments, see Licona, *The Resurrection of Jesus*, 171–82.

162. Segal, "The Resurrection: Faith or History," 137.

believer in Christianity."[163] This is simply not true. Pinchas Lapide's book was published about twenty five years earlier. He examined the historical evidence and concluded that the best explanation of the data is that Jesus rose from the dead. Lapide, however, remained an Orthodox Jew. Whether or not one agrees with Lapide, his book affirms that there is evidence for the resurrection of Jesus which may be addressed objectively.

If a supernatural event can be investigated, the next question concerns how much evidence should be required. David Hume set the bar high in an attempt to discourage the discussion of miracles.[164] Astronomer Carl Sagan provided a more concise and memorable version of this. He said: "Extraordinary claims require extraordinary evidence." This statement has become proverbial among contemporary skeptics. But, as a formal hypothesis it is remarkably vague. It is first of all not clear what is meant by "extraordinary claims." This may refer to events which are rare, unique, unusual, unprecedented, or assumed to be false. It also needs to be asked what is meant by "extraordinary evidence," and whether the word "extraordinary" is meant to have the same value in each case. For example, does it mean that a rare event (such as winning the lottery) must have evidence which itself is rare? Or, does an event that seems counterintuitive need evidence that is counterintuitive? In this vein, does a supernatural event require supernatural evidence? Depending on the values given to each variable, the equation will have different results. Sagan's words are usually (if not exclusively) used in the context of evaluating miracles and the resurrection of Jesus in particular. Without clearly defined parameters, elevated demands for evidence are questionable from the start. Biologist Jerry Coyne briefly examined the resurrection in his book, *Faith vs Fact*. Building on Sagan's words, he wrote,

> The following (and admittedly contorted) scenario would give me tentative evidence for Christianity. Suppose that a bright light appeared in the heavens, and, supported by winged angels, a being clad in a white robe and sandals descended onto my campus from the sky, accompanied by a pack of apostles bearing the names given in the Bible. Loud heavenly music, with the blaring of trumpets, is heard everywhere. The robed being, who identifies himself as Jesus, repairs to the nearby university hospital and instantly heals many severely afflicted people, including amputees. After a while Jesus and his minions, supported by angels, ascend back into the sky with another chorus of music.

163. Ibid., 136.

164. Hume said that "no testimony is sufficient to establish a miracle, unless the testimony be of such a kind, that its falsehood would be more miraculous, than the fact which it endeavors to establish" (Hume, "Of Miracles," 87).

The heavens swiftly darken, there are flashes of lightening and peals of thunder, and in an instant the skies darken.[165]

Coyne's request does not end here. He goes on to demand, among other things, that all of this be documented on video. But, such requests do not only come from those who identify as atheists. Dan Cohn-Sherbok began his study of the resurrection by saying that he believes in God. He acknowledges that this belief makes the resurrection of Jesus "theoretically possible." Yet, he finds the idea "implausible because of the findings of contemporary science."[166] It is not clear what truth from contemporary science would challenge this, especially for someone who believes in God. His requests are curiously similar to Coyne's. "If Jesus appeared surrounded by hosts of angels trailing clouds of glory and announcing his messiahship for all to see, this would certainly be compelling." This would also need to be recorded and documented "on CNN and other forms of the world's media."[167] Both Coyne and Cohn-Sherbok claimed to base their requests on rationalistic principles. But, unless a mathematical equation is formulated, or a cogent philosophical argument with clearly defined terms is articulated, such requests seem to reveal more about the subjective presuppositions of each author than their commitment to rational inquiry.

The argument for the historicity of the resurrection of Jesus, as it appears in the most sober and exhaustive works,[168] is based on an inference to the best explanation of the commonly known facts. This may prove challenging in the discussion of the historical Jesus, as there is very little agreement on much of the data. But as will be demonstrated below in chapters 4 and 5, there are a few points surrounding the resurrection that form the core of the debate. These include the crucifixion, the disciples' belief in his resurrection, the empty tomb, and Paul's transformation from persecutor to proclaimer. Those who begin with an anti-supernatural bias will naturally assume that there must be a rational explanation that better fits the evidence.

There is no shortage of naysayers to the claim that Jesus rose from the dead. Critics have been attempting to find a plausible alternative for over two hundred years. Theories come and go. Reimarus, Strauss, the Jesus Seminar, and countless others[169] made a splash in their day but are no longer

165. Coyne, *Faith vs Fact*, 119.

166. Cohn-Sherbok, "The Resurrection of Jesus, a Jewish View," 196.

167. Ibid., 198.

168. Craig, *Assessing the New Testament Evidence for the Historicity of the Resurrection of Jesus*; Wright, *The Resurrection of the Son of God*; Habermas and Licona, *The Case for the Resurrection of Jesus*.

169. Some of the recent challengers include the following: Price, *The Empty Tomb:*

relevant in the world of New Testament scholarship, even amongst the most skeptical authors. Jewish scholars have also attempted to provide alternative theories (see 4.6), with the same results. This should at least provide a caution for those who may be quick to adopt the latest counter theory.

[3.3.2] Cognitive Dissonance

There is general agreement, even amongst the most skeptical scholars, that the original followers of Jesus actually believed they had seen and encountered the risen Jesus. One of the most common explanations for this is that there must have been some type of psychological experience. Interestingly, many commentators who begin by saying that very little can be known about the historical Jesus and his world go on to provide quite sophisticated psychological evaluations of his followers. One specific theory is an appeal to *cognitive dissonance*.

The first major attempt to address this academically was made by Leon Festinger and his colleagues in their 1956 book, *When Prophecy Fails*. Their thesis was that when certain groups have strongly held beliefs, evidence to the contrary ("disconfirmation") is not only irrelevant for them but that such evidence may cause the members to continue in their mistaken belief with more fervor. The combination of the reality of disconfirmation and their insistence to the contrary causes dissonance, which the authors define as follows: "Two opinions, or beliefs, or items of knowledge are *dissonant* with each other if they do not fit together—that is, if they are inconsistent, or if, considering only the particular two items, one does not follow from the other."[170] The authors argue that it may be less painful for some to accept the dissonance than to admit they were wrong. Rationalization also may reduce dissonance.

The first chapter gives several brief examples of their hypothesis. These include millennial groups which predicted the second coming of Jesus, such as the Montanists of the second century, the Anabaptists in the sixteenth century, and the Millerites of the mid nineteenth century. A slightly different example is the movement begun by Shabbetai Tzevi (*sic*) in the seventeenth century. He had claimed to be the Messiah, but in the end was captured by the Sultan and ultimately converted to Islam. There is evidence that each group continued their beliefs—with modifications—for a brief time in spite

---

Jesus beyond the Grave; and Komarnitsky, *Doubting Jesus' Resurrection: What Happened in the Black Box?*

170. Festinger, Riecken, and Schachter, *When Prophecy Fails*, 25.

of the disconfirmation.[171] The final group to be mentioned is the disciples of Jesus, although the authors say that this example is inconclusive because they were not sure if Jesus and his disciples understood that he would die.[172] The rest of the book focuses on a UFO cult that had predicted the date of an alien invasion (along with a great flood). They had received publicity in the media and at times had many visitors, but the core group was about fifteen people.[173] There was evidence of increased fervor in the first day or two after the expected event did not happen (thus validating the hypothesis), but the remaining group quickly dwindled and even the last few hold outs had disappeared within three weeks.[174]

The theory of cognitive dissidence has since been used more commonly as a way to explain the disciples' belief in the resurrection. Jerry Coyne employs this argument, citing the work of fellow skeptic Herman Philipse. The Kingdom of God was promised to the disciples, he writes, but "unexpectedly, Jesus was crucified, ending everyone's hope for glory."[175] This is compared to modern millennialist groups who, upon realizing that the expected date had come and gone, might simply say "We got the date wrong." In the case of Jesus, he continues, "the imminent arrival of God simply morphed into a promise of eternal life, a promise supported by pretending that their leader himself had been resurrected."[176] This theory "at least seems reasonable," he says, "since it is based on well-known features of human psychology."[177] The problem is that what may seem "reasonable" in one context may not fit in a different context. The response of the millennial group was both simple and very much within their worldview. The response of the followers of Jesus, however, was complex and unprecedented. It needs to be evaluated within its own context. Alan Segal wrote quite a bit about the intersection of Second Temple Judaism, the New Testament, and the social sciences. He was intrigued by some of Festinger's work, but ultimately knew that the question was much more complex. In 1990 he wrote,

> It is difficult to say whether the experience of Christ's crucifixion can be considered a disconfirmation at all. The Gospels record the disappointment of the small group of Jesus' disciples. But, most converts to Christianity entered a post-Easter church,

171. Ibid., 3–22.
172. Ibid., 23–25.
173. Ibid., 225.
174. Ibid., 231.
175. Coyne, *Faith vs Fact*, 123.
176. Ibid.
177. Ibid.

one that proclaimed *both* the crucifixion and the resurrection of Jesus. This kerygma was formulated out of an interaction of Jewish expectations, Jesus' personal history, the experience of the early church, and the early church's use of the Hebrew Bible to understand the Easter experience.[178]

In a later work[179] he returned to this question and offered a more in-depth treatment. He began with the assumption that the disciples did have some type of psychological experience. But this notion cannot completely account for the evidence. The earliest proclamation of the new movement was already promoting the resurrection of one, individual messiah. To modern ears this may seem like a quite natural connection. But, there was no precedence for this in Second Temple Judaism (see 3.4.2). The disciples' belief was neither a simple response to their situation, nor did it correspond to any contemporary school of thought. Segal writes: "Resurrection and ascension had already entered Jewish thought in the century previous to Jesus, as a reward for the righteous martyrs of the Maccabean wars. Thus, while Christianity represents a purely Jewish reaction to a tragic series of events in Jesus' life, the reaction was at the same time absolutely novel."[180] It is also novel that the movement did not simply discontinue. Festinger's examples all lasted a very short time, usually within a matter of weeks after disconfirmation. Other would-be messiahs of the first and second centuries (most notably, Simon Bar-Giora and Simon Bar-Kochba) died violently and immediately lost their followers.[181] But, this did not happen with Jesus. There is evidence that John the Baptist had a following after his death (Acts 19:2–7), but he was never identified as the messiah.

A more recent phenomenon has furthered the discussion of cognitive dissidence theory. Menachem Mendel Schneerson was the *Rebbe* of the ultra orthodox Chabad movement (also known as the Lubavitchers, a sect of Hassidic Jews). He had been rumored to be the messiah. He died in 1994 and some in the movement speculated that he would rise from the dead. Simon Dein is a British anthropologist who has studied the Chabad movement for over two decades, beginning with the final years of Schneerson's life. His book is called *Lubavitcher Messianism, What Really Happens When Prophecy Fails?* His chief addition to Festinger's work is the importance he places on ritual and experience in helping "bolster counterintuitive cognitions."[182]

---

178. Segal, *Paul the Convert*, 297.

179. Segal, *Life after Death*, 427–28.

180. Ibid., 426.

181. See the discussion in Wright, *The Resurrection of the Son of God*, 557–59.

182. Dein, *Lubavitcher Messianism*, ix.

Specifically, he studied Chabad members in Crown Heights, Brooklyn (the movement's headquarters) and Stamford Hill, London (the largest Hasidic community in Europe). Shortly after Schneerson's death the movement split into two camps known as the *messianists* and the *anti-messianists*. The former are comprised mainly of members who joined after Schneerson's death, while the latter are usually from traditional Chabad families.[183] Extreme messianists, Dein says, appear to be a small proportion of the organization.[184] In fact, "all of the major Chabad organizations" oppose the publicizing of messianic beliefs about Schneerson.[185] The opinions of individual Chabad members are more diverse. In Stamford Hill, "millennial fervor has all but abated" since his death.[186] In Crown Heights, there is a thriving community of followers who proclaim that he is the messiah who, in some way, continues to live. Dein quotes one such member who was originally from a non-observant home.

> I have no doubt that the rebbe is the *Moshiach*. He has all the credentials for this role. I do not believe that he is really dead. Yes, he was buried but how do we know that he is inside the coffin in the *Ohel*? We cannot use the term dead to refer to the Rebbe, not in the conventional sense. At present he is concealed. We cannot see him but he is still acting in the world. He is in fact even more powerful than before his "passing." There are still miracles. He knows our thoughts and feelings. The Rebbe says that the time of our redemption has arrived and I believe him. Can you think of a better candidate for *Moshiach*?[187]

There are some parallels with Christianity and Dein dedicates a chapter to the origins of the early church's beliefs. He acknowledges that resurrection was a Jewish belief at the time, but unfortunately does not differentiate between the general concept of a corporate resurrection (which did exist at the time) and the belief in the resurrection of one individual messiah (which was an anomaly). He writes: "According to cognitive dissonance theory it would have been impossible for the disciples to hold the cognition that Jesus had a special relationship to the coming of the kingdom along with the cognition that he was dead. For his disciples dissonance was not to be reduced by abandoning faith in Jesus. Instead, they were 'forced' to modify

183. Ibid., 111.
184. Ibid., 63.
185. Ibid., 67.
186. Ibid., 84.
187. Ibid., 109.

the cognition regarding his death. The belief in resurrection was the result."[188] But, whereas millennial groups (for example) simply modified their original belief because something expected did not happen, the disciples were transformed based on something they believed actually did happen. In addition, as Segal noticed, the earliest proclamation of the new movement was too sophisticated to be the result of psychological speculation.[189]

Dein applies the same theory to Chabad. At first they had grand expectations: "Shortly after the death of Rabbi Schneerson assertions of his imminent resurrection were commonplace. Lubavitchers held that the Rebbe would be resurrected with his body intact and not just as a soul."[190] The belief that he *would be* resurrected never materialized into a claim that he actually did rise from the dead. This is an important distinction between the two groups. Nevertheless, the beliefs of the Chabad messianists are also seen through the lens of cognitive dissonance: "They made two predictions that were empirically disconfirmed: that he would recover from his illness and that he would usher in the Redemption. In accordance with cognitive dissonance theory, proselytization increased in the movement and they appealed to a number of post hoc rationalizations to ally dissonance."[191] The basic belief that actually emerged among the messianists, Dein writes, is "that Rabbi Schneerson is alive, that he is Moshiah and that the Redemption has already arrived."[192] But, this was not exactly an ad hoc theory, it already existed in Hassidic thought. For example, there is the doctrine of *hiskashrus*. This is the notion that "a spiritual leader is even more powerful following his physical death."[193] Dein explains,

> The concept of *hiskashrus* is central to Lubavitcher doctrine. Central to the hiskashrus doctrine in Chabad is the elevation of the Rebbe to super-human dimensions. If this *tzadik* somehow possesses powers of holiness that transcend normal human limitations, then a *Hasid* who connects with him can share in, or benefit from those powers. According to this doctrine an Hasid [sic] should constantly think about his rebbe—even a rebbe who has already died—and, from those thoughts, he can be

---

188. Ibid., 127.
189. See Segal's further comments below in 3.4.2 and 4.5.3.
190. Ibid., 135.
191. Ibid., 139.
192. Ibid., 140.
193. Ibid., 25.

confident that this dead Rebbe can both guide him and assure that everything will be fine for him in the future.[194]

It is not clear that there are any beliefs that emerged among the messianists after Schneerson's death that did not already exist prior to his death. Dein mentions a previous rebbe who was hailed as messiah after his death, and Schneerson spoke of his predecessor (after the latter's death) as if he was still alive.[195] Cognitive dissonance theory may have some legitimate applications. But, in the case of both the disciples of Jesus and the Chabad messianists it is not necessarily a clear fit. The former proclaimed a message that something had actually happened to their leader, an event that was counterintuitive to existing beliefs about resurrection and the messiah. The latter began with expectations of a resurrection, but no concrete claim was ever made.

The Chabad messianists have lasted longer than the adherents of the millennial or UFO cults. But, this is because Chabad was already a well-established, international organization. The messianists are a fringe minority within this group. Most Chabad members do not (or no longer) believe in Schneerson's unique role as messiah. By contrast, the resurrection of Jesus is the defining event of the movement, both then and now. The two groups each attracted followers both before and after the death of their respective leader. In this they are similar to one another, and yet apparently different to all the other groups that are usually mentioned in cognitive dissidence studies. But, the early followers of Jesus also attracted at least one person who had been adamantly opposed to their belief. The Apostle Paul is the subject of much debate, but virtually all scholars acknowledge that he originally persecuted the disciples and that for some reason came to believe their message. The most vocal opponent of Chabad's messianism has been David Berger.[196] If the Chabad messianists are to be compared with the disciples of Jesus, Berger is their Saul of Tarsus. If, for some reason, Berger begins to claim that the resurrected Schneerson appeared to him, and that he now believes wholeheartedly that Schneerson is the messiah, this would make the comparison of the two groups much more equitable. It would be a reason to take Chabad's claims that much more seriously.

194. Ibid., 29–30.
195. Ibid., 39.
196. Berger, *The Rebbe, the Messiah, and the Scandal of Orthodox Indifference*.

[3.3.3] Comparative miracles

The Jewish approach to the resurrection of Jesus may also be influenced by how this claim compares with other supernatural claims. This may appear in three ways. First, most Jewish New Testament scholars are not Orthodox, and may already have quite critical views of the miracles within the texts they embrace as their own (for example, the account of the exodus). This would certainly influence their approach to the resurrection. "If our traditions have difficulty deciding how to define or evaluate the miraculous claims in our own faiths," Michael Kogan observed, "how then are we to evaluate the miracle stories of the other's narrative?"[197] Eugene Borowitz provided a helpful suggestion. He believed it is important to distinguish "traditionalist believers from liberals within a given faith" and that debate should be conducted "only with thinkers who operate on a similar level." In other words, a discussion of the resurrection in the Jewish-Christian debate must clarify the outlook of the specific participants. Many liberal Christians see the issue in basically the same way that agnostics would. They reject the event because "modern people do not think that way." Liberal Jews, he says, would therefore agree with arguments by liberal Christians, but disagree with traditional Christian views.[198] This does not mean that only those who believe in the possibility of miracles should study the resurrection. But, those approaching the issue should be clear about their own presuppositions from the start.

Second, Jewish scholars who do believe in a literal exodus may employ a different—in a sense opposite—argument from the one just stated. It is an argument that juxtaposes the exodus with the resurrection and it was used by Judah Halevi in his classic work, *The Kuzari*. This twelfth-century book promotes the rationalism and superiority of Judaism over and against that of Christianity and Islam. It is written in the form of a dialogue, as the main character, "rabbi," presents his case to the King of the Kuzars. The exodus, he relates, was experienced and witnessed by the entire community (over 600,000 people), which leads to its authentication and truthfulness. The same cannot be said about the other two faiths which are therefore shown to be inferior.[199] Moses Mendelssohn later adopted a version of this argument. Referring to the exodus, he wrote:

> The entire nation to whom the mission was directed saw the great divine manifestation with their own eyes and heard with their own ears how God had appointed Moses His emissary and

197. Kogan, *Opening the Covenant*, 185.

198. Borowitz, *Contemporary Christolgies*, 41.

199. Halevi, *The Kuzari*, 28–30.

interpreter. Therefore, the Israelites as a whole were ocular and aural witnesses to this prophet's divine calling and required no additional testimony or proof . . . The public giving of the law was thus the strongest proof of the mission of Moses, making impossible any doubt or uncertainty that miraculous deeds could not alleviate.[200]

David Klinghoffer put a more pointed and modern spin on this argument in his bestselling book, *Why the Jews rejected Jesus*. "If it was God's habit to seek mass witness to His greatest deeds, as the Sinai event suggests," he wrote, "then why not here with Jesus' resurrection?"[201] This position assumes that God always works within a certain pattern. If true, it would mean that the resurrection of Jesus falls outside of this pattern, and therefore is not a true miracle of God. Pinchas Lapide was aware of a version of this argument as well, but did not find it convincing. God often revealed Himself supernaturally to just one person or a limited few (Lapide cites Daniel 10:7). The relatively small audience of the resurrected Jesus is in keeping with the Biblical record. Faith is always a necessary ingredient and Jewish readers, he says, should understand this. He writes: "Thus the Eternal One appeared only to Abraham; Jacob is alone when he struggles with the angel of the Lord, nobody but Moses sees the burning bush, and Elijah—in complete loneliness—hears the voice of God neither in a great and strong wind which rent the mountains . . . nor in any earthquake . . . nor in the fire . . . but in a still small voice (1 Kings 19:11ff)."[202]

A third approach to the resurrection regarding comparative miracles was pioneered by David Hume. Jesus was not the only person in antiquity to be credited with miracles, and Hume argued that competing miracles cancel each other out.[203] Offshoots of this have been used by Jewish scholars as well. Montefiore said the following about the resurrection: "If all other miracles are ill-founded, it is probable that this one is ill founded too."[204]

200. Mendelssohn, Letter to Bonnet 9 February 1770, in *Writings on Judaism, Christianity and the Bible*, 255.

201. Klinghoffer, *Why the Jews Rejected Jesus*, 88.

202. Lapide, *The Resurrection of Jesus*, 120.

203. Hume famously wrote: "Every miracle, therefore, pretended to have been wrought in any of these religions (and all of them abound in miracles), as its direct scope is to establish the particular system to which it is attributed; so has it the same force, though more indirectly, to overthrow every other system. In destroying a rival system, it likewise destroys the credit of those miracles, on which that system is established; so that all the prodigies of different religions are to be regarded as contrary facts, and the evidence of these prodigies, whether weak or strong, as opposite to each other." Hume, "Of Miracles," 91.

204. Montefiore, *The Synoptic Gospels*, 384.

Paula Fredriksen is firmly convinced that the disciples believed that Jesus rose from the dead. But, in her studies, the possibility that what they believed is what actually happened is beyond consideration for her. She writes: "Treating supernatural claims as historical data is cheating, unless we are willing to honor all supernatural claims as historical."[205] Alan Segal said: "If so, why not believe not only all the miracles of the Old Testament, including the six day creation, as well as the miraculous giving of the Quran to Muhammad? If one, then all miracles are possible, since the reports all have credible witnesses."[206] Hume's argument has been challenged by conservative scholars arguing in favor of either the miracles of Jesus[207] or specifically his resurrection.[208] They relate that, first of all, cultures that believe in the supernatural have no trouble admitting supernatural occurrences in rival religious traditions. It is the source of the power that would be questioned, not the supernatural events themselves.[209] Jesus' opponents said his miracles were not from God (Matt 12:24), but they did not deny the events. Secondly, a comparison of the miracles themselves in type, quantity and attestation reveals that not all claims of the miraculous are equal. This second point has been noticed by Jewish scholars as well, although not in the context of validating the miracles of Jesus. Three examples will be given here.

Geza Vermes said Jesus belonged to a general group of wonder workers of the day: "His roles, that is to say, as healer of the physically ill, exerciser of the possessed, and dispenser of forgiveness to sinners, must be seen in the context to which they belong, namely charismatic Judaism."[210] Vermes compares Jesus, first, with Honi. This famous character was known both as Honi the Circle Drawer in the Talmud, and Onias the Righteous by Josephus. Honi lived in the period just prior to the Roman conquest of Jerusalem in 63 BCE, and he was famous for demanding that God cause rain to fall. Some rabbis thought his attitude was too presumptuous, while others attributed it to his special (father and son-like) relationship with God.[211]

Vermes' other example is more similar to Jesus. Hanina ben Dosa lived in the mid first century in Galilee, and is described in rabbinic tradition as a

205. Fredriksen, "What You See Is What You Get: Context and Content in Current Research on the Historical Jesus," 85.

206. Segal, "The Resurrection: Faith or History?," 136.

207. Twelftree, *Jesus the Miracle Worker*, 40–43, Keener, *Miracles*, 195–8.

208. Licona, *The Resurrection of Jesus*, 135–53.

209. Examples are found in the Tanakh (Exod 7:11–12), New Testament (Matt 24:24) and the Talmud (Gittin 57a)

210. Vermes, *Jesus Was a Jew*, 58.

211. Ibid., 70.

man of "extraordinary devotion and miraculous healing talents."[212] He was renowned for his ability to heal from a distance and announce an immediate cure. The most famous of such cases involved Gamliel's son.[213] Vermes compares this with Jesus' healing of the Centurion's servant. "It is of interest to note that both Hanina and Jesus are said to have sensed the efficacy of their cures—Hanina, by means of the fluency of his prayer, and Jesus, who normally came into bodily contact with the sick, by feeling that "power had gone out of him."[214] Vermes also discussed Jesus as a teacher, prophet, messiah and "the son of man." Jesus is unique within each category and unique again in that he is the only one who could even be included in all of these categories. In the book's concluding remarks Vermes writes, "The discovery of the resemblances between the work and words of Jesus and those of the Hasidim, Honi and Hanina ben Dosa, is however by no means intended to imply that he was simply one of them and nothing more . . . no objective and enlightened student of the Gospels can help but be struck by the incomparable superiority of Jesus."[215]

Alan J. Avery-Peck wrote an article on how later rabbinic commentators viewed the achievements of these charismatic miracle workers (apart from Jesus). On one hand, the rabbinic opinion was that prophecy had ended by their day. They proposed a different model of authority, "one that rejected the charismatic holy man as a model of community leadership."[216] Yet, the rabbis spoke about Honi and Hanina as men of great piety who did miracles. Tales about them appear in the Mishnah, Tosefta and the Babylonian Talmud. Avery-Peck then discusses the time frame in which this information was documented. Although he does not specifically compare this information with the claims made about Jesus, it is relevant to this discussion.

> The problem is that, even if the materials to be discussed represent what actually was said or done by those individuals, they were collected and redacted many years after those events by people who had their own theological and social agendas . . . Consequently, we must understand the stories reviewed here about charismatic holy men who lived at the turn of the millennia to reflect more about the attitudes and theologies of the third through the sixth centuries, when the documents in which

212. Ibid., 73.
213. Ibid., 75, citing *b. Ber.* 43b.
214. Ibid., 75
215. Ibid., 224.
216. Avery-Peck, "The Galilean Charismatic and Rabbinic Piety," 150.

they are contained were edited, than about these individuals and their own historical periods.[217]

One other scholar who compared Jesus to contemporary miracle workers is Michael Mach of Tel Aviv University. His article discusses the differences between miracle workers and magicians and he begins by saying that the Gospels present Jesus differently than the other miracle workers of the day. Jesus was self-sufficient, while the magicians of the ancient world usually had some type of external help. Mach writes: "(W)e find Jesus in some cases as exorcist and in others as healer, but not as calling for the help of demons. Only the Beelzebub controversy has it differently. But here the opponents claim that Jesus is helped by the demons or their leader. It is never his own claim."[218] Mach also compares the miracles of Jesus with the rabbinic material. Examples such as walking on water, feeding the masses and changing water to wine may have parallels with stories about some of the famous rabbis. But, the ultimate meaning and purpose of the Gospel stories leads in a different direction: "To some degree these stories remind us of rabbinical narratives about the sages—with the unmarked difference, that here we have a specific notion of Jesus at the center of events."[219]

Mach does not attempt to find the historical Jesus. In fact, his working assumption is that the Gospel authors created the information according to their own needs. But, his ultimate findings about what the texts communicate help the discussion about the uniqueness of the earliest picture of Jesus. "Whatever the historical Jesus did," he wrote, "the theological Jesus was the Son of God; he hardly needed to invoke other deities and demons for his healings and exorcisms."[220] These areas of uniqueness in content, attestation and scope do not prove that Jesus did miracles. But they do raise legitimate questions. The claim of the resurrection of Jesus appears in a unique context. Not only is it not "cheating" for historians to examine the resurrection, the data seems to require it.

[3.4] RESURRECTION

The issue of resurrection has been multifaceted in Jewish history, as have the discussions in modern scholarship.[221] The combination of historical beliefs

---

217. Ibid., 152.

218. Mach, "Jesus' Miracles in Context," 191.

219. Ibid., 199.

220. Ibid., 201.

221. For a survey of these views, see Gillman, *"The Death of Death: Resurrection and*

and contemporary worldviews provides a variety of reasons to deem the resurrection of Jesus irrelevant. Eugene Borowitz wrote the following.

> Jews can see that the story of Jesus' resurrection is told against the background of Pharasaic belief. Despite this our people has never had difficulty rejecting it. Our Bible is quite clear that the chief sign of the coming of the Messiah is a world of justice and peace. No prophet says the Messiah will die and then be resurrected as a sign to all humanity. Except for the small number of converts to Christianity, Jews in ancient times did not believe Jesus had actually been resurrected. Modern Jews, who believe in the immortality of the soul or in no afterlife at all, similarly reject the Christian claim.[222]

Several reasons are given to explain why the resurrection of Jesus may not be of interest to Jews, although these say little about whether or not the event actually happened. The comment that no prophet ever proclaimed a messiah who died and was resurrected will be addressed below (3.5.3). This section will first address the question of resurrection in the Tanakh. It will then examine the beliefs of the disciples and Paul concerning the resurrection of Jesus, based on the antecedents of both the Tanakh and the literature of Second Temple Judaism. Alan Segal's work features prominently here, as he is the only scholar from this study who has written extensively on these various topics.

[3.4.1] In the Tanakh

Any discussion about resurrection within either Judaism or Christianity must begin with the question of whether or not, or to what extent, the concept appears in the documents common to each group. Alan Segal and Jon Levenson each wrote extensively on resurrection in the Tanakh and arrived at different conclusions. Segal is more cautious, and even skeptical, about resurrection in ancient Israel. While he sometimes acknowledges possible hints of resurrection in the Tanakh, he ultimately saw "no concrete narrative of the afterlife" within its pages.[223] Levenson argues in favor of resurrection in the Tanakh. He wanted to show that the concept is not merely a "Christian innovation,"[224] nor that it originated as part of Second Temple Judaism.

Immortality in Jewish Thought;" Bronner, *Journey to heaven: Exploring Jewish Views of the Afterlife*; Raphael, *Jewish Views of the Afterlife*.

222. Borowitz, *Liberal Judaism*, 216.

223. Segal, *Life After Death*, 121.

224. Levenson, *The Resurrection and the Restoration of Israel*, ix.

Rather, it "developed slowly and unevenly over the preceding centuries."[225] The vocabulary of death and what may or may not follow is examined by Segal, who sees tension in the various usages.

> "True, *refa'* ("ghost") is logically a survival of the identity of the person. But to call *nefesh* an "intermediate state" is to assume that the ancient Israelites expected an amelioration in the after-life or an intermediate state before the prophetic "end of days." There is no ancient evidence for an intermediate state; how the dead were to participate in "The day of the Lord," which the prophets sometimes predicted, is not evident."[226]

The Hebrew word *nephesh* is often translated "soul," he continues, but it did not contain the same meaning in ancient Israel as it later would in regards to determining what part of a person, if any, continues on after death.[227] The difference in word usage between the modern and the ancient is telling: "We think we have a soul; the Hebrews thought they were a soul."[228] The concept of Sheol is discussed, and Segal sees tension in the various usages. He wonders if this represents evolution in the development of monotheism, or "an alternative poetic trope" which was used by those who wrote the Psalms and prophecy.[229] For Levenson, *sheol* is more of a mystery, as it is used in a variety of ways. It may be a place from which no one returns (Psalm 88), yet God is able to restore one from that very fate (Ps 40:2). Sheol is sometimes a "universal destination" that describes those who are no longer living. It is somewhat metaphorical in that it appears in Psalms and prophetic literature but never in narrative accounts of death or legal material describing capital punishment. Sheol, according to Levenson, ultimately describes "the struggle against the powerful and malignant forces that negate life and deprive it of meaning."[230]

Both authors also addressed the historical books. Segal allows for resurrection-like experiences among certain individuals in order for God to make a point. These do not prove that resurrection was commonly believed. The narratives of Elijah and Elisha contain three accounts of "revivications," which are not the same as resurrection. The difference is that those who are merely revived return to live their normal lives and will one day die. These events are recorded as miracles, and they are meant to show "the power of

---

225. Ibid., xii.
226. Segal, *Life after Death*, 143
227. Ibid.
228. Ibid., 144.
229. Ibid., 138.
230. Levenson, *The Resurrection and Restoration of Israel*, 72.

God over death and the extent of God's favor to the prophets."[231] The fate of Elijah and Enoch, on the other hand, may provide a closer parallel with resurrection. However, they are the exceptions. For Segal, they "prove the rule by violating it in such circumstances as to clarify that they are the only two exceptions."[232] Another exception he allows for is Saul's experience with the medium at Endor. Saul was surely sinning when he sought to contact Samuel. This was a violation of law, approaching the forbidden practices of the pagan nations (Deut 18:9–14). It was forbidden, but it was possible. According to the Scriptures, he writes, "the dead can be recalled."[233] Not only that, "the dead Samuel is still a prophet and knows the outcome of the forthcoming battle."[234] For Levenson, examples such as Elisha raising a boy from the dead (2 Kings 4) provide a foreshadowing. The event is of limited scope, he agrees, and the child would again die. But, it revealed that "long before the apocalyptic framework came into existence, the resurrection of the dead was thought possible."[235]

The two authors view the poetic literature differently as well. The Book of Job, Segal argues, is clear evidence that resurrection was unknown. If there was such a thing, then Job would have had no case against God, since the final score would be settled at a later date.[236] Job 19:25, often used as evidence *for* an afterlife, is dismissed: "the text has been garbled, and we cannot tell exactly what Job intended to say."[237] Before moving on to the later prophets, Segal poses the following question: "Could it really be that God spent so much time giving His prophets messages of antagonism to the notion of Canaanite afterlife only to reverse Himself later on? Changes in the concept of the afterlife over time argue against taking it literally."[238] The book of Qohelet (Ecclesiastes) continues along the same lines as Job. According to Segal, the author "goes beyond pessimism and agnosticism about the life after death."[239]

Levenson examines the poetic imagery. The most common metaphor to explain the opposite of Sheol is that of the Temple. In many places, references to the Temple include the concept of life and even immortality (he

231. Segal, *Life after Death*, 145.

232. Ibid., 154.

233. Ibid., 126.

234. Ibid., 130.

235. Levenson, *The Death and Resurrection of Israel*, 132.

236. Segal, *Life after Death*, 147.

237. Ibid., 151.

238. Ibid., 170.

239. Ibid., 254.

cites Psalm 15; 133 and Ezek 47:1–12). In Jonah's prayer, his cry from the pit of Sheol (Jonah 2:3) is directed to God, who by contrast was in His Temple (Jonah 2:7). Levenson summarizes the Tanakh's description of the Temple as a place of care, purity, justice, security and eternity and more.[240] Nevertheless, death comes even to those who find refuge in the Temple.[241] What does live on, according to the Tanakh, is one's name and family lineage. This is important to Levenson's overall argument, as resurrection will ultimately be a corporate event regarding the house of Israel. Both the Temple and the concept of continuing lineage help point the reader to something beyond the here and now. They are more than symbols, he writes, "they are the means by which certain types of continuation despite death can be acquired."[242] Both concepts come together in Psalm 128.

It is with the prophets that clear resurrection language begins to emerge. Evidence of an afterlife appears in Ezekiel 37, the vision of the dry bones coming to life. Segal acknowledges that "no passage in the Hebrew Bible appears to be more a discussion of bodily resurrection." Yet, he sees "no evidence" that this passage is actually speaking of resurrection. Rather, he believes it uses that metaphor to proclaim national regeneration, and it speaks of the present not the future.[243] Likewise, he acknowledges that the language in Isaiah chapters 24–27 (and specifically 26:19) sounds like resurrection, but it is "not likely to be meant literally."[244] He concludes, "However, even if both these passages are taken as references to literal resurrection, they hardly affect the general tenor of Israelite religion, which emphasized life on this earth and behavior in this world . . . . But these two passages are absolutely crucial for understanding whence the language of resurrection comes."[245] The one undeniable reference to resurrection is Daniel 12:1–3. Segal sees antecedents to this passage from Ezekiel 37, Isaiah 26:19, and Isaiah 66. It is the combination of these texts, contemporary historical events, and a "dream or vision" that caused Daniel to write these words.[246] Daniel 12 therefore promises resurrection to at least some of Israel. Special rewards will also be given to martyrs, and some scholars, Segal says, see parallels between Isaiah 53 with Daniel's words about those who "make others wise."

240. Levenson, *The Death and Resurrection of Israel*, 94.
241. Ibid., 98.
242. Ibid., 122.
243. Segal, *Life after Death*, 256.
244. Ibid., 258.
245. Ibid., 261.
246. Ibid., 264.

But, Segal was not convinced that the righteous sufferer (of Isaiah 53) was a martyr, or that his death is specifically described in this passage.[247]

In Levenson's view, Jeremiah and Isaiah promised a new beginning after the exile. The dead nation will live again and hope will be renewed. "In a word," he writes, "they prophecy life in place of death."[248] This reversal of death "anticipates" the end-times resurrection of later Jewish history.[249] Ezekiel 37:14 is an example of resurrection which is "decoded" as a prediction of coming historical events.[250] Levenson rejects the common idea that Ezekiel was borrowing from Zoroastrianism. Rather, Ezekiel's words were a type of "prophetic sign act" and they more closely anticipate the later view of resurrection than the words of Isaiah.[251] It is a corporate resurrection for the people of Israel. Like Segal, Levenson recognizes that Daniel 12:1–3 is "rich in intertextual resonance."[252] The difference is that Levenson also thought the earlier prophets that are being alluded to were thinking about resurrection. Isaiah chapters 25 and 26 (like the Ezekiel passage mentioned above) are sometimes taken metaphorically as a renewal of national Israel. But, Levenson argues, if they did not believe in a literal resurrection, their choice of it as a metaphor was "highly inappropriate and self-defeating." More importantly, Daniel did not interpret it in that way.[253] Another antecedent for this passage is Isaiah's prophecy of the servant in Isaiah 53. While Segal was not convinced that Daniel was alluding to the servant, nor that the servant passage includes a description of his death, Levenson had a different perspective: "It is evident that the vision in Daniel identifies the righteous of its own time of persecution with the servant of that text and sees the language of healing and restoration after death as references to resurrection."[254]

Overall, resurrection is not a dominant issue in Tanakh. Exactly where hints may be found is a matter of debate. But, there are enough clues, metaphors and even "exceptions" to make the case that there was some type of belief in resurrection in ancient Israel.[255] The Reform movement in the early nineteenth century famously abandoned resurrection in favor of transmi-

---

247. Ibid., 266.

248. Levenson, *The Death and Resurrection of Israel*, 149.

249. Ibid 155.

250. Ibid., 157.

251. Ibid., 159.

252. Ibid., 201.

253. Ibid., 214.

254. Ibid., 213.

255. Archaeology also helps affirm this position. See Friedman and Overton, "Death and Afterlife: The Biblical Silence."

gration of the soul. This was a departure from the texts which was motivated by other factors. These included modernity,[256] and perhaps even an attempt to distance the resurrection of Jesus from the Jewish discussion.[257] Yet, the passages on resurrection in the Tanakh need to be interpreted. They are perhaps best seen as pieces of a greater whole, something to be unfolded at a later date. The New Testament offers an interpretation. Whatever else one may believe about the New Testament texts, it is clear that on every page there is a quote, paraphrase or allusion to the Tanakh. This was the main background information, along with contemporary literature, that affected the original belief that Jesus had risen from the dead. How and why this belief emerged out of such a background will be discussed immediately below.

[3.4.2] The Disciples and the Resurrection of Jesus

The original disciples were devastated by the crucifixion. Soon afterwards they had a dramatic change of heart and began to proclaim that they had seen and encountered the risen Jesus. Most scholars accept this much. What needs to be explained is how and why this particular belief emerged. The most common response, as will be seen repeatedly in Chapter 4, is an appeal to psychological explanations. But, these are usually far too simplistic and dismissive.[258] A discussion of the origin of the disciples' belief must include the historical context, and the extant literature. This means both the Tanakh and the vast writings of the Second Temple period. The former was discussed above and contains clues of the afterlife. The literature of Second Temple Judaism expanded on the Tankh's limited interest in resurrection and produced a variety of new paradigms about life after death. These may be seen in apocryphal and pseudpigraphal works, Philo, and the Dead Sea Scrolls. The literature is quite extensive.[259] There are views about martyrs, enthronement, physical resurrection, the immortality of the soul, and reward and punishment.[260] What is commonly agreed upon is that the

---

256. See Petuchowsky, "'Immortality—Yes, Resurrection—No!' 19th Century Judaism Struggles with a Traditional Belief"; Batnitzky, "From Resurrection to Immortality: Theological and Political Implications in Modern Jewish Thought."

257. Levenson wrote: "In the context of Jewish-Christian disputation, the denial of resurrection can therefore be a patent weapon in the armamentarium of the Jewish disputants." Levenson, *Resurrection and the Restoration of Israel*, 2.

258. See the discussion above on cognitive dissonance.

259. The most comprehensive single volume collection of articles about life after death in this period is Neusner, Avery-Peck, and Chilton, eds., *Judaism in Late Antiquity*, vol. 3. See also Segal, *Life after Death*, 248–350.

260. For a concise overview, see Himmelfarb, "Afterlife and Resurrection," 549–51.

disciples' belief did not fit easily or naturally with any of the existing para-digms. Amy-Jill Levine writes: "The problem was not the claim that Jesus had been raised; the problem was the claim that he *alone* had been raised. Although many expected the messiah would bring about a resurrection, a single resurrection did not prove messianic identity."[261]

The more Jesus' resurrection is seen as contrary to contemporary be-liefs, the more difficult it becomes to explain why it was accepted both by his original followers and Jews who joined the movement after the crucifix-ion. Vermes recognized this as well. Resurrection was one option regarding man's survival after death in the contemporary literature, he wrote, although this was mainly important to those who were "eschatologically motivated." The New Testament, he continues, "altered the vista and changed the per-spective" by focusing on the one individual resurrection of Jesus. He further notices that this event is said to have happened in time and space, and it began a movement that "two thousand years on is still flourishing and num-bers among its adherents a substantial portion of mankind." The Gospels also claim that Jesus repeatedly prepared his disciples for his resurrection, yet it hit them suddenly like a "bolt out of the blue." He writes: "The situa-tion is profoundly perplexing and the historian must come to grips with this puzzle."[262] One scholar who attempted to solve this puzzle was Alan Segal. His basic belief about the situation is as follows.

> Jesus' earliest disciples saw a moral and apocalyptic victory in "the Easter event." They interpreted it not just as a sign that Jesus had been resurrected from the dead but had ascended to heaven to sit next to God, inaugurating the final consummation of his-tory. The earliest Christians experienced the continued presence of Jesus in their lives, not in some attenuated form but exactly in the form of resurrected Messiah, angel of the Lord, the Son of Man (all at once) who was enthroned next to God.[263]

Segal's view of how this belief unfolded will be discussed more fully below (4.5.3). But, in short, he believed that the "visionary appearances" of the disciples began on the Sunday immediately following the crucifix-ion. The relationship between the event itself (of the resurrection) and the existing literature raises a question usually associated with the proverbial chicken and egg: *which came first?* Did the disciples come to believe in the event based on a combination of psychological factors and various "proof texts," or did they believe in the event first and use the texts to make sense

261. Levine, *The Misunderstood Jew*, 61.

262. Vermes, *The Resurrection*, 65–66.

263. Segal, *Life after Death*, 389.

of what they believed had happened? Segal begins his discussion assuming the former. There was no existing view about resurrection that provided a simple antecedent to their belief. So, creative exegesis is necessary. To make his case, Segal proposes an ingenious combination of verses from Tanakh and contemporary sources. He cites Daniel 7:9–14 and Daniel 12, along with Psalms 8 and 110 as the likely verses which, added to extra biblical sources about the role of martyrdom, "produced the kerygma of the Early Church."[264]

But, it must be remembered that Segal's vantage point was quite different than that of the disciples. He had studied this phenomenon for not just years, but decades. He was a trained historian. He had the advantage of having all of the texts from the period at his disposal to be analyzed, as well as the trials and errors of contemporary scholars who have commented on this. The disciples, by contrast, were fisherman. It is not clear which passages from the Tanakh shaped their worldview about resurrection, or how familiar they were with contemporary literature (did they even know of the Qumran community or of 2 Maccabees?). Even if they *were* aware of these texts, it is difficult to imagine that they had the time or the theological sophistication to produce such a nuanced position as the one that emerged. They were also in a crisis, their world was shattered by the death of their leader. If there was some type of psychological dissonance at play, it needs to be explained within the context of these historical factors. In the end, Segal acknowledges that the combination of psychological factors and the existing views of the afterlife is not adequate to explain the origins of the disciples' belief in the resurrection of Jesus. He writes: "It must have come from the historical experience of the events of Jesus' life, not the other way around. The early Christian community, after experiencing these events, found the Scriptures that explained the meaning of these events."[265]

[3.4.3] Paul's View of Resurrection

Paul's belief about resurrection is complex. One of the key issues of debate concerns the type of body that is to be resurrected. The exact nature of this new body has been the subject of much discussion in the early and medieval church[266] as well as with modern commentators. But, the more general question is whether it is to be a physical or non-physical body that is raised from the dead. If Paul meant the latter, that would negate the view of the Gospels

264. Ibid., 428.
265. Ibid.
266. See Bynum, *The Resurrection of the Body in Western Christianity 200–1336.*

(which were written later and proclaim a physical resurrection). Segal's view is unique, as he places Paul in a thoroughly Jewish context. He writes: "Paul's understanding of the end of time is apocalyptic. He imminently expects the end. His grasp of the resurrection is firmly mystical but in the Jewish tradition, not the Greek one. He describes his spiritual experiences in terms appropriate to a Jewish apocalyptic-mystagogue of the first century."[267]

According to Segal, Paul's understanding of the resurrection of Jesus stems first and foremost from his own experiences. He was not a convert to Christianity. Rather, his transition was from a "sophisticated and educated form of Judaism to a new, apocalyptic form of it."[268] Key among Paul's experiences is his claim in 2 Corinthians 12:1–5 that he (described in the third person) went up to heaven. In time, Paul's experiences were modified and filled with new meaning, as "Paul learned his Christianity from the community in Damascus."[269] Yet this community, too, was already influenced to some extent by Jewish apocalyptic thought. What actually happened to Paul is explained through a humanistic lens and seen as a psychological/religious experience.

> Modern science balks at the notion of physical transport to heaven, except in spaceships, whereas a heavenly journey in vision or trance is credible and understandable ... When a heavenly journey is described literally, the cause may be literary convention or the belief of the voyager; but when reconstructing the actual experience, only one type can pass modern standards of credibility.[270]

Segal wonders how such a journey could take place in Paul's mind without the Greek concept of a soul. He deduces that the body of the one who ascends and the body of the resurrected Christ must be the same. To prove this he brings in 1 Corinthians 15:44, where Paul speaks of a "spiritual body."[271] Segal will come back to this later in the chapter but it is stated here as the premise to make his current point. Segal then attempts to uncover a textual antecedent for Paul's theology of the afterlife. Along with other possibilities (Ezekiel 1, 1 Enoch, Merkaba Mysticism), the best and most precise evidence comes from Dead Sea Scrolls document 4QMA. Segal

267. Segal, *Life after Death*, 402.

268. Ibid., 401.

269. Ibid., 409.

270. Ibid., 411. This comment is misguided. Science by definition deals with the physical world, but whether or not there is something beyond the physical world is a question that goes beyond the realm of science.

271. Ibid., 412.

writes: "Along with the Angelic Liturgy this is now persuasive evidence that the mystics at the Dead Sea understood themselves to be one company with the angels, whom they call the *b'nei elohim*, which they must have achieved through some Sabbath rite of translation and transmutation."[272] Segal interacts with an impressive amount of information from apocryphal works and the Dead Sea Scrolls. His argument rests on parallels to these works in Paul's writings about his own spiritual experiences. He admits, however, that the evidence is highly speculative, both from Paul and the alleged parallel traditions. The information from 2 Corinthians 12 is "abstruse and esoteric" while our knowledge of ancient mysticism is "meager."[273]

Segal next explores the issue of transformation. Paul often expresses the plight of followers of Jesus as changed into the image of Jesus (Romans 8:29, 2 Cor 3:18). This is especially true when discussing the eternal state (Phil 3:20–21). Most commentators would agree that Paul is speaking of a radical change that takes place in the body at the resurrection. But, what exactly is the nature of this change? Segal offers the following.

> All of this suggests that the body of believers would be re-fashioned into the glorious body of Christ, a process which starts with conversion and faith but ends in the parousia, the shortly-expected culmination of history when Christ returns. It all depends on a notion of the body that is a new spiritualized substance, a new body which is not flesh and blood, which cannot inherit the kingdom (1 Cor 15:42–50).[274]

Once again, Segal has assumed a certain interpretation based on 1 Corinthians 15 to make his case. This is the keystone to most of his points. It gives strength to arguments that he admits are not quite solid. But, it is only at the end of the chapter that he addresses this crucial passage. This is the topic we will turn to now. In 1 Corinthians 15:37–50, Paul discusses the type of body that is resurrected. In 1 Corinthians 15:44 Paul uses an agricultural metaphor. The body that dies is sown a "natural body" (*soma psychikon*), while a body that is raised is a "spiritual body" (*soma pneumatikon*). These phrases, he says, do not go together in classic Platonism. Segal unpacks their meaning by appealing to Paul's worldview and Paul's own personal experiences. Ultimately, Paul was "trying to characterize his apocalyptic vision in a Hellenistic context." He writes,

272. Ibid., 414.
273. Ibid., 408.
274. Ibid., 420.

For Paul, life in its most basic sense, psychic life, was also bodily life. "Pneumatic," spiritual life is bodily as well, though Paul immediately reiterated that flesh and blood cannot inherit the kingdom of God (1 Cor 15:50). The psychic body is the ordinary body (flesh and soul); the *soma pneumatikon* is the ordinary body subsumed and transformed by the spirit.[275]

Immediately following this, Segal states his point definitively: "The body of the resurrection will not be flesh and blood."[276] This will also be his main defense in a later article which specifically addresses the historicity of the resurrection (see below, 4.5.3). Segal's approach to this subject is elaborate and intriguing. His more creative arguments are admittedly uncertain, and his final conclusion is based on two verses (1 Cor 15:44 and 50) that are never adequately explained. In the end he does little more than take their presumed face value in the English translation. He does not exegete these terms in comparison with Paul's greater argument in the same chapter, nor does he interact with what other scholars have said. The argument that Paul did not believe Jesus was raised physically is employed by others in this study as well.

Michael Cook wrote: "Since 'flesh and blood cannot inherit the kingdom of God' (1 Cor 15:50), the faithful instead would gain a new body that is essentially a transformation of the physical substance to a spiritual substance (if we can speak in such terms together, i.e., 'spiritual' and 'substance')."[277] Paula Fredrickson wrote the following: "Paul, whose testimony is late (some twenty years after these events) and admittedly secondhand ("I delivered to you as of first importance what I also received"), teaches that the Risen Christ appeared in a *pneumatikon soma*, "a spiritual body." Whatever this might be, Paul insists that this body was *not* flesh and blood."[278]

Many scholars who have analyzed Paul's words in their context have concluded that they do not argue against Paul's belief in a physical body.[279] This is not only the conclusion of committed Christians who may have a vested interest in this position. Jewish scholars have recognized this as well. As for the first verse (vere 44), Shira Lander and others have recognized[280]

275. Ibid., 430.

276. Ibid.

277. Cook, *Modern Jews Engage the New Testament*, 156.

278. Fredricksen, *Jesus of Nazareth, King of the Jews*, 262; emphasis in the original.

279. See Fee, *The First Epistle to the Corinthians*, 775–809; Gundry, "The Essential Physicality of Jesus' Resurrection according to the New Testament"; Wright, *The Resurrection of the Son of God*, 312–60.

280. Lander, "1 Corinthians, Introduction and Annotations," 312.

that the two words (*pneumatikon* and *psychikon*) are also juxtaposed earlier by Paul in the same later (1 Cor 2:14). In chapter 15 these terms are translated (in the NRSV, which is used by the *JANT*) as "natural" and "spiritual." The English word "spiritual" may be used as the opposite of physical, and this is part of the problem. But, in 2:14 the same terms are translated "unspiritual" and "spiritual." A comment on the latter passage must include a discussion of the former one. Lander comments on the earlier passage: "*Unspiritual* ("psychichos," breath-formed, or merely a living being) vs *spiritual* ("pneumatikos" or spirit formed; see 15.45 on the "first man, Adam . . . and the last Adam")."[281]

Others have commented on this as well. Vermes wrote: "As a Jew, Paul could not conceive of resurrection without envisaging some kind of body, but combining his Jewish legacy with the Hellenistic ideas of his readers, he insisted that the body would be totally different from the one that died. The risen body would be imperishable, glorious and powerful, bearing not the mortal Adam, but that of the glorious Christ."[282] Jon D. Levenson (along with co-author Kevin Madigan), wrote the following:

> In 1 Corinthians 15, Paul puts forward a defense of the resurrection of the body that derives from Jewish apocalyptic literature . . . Indeed, the very use of the image of "seeding" suggests organic growth and development; the plant is different from the seed, yet the former grows out of the latter, owing to the surpassing power of their divine creator. The body that is sown is a physical body, "it is raised," to be sure, "a spiritual body" (1 Corinthians 15:44). Nonetheless it is a body. We are not dealing here with the immortality or transmigration of the soul or anything else of that sort.[283]

The second phrase in question is 1 Corinthians 15:50, where Paul says that "flesh and blood" cannot inherit the kingdom of God. Lander noticed that this was "a common postbiblical term for the human body."[284] Paul's meaning, however, needs to take into consideration the context of the rest of the chapter. Along with the passage just discussed (about the meaning of "spiritual body"), the second half of verse 50 provides a clue as to its meaning. After saying that flesh and blood cannot inherit the kingdom, he continues: "nor can the perishable inherit the imperishable." This seems to

---

281. Ibid.; ellipsis points in the original

282. Vermes, *The Resurrection*, 127.

283. Madigan and Levenson, *Resurrection: The Power of God for Christians and Jews*, 41.

284. Lander, "1 Corinthians, Introduction and Annotations," 313.

be basic parallelism, where the second clause is defining the first clause,[285] and these terms as well do not need to imply physicality.

Claudia Setzer studied Jewish and early Christian views of the resurrection of the body. One of her objectives was to determine how such beliefs were used as boundary markers. The importance of this lies in the "peculiar utility of resurrection as a symbol in the construction of community."[286] Regarding 1 Corinthians 15:50, she does not see the necessity for a body-soul dichotomy that is sometimes espoused. She writes: ""Flesh and blood" then stands for a certain kind of bodily life that will not inherit the kingdom, but not a rejection of bodily resurrection."[287] She does not attempt to explain how or why Paul came to believe in the resurrection of Jesus. His reasons for including these passages in 1 Corinthians, she argues, had to do with overturning the "imperialistic bent" of the current political rule. Paul was trying to "replace the old pyramid of patronage" with "the crucified Jesus whom God raises in power."[288] The event itself, however, was undeniably physical: "Paul could not have been clearer that only those who believe in resurrection of the body have truly understood Jesus' resurrection."[289]

[3.5] MESSIAH

The concept of the Messiah also has a long history in Jewish tradition. The Tanakh does not specifically use the label *"the* messiah,"[290] but it nevertheless describes the concepts that later commentators would use in this discussion. Views of the messiah are quite diverse in both the Second Temple period[291] and in rabbinic and medieval literature.[292] Modern Jewish views have tended to downplay the attributes which may appear similar to the New Testament's claims about Jesus. Because of this, Jewish scholars have been less compelled to explore the question of his resurrection. Dan Cohn-Sherbok wrote: "For twenty centuries, however, Jews have steadfastly rejected the New Testament accounts of his survival after crucifixion. No doubt this was largely due to the Jewish unwillingness to grant Jesus Messianic

285. See Wright, *The Resurrection of The Son of God*, 359.

286. Setzer, *Resurrection of the Body in Early Judaism and Christianity*, 4.

287. Ibid., 64.

288. Ibid., 66.

289. Ibid., 67.

290. However, Dan 9:26 does speak about *an* anointed one.

291. Schiffman, "The Concept of Messiah in Second Temple and Rabbinic Literature."

292. Patai, *The Messiah Texts*.

status. After all, Jesus did not fulfill the traditional role of the Messiah."[293] Jewish scholarship of the last decade or two has been challenging some of the most deeply held beliefs about the identity of the messiah. Three of these will be discussed here.

[3.5.1] Pagan Messiah

The most basic characteristic of the Messiah is that he must be a Jew. In this respect, virtually all scholars would agree that Jesus fits the bill. Only those who have a perverse disposition to say otherwise would disagree.[294] But, whether or not the New Testament's portrayal of Jesus fits into a Jewish framework is a completely different question. A popular argument says that Paul created Christianity by adding pagan elements to the original Jewish message of Jesus. Jewish scholars picked up on this view as well, as seen in the pioneering work of Graetz and others who will be discussed below. This understanding allowed scholars to accept Jesus as a Jew, while keeping Paul and "Christianity" at a distance. Paul's Jewishness was often considered suspect at best. This reached its apex in the writings of Hyam Maccoby in the 1980s. According to him, Paul not only borrowed from paganism, he was thoroughly immersed in it. The title of Maccoby's most provocative book leaves no question as to his perspective: *The Mythmaker, Paul and the invention of Christianity*. Whereas Jesus was a Pharisaic rabbi, he argues, Paul was something altogether different.[295]

Maccoby relies heavily on the fourth-century writer Epiphanius, who cited the Ebionites as saying that "Paul had no Pharisaic background or training."[296] Maccoby continues down this road and make an even stronger case. Paul's theology, specifically about atonement, was borrowed from both Gnosticism and the mystery religions.[297] These would be intermingled with verses from traditional Jewish scripture. Paul's letters are used to validate this claim. "There is nothing in Paul's writing to prove that he was a Pharisee," he writes, "and much to prove that he was not."[298] Paul's very identity is questioned as well. Again following the Ebionites, Paul was a convert to Judaism, took the name Saul, and "invented" his genealogy of being from

293. Cohn-Sherbok, "The Resurrection of Jesus: A Jewish View," 191.

294. The Nazis obviously could not have a Jewish Jesus and went to great lengths to promote their own version of Jesus. See Heschel, *The Aryan Jesus*.

295. Maccoby, *The Mythmaker*, 15.

296. Ibid., 17.

297. Ibid., 16.

298. Ibid., 71.

the tribe of Benjamin. This was a "sheer bluff," which gentle converts would not be able to confirm or deny. Paul's parents were actually Gentiles who never fully converted to Judaism.[299] They were God-fearers, and because of this Paul did have some instruction in Judaism when he was young. Later in life he attempted to live as a Pharisee. He failed at this, becoming only "a member of the High Priest's band of armed thugs."[300] This biographical information is the key to understanding Paul's metamorphosis. Paul's Damascus experience, then, is "psychologically and socially understandable"[301] when these facts are recognized. Paul's experiences, both religious and psychological, would shape his theology. This is especially true of his view of the resurrection of Jesus. He wrote: "In his vivid imagination, the sacred history of the Hebrew Bible (in its Greek translation, the Septuagint) with its heroes and prophets jostles with memories of the sacred procession of the mystery god Baal-Taraz, the dying and resurrected deity who gave Tarsus its name."[302] It is not surprising that Christian scholars found this theory difficult to embrace. John T. Pawlikowski thought it had too much conjecture and too little evidence supporting it. "His rather psychological description of the Damascus-road conversion sounds as though Maccoby was a personal confidant of Paul," he wrote. "Thus, this volume cannot be accepted as a serious scholarly contribution."[303] Jewish scholars were critical as well. Ellis Rivkin wrote the following:

> But Maccoby's evidence is hard to take seriously. It rests on an account of Paul by a fourth-century chronicler, Parhanius, who drew his portrait of Paul from a hostile Ebionite source— a source which Maccoby, himself, admits is wholly unreliable. To sweep away Paul's own impassioned listing of his Pharisaic bona-fides in favor of a fourth-century disfigurement is thus to fly in the face of sound critical scholarship and simple common sense.[304]

In his next book, *Paul and Hellenism*, Maccoby continues where he left off. All of Paul's theology is given pagan origins. The death of Jesus as a means of salvation, for example, was prefigured in the stories about Dionysus, Osiris, Adonis, Attis, and Orpheus.[305] His main point was to show

299. Ibid., 96.
300. Ibid., 99.
301. Ibid., 95.
302. Ibid., 100.
303. Pawlikowski, "Review of *The Mythmaker*," 1041.
304. Rivkin, "Review of The Mythmaker," 226.
305. Maccoby, *Paul and Hellenism*, 65.

how antithetical all of this is to true Judaism. But, this line of reasoning was already waning even amongst critical scholars by the time Maccoby wrote. Amy-Jill Levine thought his views were too one sided. She acknowledged the possibility of some pagan influence in Paul's writing. Contemporary Jewish texts offer the "building blocks" for some of these ideas as well. "Moreover," she continues, "that Jews would have accepted Jesus as their Messiah, suggests that such Christological claims were not entirely alien to their world view."[306] Alan Segal's response was more direct.

> It is difficult to show that any mystery religion directly worshipping a dying and reviving God, whose death is salvific, predates Christianity. We have few texts that can be identified as using mystery vocabulary . . . It is clear that Maccoby concentrates on this long abandoned aspect of Pauline research to further his polemic against Christianity.[307]

The pagan Paul was becoming an increasingly anachronistic figure in the wider arena of New Testament scholarship. Contemporary Pauline scholarship makes a point of placing him in the context of Second Temple Judaism. Books by E. P. Sanders and James Dunn[308] are credited with pioneering this wave. What emerged is known as *The New Perspective on Paul*. It presents a radically new paradigm that has branched out in several directions. The recognition of his Jewishness has been an important step for scholarship all around, although some of the key nuances have been greatly challenged.[309] The specifically Jewish scholarship on Paul has been diverse as well. In the last twenty years, there has been a new understanding and appreciation of his Jewishness. At the same time, accusations about pagan origins remain. Both views are represented, but there does seem to be a pattern. Those who are doing groundbreaking and extensive scholarly work on Paul's theology (Segal, Boyarin, Nanos and Eisenbaum) have been concluding that it can only be understood in a thoroughly Jewish context. Conversely, those who maintain belief in pagan influences for Paul are usually writing more overtly polemical and popular works, where Maccoby remains the authority.

David Klinghoffer is one example of this latter category. He first notices the verses that affirm Paul's Jewishness (Acts 22:3, Phil 3:5–6) and wonders

306. Levine, "Review of *Paul and Hellenism*," 231.

307. Segal, "Review of Paul and Hellenism," 143.

308. Sanders, *Paul and Palestinian Judaism*; and Dunn, *The New Perspective on Paul*.

309. See Carson, *Justification and Variegated Nomism*; Gathercole, *Where is Boasting? Early Jewish Soteriology and Paul's Response in Romans 1–5*.

why Paul felt the need to be so insistent. He writes: "What does this Pharisee of Pharisees, this Hebrew of Hebrews, feel he needs to prove, and why?"[310] In the following pages, Klinghoffer questions Paul's upbringing in Tarsus, his ancestral connection to the tribe of Benjamin and his ability to read Hebrew.[311] Paul's theology is also exposed as non-Jewish. Klinghoffer makes reference to Epiphanius, the one who documented the Ebionites' view that Paul was not Jewish. The footnote[312] cites Maccoby's book *The Mythmaker* as the source. Klinghoffer continues, saying that no one ever doubted Jesus' Jewishness, but the Epiphanius passage indicates that Jews who observed the commandments (meaning the Ebionites) "found something suspect about Paul's Jewishness."[313]

Shmuley Boteach's bestselling book, *Kosher Jesus*, continues in the same vein. His view of Jesus is "profoundly shaped" by Maccoby,[314] whose name is frequently cited. For example: "It is even possible, as Hyam Maccoby maintains, that Paul was not born Jewish but converted."[315] Boteach has sections on the miracles of Jesus and even the claim that Jesus raised others from the dead, but nothing on the resurrection of Jesus. His discussion of Paul's life and theology is also devoid of any comment about the resurrection of Jesus. It is alluded to once in the book, in a paraphrase of Christian theology. After three days in a tomb, he writes, Jesus "ascended to heaven to take his place as the second part of the Christian godhead."[316]

The Jewish reclamation of Paul is a work in progress. In the popular imagination, his writings are more likely to be labeled pagan than Jewish. This makes it easy to dismiss the resurrection as borrowed mythology, rather than a potential historical event that may be analyzed. But, among scholars, such notions are largely a thing of the past.[317] Those who choose to defend the pagan view can no longer accept it as a given. It must be either defended in light of recent scholarship or abandoned.

310. Klinghoffer, *Why the Jews Rejected Jesus*, 95.

311. Ibid., 96.

312. Ibid., 231n73.

313. Ibid., 115.

314. Boteach, *Kosher Jesus*, xi.

315. Ibid., 117.

316. Ibid., 153.

317. One exception is Cook, see below 4.6.7.

[3.5.2] Divine Messiah

The most definitive theological point of tension between Judaism and Christianity is the incarnation and the related concept of the trinity. The claim that Jesus is both human and divine is, for many, a deal-breaker in the attempt to harmonize the two traditions. It is on one hand a theological issue. Based on the pre-eminence of the *Shema* (Deuteronomy 6:4), any perceived threat to monotheism is the most serious of all charges. Jewish atheists, by definition, do not agree with monotheism and are nevertheless considered part of the fold. Jews who accept Jesus are usually not considered part of the Jewish community, even though Jesus specifically said the *Shema* was the greatest commandment (Mark 12:28–29). This is clearly more than a theological issue, it is a boundary marker.[318] Yet, recent studies have brought unexpected light to this discussion as well. A number of Christian scholars have examined the boundaries of monotheism in the first century in an attempt to better understand the New Testament's claims.[319] Jewish scholars have also addressed this issue, usually in the context of Jewish-Christian relations.[320] But some have attempted to find a place for the concept of incarnation within Judaism.[321] The work of three scholars will be addressed here.

Michael Wyschogrod has studied the incarnation more than most other Jewish scholars.[322] He approached it as a modern Orthodox Jew and as a participant in Jewish-Christian dialogue. His main theological grid concerns God's election and indwelling with Israel. This covers virtually all areas of his theology, as seen in his classic work *The Body of Faith*.[323] The article that will be surveyed here specifically addresses the incarnation and its potential relevance for Judaism.

Because of the other factors of the Jewish-Christian debate, Judaism "has never really investigated this issue soberly."[324] Wyschogrod boldly seeks

---

318. This topic will be discussed further below. See 5.2.

319. See Hengel, *The Son of God*; Newman et al., *The Jewish Roots of Christological Monotheism*; Hurtado, *Lord Jesus Christ*; Bauckham, *Jesus and the God of Israel*.

320. See Katz, *Christology: A Jewish View*; Neusner, *The Incarnation of God*; Redman, "One God"; Goshen-Gottstein, "Judaism and Incarnational Theologies"; Wolfson, "Judaism and Incarnation."

321. For a profound example of this within the world of Hassidic Judaism, see Magid, *Hassidism Incarnate: Hassidism, Christianity, and the Construction of Modern Judaism*.

322. See Wyschogrod, "Christology: The Immovable Object;" and Wyschogrod, "Incarnation."

323. Wyschogrod, *The Body of Faith*.

324. Wyschogrod, "A Jewish Perspective on Incarnation," 198.

to evaluate the incarnation on its own terms and not through the lens of "two thousand years of tragic history."[325] He begins by stating that Jewish hostility to Jesus began over the issues of Messiahship and the Law. On top of these already thorny issues, the divinity of Jesus changed the debate dramatically, elevating it over the years from "reservations" to "absolute rift."[326] He cites two common Jewish responses to the divinity of Jesus. The first is biblical, and includes the problem of idolatry. This is subdivided into two parts. Idolatry may take the form of serving other gods. This means spiritual beings that had supernatural power, although inferior to the One true God of Abraham. Idolatry may also appear in what Wyschogrod terms the "sticks and stones" dimension. This refers to attributing divinity to material objects such as the golden calves.[327]

The second response is philosophical. This brings the discussion to Maimonides, who was particularly weary of assigning any corporeal attributes to God. It is because God is absolute that Maimonides strongly rejected the idea of corporeal attributes. He did notice a number of examples in the Tanakh that present the corporeal attributes of God, but these he believed should not be interpreted literally. In fact, he said that those who attribute corporeality to God are heretics. In contradiction to this, Wyschogrod affirms that the Bible does assign corporeal attributes to God. As examples, he refers to passages where God dwells in the Tabernacle, and later in the Temple and Jerusalem.[328] The God of Israel is therefore both transcendent and active in our world. Such a belief helps bridge the gap between Judaism and Christianity, at least in terms of possibilities. Wyschogrod does not rule out Christianity's claim of incarnation. It is not something that can be negated by Biblical or logical principles.

> If we can determine a priori that God could not appear in the form of a man or, to put it in more Docetistic terms, that there could never be a being who is both fully God and fully human, then we are substituting a philosophical scheme for the sovereignty of God. No Biblically oriented, responsible Jewish theologian can accept such a substitution of an ontological structure for the God of Abraham, Isaac and Jacob whose actions humanity cannot predict and whose actions are not subject to an over-reaching logical necessity to which they must conform.[329]

325. Ibid.
326. Ibid., 199.
327. Ibid., 200.
328. Ibid., 203.
329. Ibid., 204.

This understanding, Wyschogrod realizes, may appear to have "diminished" the differences between Judaism and Christianity. But, this is not necessarily the case. He continues: "The fact remains that Judaism did not encounter Jesus either as the Messiah or as God and therefore a difference remains about what God did do even if not about what God could have done."[330] Having said this, the reader might expect a discussion of what actually happened, or whether or not an incarnation, which could happen, actually did happen in the person of Jesus. But, Wyschogrod does not enter that discussion. Instead, he focuses on the Jewish rejection of Jesus. He is viewing the issue through the lens of ecclesiology. Jews and Gentiles interpret things differently. The "Gentile Christianity" that became the dominant, and then only, branch of the church, he writes, had neglected a prominent aspect of theology, namely the election of Israel. Wyschogrod acknowledges that Paul spoke of this in Romans 9–11, and that Jesus originally preached to his own Jewish people. He argues that "Jesus must not be separated from the Jewish people because he did not wish to separate himself from them."[331]

He then proposes that Christian theology must rethink its view of the Jewish people. Traditionally, the Church has held two basic views on this topic. The dominant one has been supercessionism, which says that the Church is the new Israel. The other view is based on Romans 9–11 and says that Israel has not lost its national election. Wyschogrod argues that this view would necessitate that "Jewish Christians retain their identity."[332] This is not necessarily his endorsement of Messianic Jews, but a point stressing consistency to the New Testament's message. The incarnation is ultimately placed within this matrix of Jewish-Christian relations. Jesus was a Jewish man, but he was also more than that. In Wyschogrod's words, "The church found God in this Jewish flesh."[333] This was possible, he says, because God dwells in all Jewish flesh, based on Israel's covenant and election. Perhaps, he continues to ponder, "the church" was not able to recognize God dwelling in the midst of all Israel, but was somehow able to recognize God dwelling in this one individual Jew.[334] Wyschogrod's understanding of God dwelling in Jesus may not be quite the same as the New Testament's, but it is nevertheless a unique admission coming from an orthodox Jewish scholar. For him, it seems to be a given that Jews should not believe in Jesus, but the incarnation is not a factor in this rejection.

---

330. Ibid., 205.

331. Ibid., 206.

332. Ibid., 207.

333. Ibid.

334. Ibid.

Another profoundly important work on the subject comes from Ben-jamin Sommer, professor of Bible and ancient Semitic Languages at the Jewish Theological Seminary of America. This credential places him fully within both the mainstream of Jewish thought, and the highest level of scholarship. His book is a major challenge to the traditional Jewish under-standing of monotheism, as expressed in the opening statement: "The God of the Hebrew Bible has a body, this must be stated at the outset, because so many people, including many scholars, assume otherwise."[335]

He sees evidence for his thesis throughout the Tanakh. Some of these passages "point toward a non-material anthropomorphism," he says, but "others reflect a more concrete conception of God's body."[336] The fact that God cannot be seen is often taken to mean He has no body. But, he argues, Exodus 33:20 says that no one can see God and live. This does not mean that God has no physical form.[337] There are also references that explicitly say that God was seen (Isaiah 6:1, 5; Amos 9:1; Gen 3:8–9; Ex 33:11). Many scholars tend to avoid, or at best, downplay such passages. It is a common problem: "the habit of assuming that because we all know the Hebrew Bible's God has no body, evidence to the contrary must be denied or, if that is not possible, explained away."[338] Sommer defines body as "something located in a particular place at a particular time, whatever its shape or substance."[339] Common words found in the Scriptures, such as glory (*kavod*) and name (*shem*) provide unique opportunities to explain God dwelling among His people.[340] The Tabernacle and the Temple, are also obvious examples of this. Later, in the rabbinic period, the notion of the *Shekhinah* is employed to suggest "something resembling the multiplicity of divine embodiment."[341] Jewish mysticism adds to the discussion as well. The concept of the *sephirot* in Kabbalah reveals that "the divine can fragment itself into multiple selves that nonetheless remain parts of a unified whole."[342]

At the end of the book he comes to practical considerations, including the relationship of all this with Christianity. Despite all that has been said so far, his ultimate stance is quite traditional. Jews, he says, should repudiate Christianity because it includes a commitment to one who has been deemed

---

335. Sommer, *The Bodies of God and the World of Ancient Israel*, 1.

336. Ibid., 2.

337. Ibid., 3.

338. Ibid., 5.

339. Ibid., 80.

340. Ibid., 58–60.

341. Ibid., 127.

342. Ibid., 129.

by Judaism as a false messiah.[343] As with Wyschogrod, the big problem is not the incarnation per se. It is the further step of Christianity's "revival of a dying and rising god, a category ancient Israel rejects."[344] But, this seems just as dismissive as the people he argued against (above) who dismissed the incarnation because of what is commonly assumed. Even if parallels are found, it needs to be demonstrated that Israelite rejection was based on the concept of resurrection itself, or simply because these other deities were, in fact, pagan examples of this. This is important given the fact that Sommer places the incarnation of Jesus in purely Jewish terms, while rejecting forms of incarnation that exist in pagan literature.

Again, the incarnation in itself is not the problem for him. God is able to be in more than one place at a time. "That a deity came down did not mean the deity did not remain up," he writes. "The presence of God and of God-as-Jesus on earth is nothing more than a particular form of this old idea of multiple embodiment."[345] He concludes: "No Jew sensitive to Judaism's own classical sources, however, can fault the theological model Christianity employs when it avows belief in a God who has an earthly body as well as a Holy Spirit and a heavenly manifestation, for that model, we have seen, is a perfectly Jewish one."[346]

Daniel Boyarin is professor of Talmud and Near Eastern Studies at Berkeley. He has written extensively on early Judaism, early Christianity, and their overlapping worldviews. In his book, *Borderlines*, he traces the concept of the logos. Even before the Gospel of John, he explains, this word was used to explain that there was "a second divine entity, God's Word (Logos) or God's Wisdom, who mediates between fully transcendent Godhead and the material world."[347] Boyarin traces the history of this concept from its broad use in Philo to its original polemical use by Justin Martyr. He concludes: "This doctrine was widely held by Jews in the pre-Christian era and after the beginnings of Christianity was widely held and widely contested in Christian circles. By the fourth century, Jews who held such a doctrine and Christians who rejected it were defined as "neither Jews nor Christians" but heretics."[348]

A few years later, he continued his study of first-century Jewish beliefs in the book, *The Jewish Gospels*. Jesus was a Jewish man, virtually everyone

343. Ibid., 135.
344. Ibid., 136.
345. Ibid., 133.
346. Ibid., 135.
347. Boyarin, *Border Lines: The Partition of Judaeo-Christianity*, 31.
348. Ibid.

agrees on this. Boyarin attempted to go beyond this commonly held view and enter a more daring thesis. He writes: "I wish us to see that Christ too—the Divine Messiah—is a Jew. Christology, or the early ideas about Christ, is also a Jewish discourse and not—until much later—an anti-Jewish discourse at all."[349] He begins with some definitions. While many people have assumed "Son of God" was a reference to divinity and "Son of man" a reference to humanity, Boyarin turns this on its head. The former term actually indicates Jesus as the King Messiah, the latter one is a reference to divinity.[350] Daniel 7 is an important antecedent for the use of this term, as is *1 Enoch* and *4 Ezra*, each of these and their parallels to the Gospels is discussed in detail.

Throughout the book he addresses theology and takes many of the New Testament claims at face value. He does not affirm or deny historical claims, until the final few pages. At this point, the resurrection becomes an issue. He first says that the resurrection "seems to me so unlikely as to be incredible."[351] In his view, the resurrection and the disciples' experiences are not what actually happened.[352] However, in the spirit of ecumenicism, he does not want to invalidate the faith of others who believe this. He therefore adds the following in a footnote: "Let me make myself clear here: I am not denying the validity of the religious Christian view of matters. That is surely a matter of faith, not scholarship. I am denying it as a historical, scholarly, critical explanation."[353] Perhaps some of Jesus' followers, he writes, "saw him arisen." But this "must be" because they had a narrative that caused that expectation. Jesus fulfills the role of both the divine figure from Daniel and the Messianic King. The real Jesus—prophet, magician, charismatic teacher—was transformed by the belief, whether his own or that of the people, that he was the coming one. Boyarin concludes: "Details of his life, his prerogatives, his powers, and even his suffering and death before triumph are all developed out of close midrashic reading of the biblical materials and fulfilled in his life and death. The exaltation and resurrection experiences of his followers are a product of the narrative, not a cause of it."[354]

Like Sommer, Boyarin recognizes that the central claim about Jesus' identity is not outside the boundaries of Jewish thought. The former affirms the concept of incarnation while the latter allows for the concept of a divine messiah. But Boyarin, again like Sommer, has a problem with the historicity

349. Boyarin, *The Jewish Gospels*, 6.
350. Ibid., 26.
351. Ibid., 159.
352. Ibid., 160.
353. Ibid.
354. Ibid.

of the resurrection. While he denies it on "historical, scholarly, critical" grounds, the only piece of evidence against it is that he personally finds it incredible and therefore unlikely. Boyarin's work is important not only because of his specific conclusions about the possibility of a divine messiah, as some of these may be challenged.[355] Rather, his willingness to follow the evidence even when it goes beyond the traditional boundaries is both commendable and absolutely vital for the advancement of scholarship itself. As Eisenbaum concluded in her review of Boyarin's book, "the opportunity to acknowledge overlap and resonance with another faith once conceived in diametrical opposition would not be a bad thing."[356]

[3.5.3] Dying Messiah

The problem of a resurrected Messiah, for many, is the notion that the messiah would die in the first place. After Menachem Schneerson died, some of his followers continued to believe that he was the messiah and that he might rise from the dead. David Berger was particularly upset by this, saying that "there is no more fundamental messianic belief in Judaism than the conviction that the Davidic Messiah who appears at the end of days will not die before completing his mission."[357] A dying messiah is not only beyond the traditional boundaries of Judaism, but the negation of the concept is here declared a fundamental belief. This surely has implications for the Jewish study of the resurrection of Jesus. However, the idea of a suffering and dying messiah actually has a long history within Judaism. This brings us to Isaiah 53,[358] a passage that has been well rehearsed.[359]

There have been two dominant interpretations of Isaiah 53 within Judaism. One is that it speaks of an individual, perhaps the messiah, and the

355. For a critical review, see Schafer, "*The Jew Who Would Be God.*"

356. Eisenbaum, "They Don't Make Jews Like Jesus Anymore," 72.

357. Berger, *The Rebbe, the Messiah and the Scandal of Orthodox Indifference,* 11–12. Berger was careful to say the "Davidic" Messiah, differentiating this figure with the "Messiah son of Joseph" who is also known as the "Ephramite Messiah." This figure appears in rabbinic literature and is known for dying prior to the coming of the Davidic Messiah. But, the two are not mutually exclusive. Himmelfarb wrote: "It is also worth noting that the one certain case of a messiah named Ephraim in Jewish literature (*Pesiqta Rabbati* 34, 36, 37) is indeed a suffering messiah, but he is also a Davidic messiah." Himmelfarb, "The Messiah Son of Joseph in Ancient Judaism," 779.

358. This passage actually includes Isa 52:13—53:12.

359. See Bellinger and Farmer, *Jesus and the Suffering Servant;* Stuhlmacher and Janowski, *The Suffering Servant: Isaiah 53 in Jewish and Christian Sources;* Bock & Glaser, *The Gosepl according to Isaiah 53;* Horowitz, "Isaiah's Suffering Servant and the Jews: From the Nineteenth Century to the Ninth."

other is that it speaks about the nation of Israel as a whole. The discussion begins in the rabbinic period. The Jerusalem Talmud (Shekalim 5:1) applies Isaiah 53:12 to Rabbi Akiva, and the Babylonian Talmud applies 53:4 to Messiah in Sanhedrin 98b. Nowhere does either Talmud ascribe any portion of Isaiah 53 to Israel. Midrash Rabbah interprets 53:5 as the Messiah in Ruth Rabbah 2:14, however Numbers Rabbah 13:2 interprets 53:12 with reference to Israel in exile. Perhaps the earliest reference to Isaiah 53 as Israel comes, ironically, from a Christian source. The Church Father, Origen, mentions that this response was given in a dispute he had with a group of Jews.[360] Over the years, both main interpretations appear within Jewish texts.[361]

The reasons for the various interpretations include both exegesis and social factors. Joel E. Rembaum documented the shifting nature of these interpretations in a 1982 article in *Harvard Theological Review*. He saw three factors that led to Judaism's shift away from the messianic interpretation and towards the national interpretation. The first was a response to Christian propaganda that said that the exile is punishment. This created the Jewish belief that in exile the Jews were actually functioning as a "light to the nations." The second was in response to Christian missionizing. Because of this, most Jews responded by "avoiding the messianic interpretation altogether." The third was in response to the Crusades. In the midst of the terrible situation, Isaiah 53 came to be seen as the Jewish people, whose suffering "was part of the divine plan."[362] The simple dismissal of the messianic interpretation is too hasty. The national interpretation was not the dominant one. Daniel Boyarin wrote: "Quite the contrary, we now know that many Jewish authorities, maybe even most, until nearly the modern period have read Isaiah 53 as being about the Messiah; until the last few centuries, the allegorical interpretation was a minority."[363] At the very least, the messianic interpretation can no longer be discarded without discussion.

The servant of Isaiah is said to suffer, but whether or not this figure was to die—and be resurrected—has also been an area of dispute. Levenson and Segal each addressed this in their respective evaluations of resurrection in the Tanakh (3.4.1). Levenson said that the servant not only dies, but that the language used by Daniel in his clear reference to resurrection (chapter 12) includes antecedents from Isaiah 53. Segal, on the other hand, was not

360. Origen, *Contra Celsum* 1.55.

361. Driver and Neubauer, *The Fifty-Third Chapter of Isaiah according to Jewish Interpreters.*

362. Rembaum, "The Development of a Jewish Exegetical Tradition Regarding Isaiah 53," 292–95.

363. Boyarin, *The Jewish Gospels,* 152.

convinced that the servant was a martyr or that he would die. This is a curious opinion. Even apart from Daniel's use of the servant passage, the narrative of Isaiah 53 leaves little room to suggest that the servant did not die. Verse 8 says that he was "cut off from the land of the living," a phrase which could possibly be taken metaphorically. But, the passage also says that the servant was like a lamb that is led to slaughter (verse 7), and that he was assigned a grave (verse 9). In the remaining verses, the servant continues to function after death. As David Flusser noticed, it is not a stretch to see this as implying resurrection.

> Though the Servant "was pierced for our transgressions, tortured for our iniquities" (v.5), he "shall enjoy long life and see his children's children" (v.10). So Isa. LIII could be understood not only as speaking about the death of the Servant (see also v.8 and 9), but implicitly also about his resurrection.[364]

The New Testament cites Isaiah 53 directly in several places.[365] The earliest *allusion* is found in 1 Corinthians 15:3, which says that Jesus "died for our sins." Shira Lander said this verse is "perhaps invoking Isaiah 53."[366] The suffering servant passage is directly ascribed to Jesus in 1 Peter 2. Claudia Setzer comments: "The text weaves in images from Isaiah 53:3–9, where Israel is like the sacrificial lamb, suffering on behalf of others who are straying like sheep. Probably emerging from the period after Israel's exile, the passage gives meaning to Israel's suffering as redemptive or instructive."[367] The national interpretation is assumed here, and it is perhaps implied that the New Testament is using Isaiah 53 in a way that runs counter to its original meaning. Yet, it needs to be remembered that the New Testament documents—however late one may choose to date them—appear before rabbinic literature. There does not seem to be any source from Second Temple Judaism that equates the servant with Israel, and the earliest rabbinic commentaries on Isaiah 53 focus on the messianic or at least the individual interpretation. Whether or not there are Second Temple sources that refer to a suffering and dying messiah, however, has been a matter of debate.[368]

Both positions have been used in the discussion of the resurrection of Jesus. If the national interpretation of Isaiah 53 did exist in the first century

---

364. Flusser, *Judaism and the Origins of Christianity*, 423.

365. Matt 8:17, Mark 15:28, Luke 22:37, John 12:38, Acts 8:32, Rom 10:16.

366. Lander, "1 Corinthians, Introduction and Annotations," 310.

367. Setzer, "1 Peter, Introduction and Annotations," 440.

368. David Mitchell has argued strenuously for this position. See, for example, "A Dying and Rising Josephite Messiah in 4Q372." Martha Himmelfarb has argued that Mitchell's scholarship is "compromised by his zeal to make the evidence fit his picture." See her discussion in "The Messiah Son of Joseph in Ancient Judaism," 774

then the claims about Jesus may easily be discarded as un-Jewish and there-fore irrelevant. Although, from the historical point of view, it becomes more difficult to explain why the original disciples and other Jews would have believed something that was antithetical to contemporary Jewish thought.

On the other hand, perhaps there was a preexisting view about a suffer-ing and dying messiah. It may then be suggested that Jesus simply borrowed the idea. This was the starting point for Hugh Schonfield's book, *The Pass-over Plot* (see below, 4.6.2). A similar suggestion was made by Israel Knohl of Hebrew University. In 2009 he wrote *The Gabriel Revelation*, based on a newly discovered apocalyptic work written at the turn of the first century. It speaks of a messianic figure dying and rising after three days. The discovery, he wrote, was dramatic, and would "change the way we view the histori-cal Jesus and the birth of Christianity."[369] Since then, however, he himself has acknowledged that the text does not actually say what was originally thought.[370] What is important for our purpose is how Knohl made use of his original discovery. With minimal interaction with either the New Testament or the historical Jesus, Knohl offers an alternative to the canonical narrative. On Jesus' last night on earth, he writes, "the inner struggle within Jesus' soul reached a climax."[371] He pleaded with God, but ultimately chose to stay on course. He "opted to stay in Jerusalem and follow the path of suffering, death and resurrection on the third day, a messianic path devised in *The Gabriel Revelation*."[372] Even if this text actually said what Knohl originally thought, it would still need to be explained how this "path" materialized and led to the disciples belief that Jesus actually rose from the dead. The idea of a dying messiah, then, has been used to dismiss the historicity of the resurrection from both sides of the coin—for some it is a foreign concept not worthy of Jewish discussion, and for at least two others it provided the basis for a counter theory. Neither view, however, has been able to provide a cogent reason for historians to dismiss the study of the resurrection of Jesus.

[3.6] DUAL COVENANT THEOLOGY

The dominant theological grid that has characterized the Christian approach to the Jews is *supercessionism*, or what is also called "replacement theology." This view says that with the coming of Jesus, God is finished with the Jewish

369. Knohl, *The Messiah and Resurrection in the Gabriel Revelation*, xi.

370. See the discussions in Himmelfarb, "The Messiah Son of Joseph in Ancient Judaism," 778–79; Elgvin, "Eschatology and Messianism in the Gabriel Inscription."

371. Knohl, *The Messiah and Resurrection in the Gabriel Revelation*, 93.

372. Ibid.

people and works instead only through the Church.[373] This view developed early in church history and dominated at least until the Second World War. It continues today. But, after the holocaust, Christians began to rethink the Church's teaching on this subject,[374] and more importantly the church's actions as a result of this teaching. This led to Dual Covenant theology, which emerged as a corrective. This view has become popular in Jewish circles as well. It says that Jews and Christians each have a separate and equally valid covenant with God (or, perhaps a different version of the same covenant).[375] This provides a good fit for the modern, pluralistic worldview. By the end of the century, however, dual covenant theology began to be challenged. The more that Jesus and Paul are recognized as (good) Jews, the more difficult it becomes to say that their message has no relevance for Jews.[376] This has led to more nuanced views than the extremes of either *supercessionism* or dual covenant theology.[377]

The resurrection of Jesus is a unique factor in this discussion. It is not only a theoretical concept which may be believed by one group and not the other. It is an event which either happened or did not happen. This section will focus on the Jewish use of dual covenant theology as it may be relevant to the resurrection. These issues do not directly affect the historicity of the event, but may contribute to a general lack of interest in the subject.

[3.6.1] Atonement

The question of soteriology is a difficult one in Jewish-Christian relations. Terms such as redemption, salvation, justification and atonement may have different meanings even within each tradition, and may have connotations that are singular or plural, present or future. For this reason, some have suggested the two traditions are simply too different to discuss coherently.[378]

---

373. Brand, *Perspectives on Israel and the Church, 4 Views.* Vlach, *Has the Church Replaced Israel? A Theological Evaluation.*

374. Smith, "The Effect of the Holocaust on Jewish-Christian Relations." Kessler, *An Introduction to Jewish-Christian Relations,* 124–47.

375. The most well-known work from a Jewish perspective is Franz Rosenzweig's book, *The Star of Redemption.*

376. See Borowitz, "Jesus the Jew in Light of the Jewish-Christian Dialogue"; Cox, Rabbi Yeshua ben Joseph: Reflections on Jesus' Jewishness and the Interfatih Dialogue"; Catchpole, "The Role of the Historical Jesus in Jewish-Christian Dialogue."

377. See Soulen, *The God of Israel and Christian Theology*; Fruchtenbaum, *Israelogy*; Rudolph, *A Jew to the Jews: Jewish Contours of Pauline Flexibility in 1 Corinthians 9:19–23.*

378. Kellner, "How Ought a Jew View Christian Beliefs about Redemption?";

But, on a more basic level, each tradition recognizes the need for forgiveness of sin and being made right with God. The New Testament presents the death and resurrection of Jesus as the means to this end (1 Cor 15:17; Romans 10:9).

Traditional Judaism provides a different solution, as summarized here by the Encyclopedia Judaica: "After the destruction of the Temple and the consequent cessation of sacrifices, the rabbis declared: "Prayer, repentance, and charity avert the evil decree" (TJ, Ta'an.2:1, 65b). Suffering is also regarded as a means of atonement and is considered more effective than sacrifice to win God's favor (Ber. 5a). Exile and the destruction of the Temple (Sanh. 37b, Ex. R. 31:10) were also reputed to bring about the same effect."[379] Given this, the traditional Jewish response to the New Testament's central claim is quite understandable. Amy-Jill Levine explains: "For Jews, Jesus is unnecessary or a redundancy; he is not needed to save from sin or death, since Judaism proclaims a deity ready to forgive repentant sinners and since it asserts that "all Israel has a share in the world to come" (Mishnah *Sanhedrin* 10:1)."[380]

There is no doubt that Rabbinic Judaism promoted this view after the destruction of the Temple. Beginning with the Mishnah (as Levine quotes here) this view has gone virtually unchallenged in the Jewish world. A question that needs to be addressed is whether or not such a position is directly stated, or even alluded to, in the Tanakh. The Law of Moses presents the sacrificial system as the means of atonement (although that was not the only purpose of sacrifices). Exceptions to this are not necessarily as clear. This discussion has been especially prominent in recent decades with the rise of the Messianic Jewish movement. As more Jewish people have come to believe in Jesus as the Messiah, the traditional response has had to interact more vigorously with this subject. The debate is between, as they are often called, "missionaries" versus "anti-missionaries." One of the first books to defend the traditional position came from David Berger and Michael Wyschogrod, both Orthodox Jewish scholars. They do not condemn the sacrificial system, but see its efficacy as situational. They write: "When sacrifice is possible it is necessary, though useless without repentance (the "broken spirit" and "wounded heart"). When sacrifice is not possible, God forgives those who sincerely repent."[381]

Neusner, "The Absoluteness of Christianity and the Uniqueness of Judaism: Why Salvation Is Not of the Jews." See also Gurtner, *This World and the World to Come: Soteriology in Early Judaism*.

379. Roth, "Atonement," 830–31.

380. Levine, *The Misunderstood Jew*, 18.

381. Berger and Wyschogrod, *Jews and Jewish Christianity*, 58–59. See also

The most exhaustive discussion on this subject, and one that counters the traditional view, comes from Michael Brown. He is a Messianic Jew, although his proficiency in the area of atonement in the Tanakh has been recognized by leading Jewish scholars.[382] He responds to the verses and arguments commonly used in the debate, and he concludes that the Tanakh *does not* allow for atonement without a blood sacrifice. The idea that God forgave sin "when sacrifice is not possible" is a problematic view, he argues.

> Just consider how hopeless the anti-missionary argument is that with the Temple destroyed, God ordained that prayer would replace sacrifice. The Temple was destroyed because of our sins as a people, sins that were so grievous to God that he said, "Enough! No amount of prayer, sacrifice, or fasting will stop me. I will reject my city and my sanctuary, and I will judge my people, banishing them from my presence." How ludicrous to say then, "Now that the Temple has been sacked and we can no longer offer sacrifices, God will accept our prayers instead."[383]

The need for blood atonement has also been noticed by some traditional Jewish scholars. In other words, it is not just an idea employed by Christians and Messianic Jews who are reading New Testament theology back into the Tanakh. Brown cites Geza Vermes: "according to Jewish theology, there can be no expiation without the shedding of blood: *"en kappareh "ella" bedam.""*[384] This position is also found in classical texts of Traditional Judaism. Brown continues,

> Rashi states that "the fundamental principle (*'iqqar*) of atonement is in the blood" (b.Yoma 5a). Tosafot, also discussing the Talmudic statement that there is no atonement without the blood, makes reference to a passage found elsewhere in the Talmud (b. Pesahim 59b) that indicated that the priest had to eat certain specified sacrifices if those offerings were to have their atoning affect. Tosafot then concludes, "But in any case, the fundamental principle [again, *'iqqar*] of atonement doesn't exist without the blood" (b. Zevahim 6a).[385]

Wyschogrod, "Sin and Atonement in Judaism"; Singer, *Let's Get Biblical*, 12–21.

382. Brown, "*Kipper* and Atonement in the Book of Isaiah." This article appeared in a tribute book for Baruch A. Levine.

383. Brown, *Answering Jewish Objections to Jesus*, 2:101.

384. Vermes, "Redemption and Genesis xxii: The Binding of Isaac and the Sacrifice of Jesus," 205, cited in Brown, *Answering Jewish Objections to Jesus*, 2:109.

385. Brown, *Answering Jewish Objections to Jesus*, 2:109.

This debate is too detailed to unpack here, apart from presenting each side's general position. Conclusions usually fall down party lines and each side accuses the other of taking passages out of context. The arguments for and against are found in the works just cited, and they are readily available to all. For now, it is enough to identify this issue as one that might prematurely dismiss the resurrection of Jesus.

The traditional view, however, is not the only mainstream Jewish position on atonement in the modern world. The Reform movement of the early nineteenth century in Germany challenged many traditional Jewish beliefs. These include the role of the messiah (which became an era rather than a person), the notion of resurrection (which was replaced by the transmigration of the soul), and even the means—and in some cases the need—for atonement. Reform pioneer Isaac M. Wise wrote a book about Jesus in the nineteenth century that asserted that the crucifixion never happened. This was partly a response to the charge that Jews killed Jesus, arguing that if he was never killed there is no one to blame. But, he was also against the theological position of a vicarious sacrifice. As an "enlightened" man, he saw this as archaic and barbaric.[386] This view persists today.[387] But, whatever Wise's presuppositions may have been about the meaning of the crucifixion, he did not succeed in providing a cogent historical alternative for his position. This is perhaps also relevant in the discussion of the historicity of the resurrection—questions about the implications of a certain event do not necessarily comment on its historicity.

[3.6.2] Pluralism and Jesus

The dual covenant theory provides a convenient response to the resurrection. If the implications of the event are not for the Jewish people, than the event itself becomes a non-issue. In this context, some Jewish scholars go so far as to say that the resurrection actually happened—as long as it is made clear that there are no implications for Jews. Four pluralistic examples will be given, two of which affirm the historicity of the event in one way or

386. See the discussion below, 4.6.1.

387. Telushkin summarized modern views of the Temple: "Reform Judaism simply has dropped reference to the entire subject from its prayerbook: It views sacrifices as a primitive stage in Jewish religious development, one in which there is no reason to take pride. The Orthodox prayerbook, on the other hand, repeatedly reiterates the hope that the Temple will be rebuilt, and sacrifices offered there again. The Conservative prayerbook has changed all the future references to sacrifices to the past tense: It speaks proudly of the sacrifices that once were brought before God at the Temple, but expresses no desire to have them reinstituted." Telushkin, *Jewish Literacy*, 62.

another. The difficult part, as will be seen, is to simultaneously affirm the Jewishness of Jesus and make a case from the New Testament that Jesus is for Gentiles only. Irving "Yitz" Greenberg, has been on the forefront of the Jewish-Christian dialogue movement for many years. A modern Orthodox Rabbi and professor, his views have challenged both liberals and conservatives, both Jewish and Christian. His book, *For the Sake of Heaven and Earth*, is a collection of his essays on Judaism and Christianity that span four decades. He shows respect for Christianity and has sought to find a positive place for it, while maintaining Jewish distinctives.

While some Jews have called Jesus a "false messiah," Greenberg prefers the term "failed messiah." The difference is that "[a] failed Messiah is one who has the right values and upholds the covenant, but does not attain the goal."[388] Greenberg sees a place for Jesus in line with Jewish history and Jewish teaching. It is through the lens of God's covenant with Israel that he will make his case. First, God chose Abraham and his descendants. At Sinai, God gave further revelation and created a nation. After that, additional revelation was given and a new group was formed. "The group that would bring the message of redemption to the rest of the nations had to grow out of the family and covenanted community of Israel."[389] Christianity, then, is both an offshoot and a continuation of God's covenant with Israel. It is acceptable for Gentiles. But, in what way did Jesus fail? For Greenberg, and most traditional Jews, the Messiah will be recognized by the changes he brings. These include overcoming sickness, poverty and oppression, along with re-establishing "political, economic and social structures" that "support and nurture the perfection of life."[390] Greenberg is nonetheless conciliatory. Although Jesus did not finish the job, "his work is not in vain."[391] He is then compared with other great figures in Jewish history. Abraham, Moses and Jeremiah had their failures but were clearly part of God's plan.

Greenberg draws a more direct parallel between Jesus and the Messiah ben Joseph of rabbinic tradition. This figure is a good example of a "failed but true messiah." The Messiah ben Joseph comes first and eventually dies. He paves the way for the Messiah ben David who will bring about the "final restoration."[392] But, the death of the *Messiah ben Joseph* is not in fact a failure. It is an act of completion, ordained by God, which leads to the coming of the *Messiah ben David*. In the same way, others would argue, the death

---

388. Greenberg, *For the Sake of Heaven and Earth*, 153.

389. Ibid., 21.

390. Ibid., 147.

391. Ibid., 177.

392. Ibid., 153.

of Jesus should not automatically be labeled a failure (at least not without interacting with the resurrection and its implications).

Greenberg writes almost nothing about the historical Jesus. It is beyond his scope of interest. He is more concerned with the relationship between the two religious groups. Jesus is deemed a failure because he did not do what Orthodox Judaism expected, at least not in the proper timetable. This raises the question of what Jesus actually did, or why anyone should follow him at all. According to Greenberg, God literally spoke to and called Abraham. The Exodus, too, was a real historical event. The next revelation must also have a historical basis. "Christianity is a commentary on the original Exodus, in which the later event—the Christ event—is a manifest, "biblically" ordained miraculous event."[393] But, what exactly is the "Christ event" mentioned here? Something important must have happened. In one of his only statements on the historical Jesus, he offers the following words.

> Then they received another, activating signal: an empty tomb. The fact that Jesus did not even attain the minimal dignity of a final resting place—an undisturbed grave—should have been the final nail in the crucifixion of their faith. Instead they increased hope and trust in God. Soon they experienced the same (or greater) presence in their midst as before. Once faith supplied the key of understanding, the empty tomb yielded the message of the resurrection. Whether they received this message within three days, as the Gospel story indicates, or within three decades, as the most probable scholarly account has it, is of secondary importance.[394]

Greenberg is not concerned with historical details (although he alludes to the theory that says the empty tomb account was a later invention rather than a historical reality). For him, it is irrelevant whether or not the resurrection actually happened, since this does not fit into his scheme of Jesus as a failed messiah. But, this position has consequences for Jewish-Christian dialogue, the very thing Greenberg set out to accomplish. For most Christians (along with Paul in 1 Cor 15:17), the resurrection is the essential ingredient of their faith. It determines whether or not Jesus is the true Messiah or a false messiah. The idea of a "failed messiah" is counterproductive in dialogue with those whose faith is based on this event. By calling Jesus a messiah (albeit a failed one), Greenberg has offered a radical new paradigm. But the title sends mixed signals; such was the conclusion of Shaul Magid. Greenberg was not trying to reclaim Jesus, Magid wrote,

393. Ibid., 156.
394. Ibid., 222.

"as much as complicate the very notion of the Messiah in order to meet his Christian interlocutors half way."[395]

A second pluralistic offering comes from Michael S. Kogan, in his book, *Opening the Covenant: A Jewish theology of Christianity*. He begins by saying that each side must "give up long-standing convictions of their own exclusive possession of truth."[396] Christians must "re-examine" the exclusive claim that Jesus alone provides salvation, and Jews must acknowledge that God was "involved with" the life of Jesus.[397] This approach places dialogue above the actual beliefs of each group. Later in the book, however, he will explain that neither side should ask the other to give up core doctrines.[398] For most of the book, Kogan attempts to navigate the fine line between truth claims and pluralism. He surveys the passages from the Tanakh that are typically part of the discussion of messiahship. He does not directly discredit Jesus, but this is often implied in his evaluations. For example, speaking of Jeremiah's new covenant (Jr 31:31–34) he concludes: "All this will be accomplished directly by God, with no mention of (or, seemingly, need for) a Messianic figure."[399] Traditionally, such conclusions would be used to disqualify Jesus as the Messiah. But, for Kogan that is the wrong question.

His view of Jesus is likewise pluralistic. There were many messianic groups in Second Temple Judaism, he acknowledges, and the earliest followers of Jesus should legitimately be counted among them. This leads him to conclude the following about Jesus: "He was *a* Jewish Messiah." But, although Kogan views this as a legitimate form of Judaism in its day, the fact that Jesus "dies for the redemption of the world" places his mission in a different category. Jesus has "broken out of his original Israelite context."[400] The specific event of the resurrection is discussed as well. He mentions a conversation he had with a liberal Christian who denied the historicity of the resurrection, assuming this would put him and Kogan on common ground. But, Kogan's response surprised the liberal Christian. Kogan said: ""Following the death of Jesus his followers continued to have experience of him in his bodily form. I have no reason to doubt the authenticity of that experience.""[401] He then explains that religious events should not be discussed in the same

395. Magid, "The New Jewish Reclamation of Jesus in Late Twentieth-Century America: Realigning and Rethinking Jesus the Jew," 366.

396. Kogan, *Opening the Covenant*, xii.

397. Ibid., xiii.

398. Ibid., 102.

399. Ibid., 45.

400. Ibid., 68.

401. Ibid., 102.

light as historical events. The former involves the "breaking of the infinite into the finite" and therefore there will always be "an irreducible element of objective uncertainty."[402] Later in the book, Kogan addresses three "central propositions" of the Christian faith. These include the incarnation, vicarious atonement and, again, the resurrection. The question is: how can Jews reject these things and yet affirm them for their Christian friends and neighbors in a positive way? He writes:

> I believe that, *while we cannot affirm the truth of these propositions, we need no longer insist on their falsity.* We cannot affirm their truth because that can only be done from the standpoint of Christian faith, a standpoint we do not share. Nevertheless, we need no longer insist on their falsity, because their message is not now being used by mainstream churches to undermine our faith and because the logic of our view that the divine hand guides Christianity as well as Judaism leads us to entertain the possibility of their being true.[403]

He then offers reasons that would seem to lead in the direction of denying the historicity of the resurrection. First, most Jews at the time "saw no reason" to believe it, and those who saw the risen Christ were already his followers. Paul, he says, "was perhaps the exception," but he had "a religious experience quite different from the resurrection appearances described elsewhere." Second, although resurrection of the body was a Jewish belief, they would have rejected the idea that "the man Jesus had, in fact, already been raised."[404] He does not interact with the question of why at least some Jews did believe that Jesus alone rose from the dead, nor why a committed adversary like Paul would have had a religious experience that caused him to embrace Jesus. It is also not clear how the challenges he presents here relate to his statement above that he does not doubt the authenticity of the disciples' experiences. In the end, he is dogmatic about only one thing: if the resurrection did happen, he assures his fellow Jews, "it neither speaks to us directly nor threatens us in any way."[405]

The resurrection of Jesus is the defining event of the New Testament, just as the exodus is the defining event of the Tanakh. Conservative Rabbi Michael Goldberg recognizes the importance of each. In his 1985 book, *Getting Our Stories Straight*, he explains that Jews and Christians need to understand and appreciate how each of these contributes to what he calls

402. Ibid., 114.
403. Ibid., 115; emphasis in the original.
404. This seems to be delineating a corporate resurrection from an individual one.
405. Ibid., 118.

"master stories." These master stories "offer us both a model for understanding the world and a guide for acting in it." They not only inform us, he says, "but more crucially, they form us."[406] In the first half of the book he traces the origins and calling of the Jewish people. This will be compared and contrasted with the life of Jesus, which is the focus of the second half. Each master story has its own view of God and the world we live in. "Obviously," he writes, "if none of these events, whether natural or supernatural, ever really happened, then all our narrative based claims about God and everything else would simply stand unjustified."[407] In each case Goldberg assumes the texts are reliable, or at least conform to a "general historicity."[408] He offers a non-critical summary.

For Goldberg, the Jewish master story is about one group of people, yet it "holds out a future vision of how the life of all peoples may be sustained—and even transformed!—in the future."[409] For his study of the life of Jesus, Goldberg uses the Gospel of Matthew. He begins with the genealogy in Matthew 1 and recognizes that "this story is related to another that starts with Abraham and runs through David."[410] Clearly, the New Testament is claiming to be a continuation of the Jewish master story. But as the events unfold, Goldberg notices something amazing in the teachings of Jesus. "Jesus is no longer merely a teller of parables of God, but is instead the parable of God himself; he is the transcendent touching the worldly in and through ordinary life"[411] Goldberg recognizes that Jesus is claiming to be much more than just a good teacher. He is making powerful claims about himself, and also about God's plan. This is seen at his final Passover celebration. Here, his words "point not merely to the transformation of the seder, but ultimately to the transformation of the covenant itself."[412] After Jesus' resurrection, "a new relationship with God is offered."[413] The resurrection is recorded as a historical event and it is explained quite definitively: "For the resurrected Jesus, alive in body as well as spirit, provides the most impressive kind of evidence—physical evidence!—that God does save where nothing else can."[414]

---

406. Ibid., 13.
407. Ibid., 112.
408. Ibid., 220.
409. Ibid., 127.
410. Ibid., 135.
411. Ibid., 163.
412. Ibid., 174.
413. Ibid., 204.
414. Ibid., 210.

Like Pinchas Lapide, Goldberg affirms the resurrection of Jesus. But, whereas Lapide was specifically investigating the historicity of the event, Goldberg seems to acknowledge it merely for the sake of his argument. He can readily say that Jesus rose from the dead, or even that he claimed equality with God. As long as these things are designated a foreign (non-Jewish) story, it becomes irrelevant whether they are true or false. It is merely someone else's story. By using the expression "master story" (as opposed to covenant), the issue becomes one of preference. Each group is entitled to believe what they choose. This fits well with modern notions of ecumenicism, but it creates problems in logic. Specifically, how can Jesus be a covenant breaker to some and yet at the same time be the God-ordained savior to others? Either he is the fulfillment of the Tanakh, as Matthew—the text Goldberg was using—explicitly proclaims throughout his Gospel, or he is not.

The resurrection of Jesus is often the subject of debate, usually between an evangelical Christian and an atheist (or agnostic). Sometimes it is between a Christian and a Muslim. Whether or not Jesus rose from the dead is important to all involved. If the event did not happen, Christians lose the foundation of their faith. If it did happen, the worldview of both the atheist and the Muslim are severely shattered as well.[415] Jewish scholars rarely engage in this debate, as it does not seem to be immediately relevant. There was, however, one example of a dialogue amongst Jews and Christians which approached this subject. Peter Zass is a New Testament scholar who wrote the commentary for Colossians in the *JANT*.[416] He participated in a friendly debate/discussion with Christian apologist, William Lane Craig. The transcript of the actual event is brief. At one point, Craig explained why he believed in the historicity of the resurrection and asked for a response. Zass offered the following somewhat surprising statement: "I don't dispute the fact of the resurrection. It's not something I'm involved in, but it doesn't seem to be an event that's made much positive difference to Jewish history."[417] Zass seems to acknowledge the historicity of the resurrection, and it would be interesting to know how and why he came to this conclusion. His dismissal of the discussion (at least as it is recorded in this book) is odd. He is not "involved" in the resurrection because it apparently has no personal interest for him. Yet, he is a New Testament scholar, and specifically he was in a discussion where the resurrection was sure to be an issue. Perhaps in a later work his belief will be clarified.

---

415. The official Muslim view is that Jesus did not die on the cross, *Sura* 355.

416. Zass, "Colossians, Introduction and Annotations."

417. Copan and Evans, *Who Was Jesus?*, 38.

[3.6.3] Pluralism and Paul

Dual covenant theology has been an attractive option for many. But, since a plain reading of the New Testament speaks against this view, theories have by necessity become much more sophisticated and this has spilled over to discussions about Paul. Kirster Stendahl was one of the first major voices to promote a Jewish Paul whose message was not for Jews.[418] One of his students at Harvard was Pamela Eisenbaum. She furthered some of his arguments and added nuances based on her own Jewish perspective. She rightly places Paul in his Jewish context in her book, *Paul was not a Christian*. In fact, she writes, "Paul's letters would have been regarded as Jewish by other Jews of the time, including Pharisees."[419] One of the keys to interpret Paul, she writes, is an understanding that his letters are specifically addressed to Gentiles.[420] She argues that Paul does not believe that Jews need Jesus. His resurrection from the dead therefore has no direct value for Jews.

> The death and resurrection of Jesus has achieved the reconciliation between Gentiles and God that was envisioned by Israel's prophets. To put it boldly, Jesus saves, but he only saves Gentiles. By that I do not mean that Paul believed that Jesus is irrelevant for Jews. Paul hoped his fellow Jews would eventually recognize the cosmic significance of Jesus as marking the beginning of the messianic age. But the significance was not that Jews needed to be saved from their sins. The efficacy of Jesus' sacrificial death was for the forgiveness of the sins of the nations.[421]

What makes Eisenbaum's study unique is that she came to these conclusions without a discussion of Romans chapters 9—11. She acknowledges that these chapters are the "*locus classicus*" for those who embrace the New Perspective on Paul, yet an examination of these passages, she says, "would have required another book."[422] She nevertheless concludes: "There is nothing that forces a reader to understand Paul as saying Israel—that is, Jews—must convert to Christianity to be saved."[423] She is correct if she means that Paul argued that Jews do not need to stop being Jews to be saved. But, whether or not Paul believed Jews need Jesus to be "saved" is a different

---

418. See Stendahl, "The Apostle Paul and the Introspective Conscience of the West"; and Stendahl, *Paul among Jews and Gentiles*.

419. Eisenbaum, *Paul Was Not a Christian*, 8.

420. Ibid., 61.

421. Ibid., 242.

422. Ibid., 251.

423. Ibid., 255.

matter, and a discussion of these key chapters would have helped the reader know that her conclusions were thoughtfully weighed.

Jon D. Levenson arrived at a similar conclusion. He teamed up with fellow Harvard professor Kevin Madigan to discuss both the resurrection of Jesus as well as the end-times resurrection of traditional Judaism. This was the focus of their book, *Resurrection: The Power of God for Christians and Jews*. It is an affirming and complementary study. The opening words of the foreword declare it to be "a book by a Christian and a Jew," and the authors write with one voice. Madigan and Levenson acknowledge that the first disciples, along with Paul, clearly believed in the importance of the resurrection as an actual, physical, historical event. This was so important to Paul that, if it did not happen, "every Christian's faith would be in vain."[424] The authors do not share their personal beliefs directly, but some inferences may be drawn. Madigan identifies as a Christian, and therefore (one would assume) he believes that the resurrection is a historical event. It would be hard to conclude otherwise given what the authors have said about Paul's view of the resurrection. There would simply be no reason for him to identify as a Christian without believing in the resurrection of Jesus.

Levenson's opinion of the resurrection of Jesus is likewise not stated. But according to the authors, this is irrelevant. Paul's theology provides an exception for Jews. To uphold this understanding, the authors provide a hermeneutic which seems ultimately devised for the sole purpose of using Romans 11:26 ("all Israel will be saved") as their capstone. The earliest Christian communities, they write, conceived of themselves as the new Israel (implying a form of supercessionism). Passages from Acts 1–5 are cited to demonstrate this. However, the term "Christian communities" (especially as it is used here) is anachronistic prior to Acts 11:26. The earliest followers of Jesus were Jews. The authors consistently speak of two groups: Jews and the church. The impression given—although surely the authors know otherwise—is that Jews were never part (or perhaps were only an insignificant part) of the community of believers in Jesus. This construction enables them to conclude as follows.

> Paul thought in terms of three groups: Jews, Pagans and the Church. For the Pagans of that world, the only hope was to cease to be Pagans and to become sons of Abraham ... For Christians, Paul thought that this adoption would be affected through

424. Madigan and Levenson, *Resurrection: The Power of God for Christians and Jews*, 25.

baptism; for Jews, it had been accomplished through circumcision, and so Israel and the sons of Abraham would be saved.[425]

These words are then followed by a quote from Romans 11:25–27. All Israel will be saved, they reason, since Paul thought in these three categories. But, this is not an accurate representation of either the early Church or Paul's ecclesiology in Romans. In truth, Paul thought in terms of four groups. These include Jews (those who believed, and those who did not) and Gentiles (those who believed and those who did not). It is by denying the historical reality of Jewish Christians in the first century that the authors are able to devise a plan which excludes Jews from needing Jesus today. Madigan and Levenson do not believe that Paul was a universalist, apart from an exemption for Jews. Paul clearly believed that all have sinned and that Jesus provides a very real solution to a very real problem. They make this point definitively and offer several verses as proof. One of them, ironically, is Romans 1:16. The first part of the verse is quoted, which says that the gospel is the power of God to all who believe. "Paul," they write, "links one's eternal destiny to one's willingness to believe in the Christian message."[426] The remaining part of the verse, however (which they do not quote), says that this same gospel is to the Jew first. Madigan and Levenson have produced a well-meaning, but at best incomplete, study of the resurrection of Jesus. Other scholars who have addressed these key passages more closely have arrived at very different conclusions. Michael Cook wrote,

> Unless he believes that accepting Christ is a *sine qua non* for Israel herself to be saved, why is Paul so exercised by his fellow Jews' recalcitrance, or why would he seek refuge in the contorted fantasy that Israel's *jealousy* will motivate her to accept Christ? No, for Paul faith that Jesus is the Christ—in the sense that Paul characteristically defines him—is the *sole* avenue to redemption for Jews as well as Gentiles.[427]

Mark Nanos has written significantly on the book of Romans. It is difficult to state his views concisely, as he has commented on and challenged a number of relevant issues. This was noticed in Amy-Jill Levine's review of his book, *The Mystery of Romans*. "Should he be correct," she wrote, "his work requires a rethinking not just of the epistle but also of the history of the Romans church, of Pauline soteriology, and potentially of contemporary

---

425. Ibid., 32.
426. Ibid., 34.
427. Cook, *Modern Jews Engage the New Testament*, 105; emphasis in the original.

Jewish-Christian dialogue."[428] Most importantly for Nanos, Paul was a Jew and his message does not exclude Jews. In a discussion of Romans Chapters 9—11, he argues: "In fact, while the proponents of this explicitly seek to propose a modern view that is respectful of Jews and Judaism in Paul's theology, paradoxically, their position excludes Jews from Christ and makes little sense of the situation of Paul and other Christian Jews, their mission, or their suffering for their confession that Jesus was Israel's Messiah."[429] Nanos's own unique interpretation sees all references to "salvation" in Romans not as a solution to sin, but as Jews needing to be restored to their role as God's messengers. In his comment on Romans 11:26 he writes: "Paul's argument is based not on being in need of restoration to the covenant, but of being disciplined because they have not undertaken the covenant obligation of being entrusted with God's oracles to the nations."[430] Finally, Alan Segal was sympathetic to the dual covenant position, but ultimately recognized that Paul was not saying what many people would like him to say.

> As a believing Jew and a twentieth-century humanist, I could have hoped for a different outcome of Paul's interpretation of these passages. The theology outlined by Stendahl, Gaston and Gager makes more sense for today than does Paul's actual conclusion. It would have been easier for today's Christianity had Paul embraced cultural pluralism more fully.[431]

Paul's message was for Jews and Gentiles, and there has not yet been a cogent alternative to this fact based on his writings. His teaching is inextricably linked to his belief in the resurrection of Jesus. The historicity of this event is not a side issue. Everything Paul wrote about the law—or anything else—is predicated on his belief that Jesus rose from the dead. If this event did not happen, it is at least worth pondering what *did* happen to cause the early movement of disciples (and at least one "converted" skeptic) to unfold in a way that seems exactly as if a resurrection actually occurred. This will be the subject of the next chapter.

---

428. Levine, "Review of The Mystery of Romans," 222.

429. Nanos, *The Mystery of Romans*, 258.

430. Nanos, "Romans, Introduction and Annotations," 278.

431. Segal, *Paul the Convert*, 281.

CHAPTER FOUR

JEWISH VIEWS OF THE RESURRECTION OF JESUS

THE RESURRECTION OF JESUS is the main focus of the Gospels, the content of proclamation in the Book of Acts, and the foundational event to all of Paul's theology. To ignore this event is to ignore the central claim of the New Testament. This does not mean that every study of New Testament subjects needs to provide an opinion about the historicity of the event. Scholars who focus on textual as opposed to historical issues may have no need to comment on this one way or the other. This may include literary comparisons with traditional Jewish texts[1] or examinations of a given Gospel's perspective on social or political concerns.[2] But, for those focusing on the historical Jesus or the origins of Christianity, the resurrection needs to be addressed. Comments on the historicity of the resurrection may appear in a variety of forms, ranging from casual and dismissive comments to more detailed studies. For this reason, the case studies of this chapter are divided into several categories.

The first category is perhaps best described as anecdotal, and includes works of historical fiction about the life of Jesus. These may say more about the general Jewish interest in the resurrection of Jesus than about the historicity of the event itself. But, this adds to the study as well. The next category includes comments made within greater works on Jewish history. It is understandable that these may not include exhaustive comments on the resurrection, nevertheless they provide some valuable insight as well. The next section, on the biographies of Jesus, is perhaps where it is most

---

1. Daube, *The New Testament and Rabbinic Judaism*; Montefiore, *Rabbinic Literature and Gospel Teaching*.

2. Reinhartz, *Befriending the Beloved Disciple*; Levine, *The Social and Ethnic Dimension of Matthean Salvation History*.

noticeable that Jewish scholars are not always enthusiastic about discussing the resurrection. These works were specifically focusing on the life of Jesus, yet most of them had extremely little to say about what happened after the crucifixion. The final three sections include the scholarship that more directly focuses on the resurrection in one way or another. These include articles dedicated to at least one aspect of the resurrection, a section on the three scholars who wrote exhaustively on the subject, and finally a series of works which provide alternative historical theories to the New Testament narrative. What is of interest is how the authors approach the historicity of the resurrection, what events they acknowledge as historical, and whether or not they offer an alternative. Many of the alternative suggestions, whether minor or more elaborate, were already discussed in general in the previous chapter. Only when unique challenges are made in this chapter will there be a brief response.

[4.1] IN HISTORICAL FICTION

The books discussed in this section are similar to the "biographies" of Jesus listed below. The difference is that these works may include fictional elements, usually new characters, alongside the reconstruction of the life of Jesus. A couple of the authors take the story into the world of fantasy. Asch has characters who were reincarnated, and Fleg employed a mythical medieval figure. But, in each case the fantastic (and supernatural) elements are designed merely to set the stage for how the story will be told. Once underway, these narratives are both lucid and historically well researched. In some ways, these works are more sober than some of the authors below who were professing to write serious scholarship.[3] The four authors in this category were basically trying to understand what it means that Jesus was a Jew, and their views of the resurrection reflect this.

[4.1.1] Joseph Jacobs

Meshullam ben Zadok was a member of the Sanhedrin at the time of Jesus. About twenty-five years later he writes to his friend (Aglaophonos) to reveal his thoughts about the man from Nazareth. This is the theme of Joseph Jacobs' novel, *As Others saw Him*. Originally published anonymously in 1895,

---

3. See Klausner's explanation of Joseph of Arimathea's reasons for reburying Jesus or his speculation about Paul's conversion (4.3.4). See also Maccoby's writings about Paul (3.5.1 and 4.6.5). Schonfield's book *The Passover Plot* is also a work of fiction and could have been discussed here, but will be addressed below (4.6.2).

it was a pioneering effort in the field of Jewish historical fiction in the days of Jesus. Written in the first person by Meshullam, he states: "For I was at Jerusalem all the time he passed for a leader of men up to his shameful death. At first I admired him for his greatness of soul and goodness of life, but in the end I was persuaded to believe that he was a danger to our nation, and, though willingly, I was of those who voted for his death in the council of Twenty-Three."[4]

It is not surprising that Jacobs' name was not at first attached to this work. He was a Jewish scholar, who also had great success in writing (and re-writing) children's stories. The views expressed in his book are quite tame by today's standards. But just prior to the twentieth century, he would have faced difficulties from both his Jewish peers as well as many Christians. The former might have seen his portrayal as too sympathetic; the latter might have resented a portrayal which went against canonical tradition. The main events of Jesus' life are described from Meshullam's vantage point. These include reactions to the scandalous birth, his baptism by his cousin (where Jesus first believed that God called him His beloved son), and his teaching in both the synagogue and the Temple. This teaching was similar to what other Jewish sages had spoken, yet was also quite different. Meshullam admits being captivated by his teaching. The words of Jesus, he wrote, "seemed to know all my secret thoughts and sins; and yet I felt not ashamed, for they saw the sins, so they seemed to speak forgiveness of them."[5]

The most radical—and disagreeable—aspect of his teaching concerned Jesus' own view of himself. Meshullam could not understand how such a one could display "a wisdom and a sound sense equal to the greatest sages," and yet say such "mad" things about himself.[6] To be sure, this Jesus was claiming to be God, not just a messenger. This was too much, and it clearly went beyond acceptable boundaries. He explains: "While we see the Deity everywhere, we localize him nowhere."[7] The ministry of Jesus continued, leading to much speculation and discussion. Some wondered if he could be the Messiah. Others pointed to the lack of signs that were supposed to accompany the Messiah's arrival. Some countered that perhaps he was the Messiah ben Joseph, "who shall be slain before the other cometh."[8] All of this produced a mood of excitement at his entry into Jerusalem for Passover. Meshullam was one of the onlookers. Jesus, he writes, displayed no signs of

4. Jacobs, *As Others Saw Him*, vi.

5. Ibid., 49.

6. Ibid., 112.

7. Ibid., 113.

8. Ibid., 116.

a coming triumph. Rather, he is seen with "his eyes downcast" and his "face all sad."[9]

Nevertheless, Jesus was creating quite a stir and the High Priest called a special meeting. Whoever Jesus was—or claimed to be—any type of rebellion could bring Pilate's wrath on the Jewish nation. This needed to be addressed. Jesus was brought in and asked if he was the Messiah, to which he responded in the affirmative. This was all they needed to hear. A vote was taken to decide if he should be sent to Pilate. Meshullam hesitated but ultimately agreed. Jesus was taken to Pilate and then to Golgotha, as Meshullam watched from a distance. The story ends with Meshullam's musings—perhaps still wondering if he did the right thing. Jesus was so good and wise, yet he also went too far: "He spoke as one having authority, and it seemed to us arrogance."[10]

There is no mention of the resurrection after the crucifixion. There is, however, one hint earlier in the narrative regarding a possible explanation. Meshullam describes a time he was studying Torah and had an unusual experience: "I looked up from my sacred scroll, and lo! Jesus the Nazarene stood before me, gazing upon me with those piercing eyes I can never forget."[11] He reports that Jesus said: "Awake thou that sleepest, arise from the dead, and the Christ shall shine upon you." But, when Meshullam looked up again Jesus was gone. There was no one standing there. He then went outside and saw Jesus walking with some of his friends. Surely he could not be in two places at once. It was a riddle, but perhaps one that would also explain later events. "I know not what to think; but I have heard that, even after his death, those who were nearest and dearest to Jesus saw him and heard him even as I did."[12]

[4.1.2] Edmund Fleg

One of the most creative approaches to the life of Jesus comes from Edmund Fleg, a French author and playwright. The book opens with Fleg himself at the Mount of Olives in Jerusalem. He is asking questions to himself, trying to understand the ancient story of Jesus. He is met by an odd character who, to Fleg's surprise, spoke perfect French. The stranger would turn out to be even more extraordinary. He is the Wandering Jew, the medieval mythical figure who is destined to roam the earth, cursed, until Jesus returns. Fleg

9. Ibid., 124.
10. Ibid., 202.
11. Ibid., 89.
12. Ibid., 92.

thought this was just a tale. But he then embarks on a tour of what really happened 2,000 years ago as told by this strange figure, one who was actually on the scene in the days of Jesus.

Fleg begins by poking fun at himself as the Wandering Jew questions both his Jewish allegiance as a liberal Jew and his desire to add to the literature on the historical Jesus. The Wandering Jew says: "But, between ourselves, if Judaism had only Jews of the same caliber as yourself to rise in its defense, there would be no more anti-Semites—and why? Because there would be no more Jews! . . . And now, like everyone else, you are going to write a life of Jesus?"[13] The wandering Jew becomes Fleg's guide. He had been an eyewitness to the final days of Jesus. He alludes to being the man recorded in the Gospel Mark who fled quickly and left his cloak.[14] He followed the arrest of Jesus, but wished he had not. As he leads Fleg on this tour of a lifetime, he constantly questions his ultimate betrayal of Jesus. There were reasons to question Jesus' messianic claims, and yet there was much that caused him to ponder otherwise.

> And yet . . . the prophecies that he fulfilled in his lifetime may have been imitative, but what of those other prophecies, his own, that have been fulfilled after his death? . . . Was not Jerusalem destroyed, as he had foretold? Was not Israel led captive into all the peoples? . . . Did not the Twelve receive the Holy Ghost, as he had promised? Cowards though they were, did they not conquer the earth? . . . Is not his Gospel preached to all nations? And, exalted on his cross, did he not draw all men up to him?[15]

As he tells the story, Judas was the one to betray Jesus based on a plan by the Sanhedrin to appease the Romans by handing over one trouble maker. The Wandering Jew also had relatives who were arrested. When Jesus was on the way to his crucifixion he asked the Wandering Jew to help him carry his cross. Because of ambivalence, and then seeing two of his own relatives carrying their own crosses, he went to help them instead. Simon of Cyrene helped Jesus with the cross while the Wandering Jew attended to his relatives (who would be crucified on either side of Jesus).[16] The body of Jesus was placed in a tomb by Joseph of Aramathea.

When he had refused to help carry the cross, the following words began to ring in his ear: *you shall walk until I come again.*[17] These words would

13. Fleg, *Jesus: Told by the Wandering Jew*, 16; ellipsis points in original.

14. Ibid., 262.

15. Ibid., 266; ellipsis points in original.

16. Ibid 277–78.

17. Ibid., 295.

be his constant companion over the centuries. But, what had happened to the body after it was placed in the tomb? He relates several events, trying to make sense of them. First, Mary from Magdala discovered the empty tomb. When he goes there to see for himself a guard tells him that the disciples took the body and gave them a bribe. Another guard said that such a story is not possible and a debate ensued.[18] He continued to investigate. One guard saw an angel, another saw nothing. One witness said there were two angels. John and Peter arrived at the tomb. They did not believe the story of the women, and came to see for themselves. They acknowledged that the tomb was empty.[19] He then finds two others who were on their way to Emmaus. They had spent time with the risen Jesus and were a more credible witness than the woman, he argues to himself.[20] Then there was an appearance to Peter and a week later even Thomas believed. But, he himself had no experience. *"Why should I seek him if he had hidden himself from me?"*[21] He continues to ponder the issue: *"*"They have seen something-so much is certain," I thought as I walked. "But what have they seen" Is it a figment of their imagination? Yet how could they all imagine the same thing simultaneously? They touched him. They saw him eat! Can you handle a dream? Do you offer food to a dream?"[22]

His walking took him to the Sea of Galilee, where the disciples had assembled. Thomas tells him of the importance of just believing, and John explained that Jesus is the word who became flesh.[23] There was even a group of five hundred who saw and believed. But, he himself did not have an experience. In the end, the question of the resurrection is reduced to personal experience, even in the midst of confirmation from others. Fleg was writing just a few years before the beginning of World War Two, which was perhaps the greatest influence on his perspective. In the end, the wandering Jew becomes a preacher, and even somewhat of a prophet, envisioning what God would say about how both Christians and Jews handled their respective inheritances. To the former he says:

> In two thousand years what have you done with it, you Christians, children of the Gentiles? What have you done with my Jews whom I have forgiven? What have you done with my poor

18. Ibid., 297.

19. Ibid., 301.

20. Ibid., 304.

21. Ibid., 305.

22. Ibid., 306.

23. Ibid., 308.

in whom I incarcerated myself? What have you done with my peace for which I died?[24]

To the latter group he says the following:

> You will say: "we have remained faithful to thee for centuries and centuries. We have waited, amidst torture and persecution, for the true Messiah whom thou hast promised us!" He will reply: "to wait is not enough! What have you done to bring about his coming? I scattered you amongst the people that you might be as links between them. But instead of linking them together, you have clung to their idols, shared in their luxuries, and taken part with them in their conflicts."[25]

The final section is an appeal for world peace. Paraphrasing the teachings of Jesus, the Wandering Jew pronounces woes on those who make arms, and "blessed are those" who refuse to bear arms. The last words that Fleg hears from this character are: "Blessed are those who die for peace, for they shall see God!"[26]

[4.1.3] Scholem Asch

In the 1930s, Pan Viadomsky was an elderly, sickly, anti-Semitic professor of ancient history. Having obtained a first-century document that he believed was written by *Judah Ish-Kiriot*, he employs the help of a young Jewish scholar to help with translation. So begins Sholem Asch's novel, *The Nazarene*, which was originally written in Yiddish. Asch was famously ostracized in the Jewish community. He never made any type of faith commitment to Jesus, although he was accused of being a missionary simply because he approached the subject.[27] *The Nazarene* tells the story of Jesus from three perspectives. Viadomsky, it turns out, is a reincarnation of someone called Hegemon Cornelius, who was a centurion in Pilate's Jerusalem guard. The document itself also adds to the narrative. Finally, the young Jewish scholar learns that he himself is some type of reincarnated version of a man named Josephus, a disciple of *Nicodemon*. Apart from the supernatural elements to establish the characters, the narrative portrays a very Jewish Yeshua (as he is here called).

24. Ibid., 312.
25. Ibid., 313.
26. Ibid., 316.
27. Lieberman, *The Christianity of Sholem Asch*.

The story goes back and forth between the two modern scholars and the events of the life of Yeshua. After the crucifixion, Yeshua is buried by Joseph of Arimathea and *Nicodemon*. Judah hangs himself. The narrative then returns to the "present." Viadomsky at this point had grown more sickly, but he sat up and wondered what happened next. He was surprised that the student did not continue the story, did he not know of what happened after Yeshua's death? The student had little interest in the following events, but he complied with Viadomsky's wish to hear the remainder of the story. He said that Yeshua had disappeared from his grave and went to his disciples. He told them he was the messiah, that he was now with God in Heaven and that he would soon come to earth "in order to judge the living and to begin the kingdom of heaven."[28]

Viadomsky asked if there were many followers, which the student replied: "I do not know. I took no interest in the matter."[29] He then said that some of his own circle joined the sect of "messianists." This included Joseph of Arimathea. *Nicodemon*, however, did not follow them at first. He believed, "It is enough that rabbi Yeshua lived like a righteous man, sought after God, drew men nearer to heaven, and died in utter purity."[30] At this Viadomsky asked how he felt about the new movement. The student's response sounds very much like a modern appeal to ecumenicism and not particularly like what might have been said in the first century. He began by saying that what is important is to wait for the messiah and that the very act of waiting is "the fountainhead of faith." He continues: "The only difference between us was that in their belief the Messiah had already been once on earth, and was due to return, and we said that this could not be, that the Messiah could not have been on earth and mankind remain unredeemed from evil, but full of wickedness. Our belief was that the Messiah was yet to come, theirs that he was to come again."[31]

[4.1.4] Rolf Gompertz

In 1977, Rolf Gomperz wrote *My Jewish Brother Jesus*. It is a brief, standard historical novel which was later republished as *A Jewish Novel about Jesus*. One interesting twist is a budding romance between Mary Magdalene and Judas, one that ended when each had to follow their separate destinies. Gompertz's main reason for writing was simply to reveal Jesus as a Jew. "He

28. Asch, *The Nazarene*, 692.

29. Ibid.

30. Ibid.

31. Ibid., 693.

was born a Jew, he lived as a Jew, and he died a Jew."[32] This book, he tells his readers, ends with the death of Jesus. "What happened three days later and after," he says," is the beginning of another book I hope to write some day."[33] This story starts with Judas, who is interested in becoming a zealot. But, after witnessing a crucifixion realizes he does not have it in him to be a man of violence. The next day he meets Jesus and finds a new purpose in life.

The message of this Galilean preacher is all about love, as he reveals in a later conversation with Judas. ""We must make others see!" Jesus exclaimed, as if driven by some inner calling. "Once they see, it will change their lives, Judas! Once they see what alone can make them happy, once they see what really makes them happy, they will change, they will become happier human beings. They will infect each other with love, Judas."[34]Jesus reveals to Judas that he is the Messiah.[35] Later, because of the commotion surrounding his message and the misunderstandings, Pilate tells Caiphas to call for Jesus' death. As others began to back away from Jesus, Judas also questioned his own commitment and eventually helped Caiphas by betraying Jesus. The book ends with the death—as promised—although there is a one page epilogue which includes these words: "Following his death, the body of Jesus was placed in a tomb. Three days later the body was missing. From this day on, there were reports of a resurrected Jesus appearing to his followers. Despair was turned into hope, defeat into victory."[36]

[4.2] IN THE WRITING OF JEWISH HISTORY

Since the *Haskalah*, or Jewish Enlightenment, Jewish scholars have been interested in reconstructing their own history from a secular point of view.[37] The needs of modernity presented challenges to Jewish self-understanding, as well as Jewish interaction with the new world and Christianity. It is impossible to write a Jewish history without mentioning the (almost completely negative) role of European Christendom. The emergence of the Christian movement also needs to be explained. It clearly began within the boundaries of Second Temple Judaism, and yet the origins are inextricably linked to the claim of resurrection on the part of the original disciples and/or Paul.

32. Gompertz, *My Jewish Brother Jesus*, xi.
33. Ibid.
34. Ibid., 31.
35. Ibid., 33.
36. Ibid., 185.
37. See Feiner, *Haskalah and History, The Emergence of a Modern Jewish Historical Consciousness*; Rosman, *How Jewish Is Jewish History?*.

Even within such a sweeping historical overview, a response to the resurrection is required. These works offer a peripheral view of the resurrection of Jesus and potential explanations.

[4.2.1] Heinrich Graetz

The first complete study of Jewish history came from Heinrich Graetz in the mid-nineteenth century. It was published in six volumes and has continually been in print. Graetz had mixed feelings about Jesus, and was heavily influenced by the German critical scholarship of the day. But for a Jewish scholar his study was groundbreaking. His section on the life of Jesus is over ten pages and begins by commenting on Jesus' character. Because of his Galilean origins and his native Aramaic, Graetz wrote, Jesus could not have been steeped in the Law. But he had other positive qualities: "High-minded earnestness and spotless moral purity were his undeniable attributes: they stand out in all the authentic accounts of his life that have reached us, and appear even in those garbled teachings which his followers placed in his mouth."[38]

Jesus is described as an Essene although this is said to be speculation. It was to the poor and needy, the outcasts, that he would bring "the great healing truths of Judaism."[39] He had no plan to change Judaism, his goal was to "redeem the sinner" and prepare him for the "approaching Messianic time."[40] But, he was more than a teacher. He was a worker of miracles. Such stories of "extraordinary events" and cures may certainly have been exaggerated, he writes. Yet, they "must doubtless have had some foundation in fact."[41] Messianic speculation grew and he was forced to go to Jerusalem. The triumphal entry is said to be an invention and the trial before the Sanhedrin is questionable. But, eventually, Jesus appeared before Pilate and then went to the cross. Graetz mourns his death, as one who attempted to bring so much good into the world. Yet, this death would also bring severe consequences for the Jewish people. The disciples gathered together to mourn for their master. They continued in their faith and were even joined by others. The only problem was the "shameful death" that he endured. A suffering Messiah was a stumbling block to their movement. It was because

38. Graetz, *History of the Jews*, 149.

39. Ibid., 152.

40. Ibid., 155.

41. Ibid., 156.

of this that one of the followers referred to Isaiah 53 to make the events fit the prophecy.[42]

After a very brief discussion of the new movement in its earliest form, he comes to Paul. His view was typical of the day, in that he applauded Jesus as a Jew, but had much stronger language reserved for Paul. This trend would dominate in Jewish scholarship for over a hundred years, and can still be found today. For Graetz, Paul was "excitable and vehement," bitter in his treatment of others who disagreed with him. His Jewishness was spurious as well: "He had limited knowledge of Judean writings, and was only familiar with the Scriptures through the Greek translation; enthusiastic and fanciful, he believed in the visions of his imagination and allowed himself to be guided by them."[43] Paul persecuted the early followers because they broke with Pharisaic doctrines. In Damascus, he learned that many heathens had gone over to Judaism. This might have caused Paul to wonder if the time was at hand when all nations would recognize the God of Israel. But, Jewish law would be too burdensome for Gentiles. However, his teachers may have told him that the Law was only binding until the Messiah comes. So, if the Messiah had already come, the law would not be necessary for Gentiles.[44] This reasoning, combined with Paul's temperament caused him to believe that "Jesus had made himself manifest to him."[45] But, if Jesus had died, how could such a manifestation occur? This led to his belief that Jesus had risen from the dead. This, in turn, lead Paul to believe Jesus was their Messiah, a belief he would passionately bring to the Gentiles along with the claim that they no longer need the law.[46]

[4.2.2] The Jewish Encyclopedia

The Jewish Encyclopedia was the first monumental work of Jewish scholarship to be written in English. It was published between 1901 and 1906 and it included a section on Jesus of Nazareth, divided into three subsections: in history, theology, and Jewish legend. Isadore Singer edited the entire project, but Reform leader, Kaufmann Kohler, wrote the section on Jewish history. The historical section gives a basic overview of the story. Jesus was more Jewish than John the Baptist, and he did not directly claim to be the Messiah. In Passover of the year 29 C.E. he went to Jerusalem. After the

42. Ibid., 166.
43. Ibid., 223.
44. Ibid., 224–25.
45. Ibid., 225.
46. Ibid., 226.

Passover meal, there was no actual Jewish trial, although Jesus was handed over to Pilate by some priests. He was sent to the cross, where he died. This ends the section on history. However, the resurrection is addressed in the immediately following section on theology. The disciples and the women, it says, "beheld him in their entranced state." The apparitions that occurred after the crucifixion were placed within his lifetime as part of the final editing of the Gospels. These include the transfiguration and walking at night as a spirit on the lake. Visions were also experienced of seeing Jesus in the clouds. The reason for such experiences is not explained. But, the theological source of Jesus' teaching is given: "And so it came about that, consciously or unconsciously, the crystallized thought of generations of Essenes and entire chapters taken from their apocalyptic literature (Matt. xxiv.–xxv.) were put into the mouth of Jesus, the acme and the highest type of Essenism."[47]

There is also an entry for Paul. Like Graetz, the *Jewish Encyclopedia* takes a negative approach to the man from Tarsus. His use of the Septuagint led the writer to say that he had no familiarity with the Hebrew texts. Throughout his writings there is "an irrational or pathological element which could not but repel the disciples of the Rabbis." His "epilepsy" often put him in a state of ecstasy that similarly caused him to be estranged from the Jews. Ultimately, Paul is declared completely un-Jewish. This is adduced by his Hellenistic upbringing and his "unparalleled animosity and hostility to Judaism." Paul's theology is then summarized—"a system of belief which endeavored to unite all men, but at the expense of sound reason and common sense." Regarding the Damascus experience, "there is possibly a historical kernel to the story." No details are given. But, Paul apparently had a vision of Jesus who called to him. This stirred up previously held convictions: "Evidently Paul entertained long before his vision those notions of the Son of God which he afterward expressed; but the identification of his Gnostic Christ with the crucified Jesus of the church he had formerly antagonized was possibly the result of a mental paroxysm experienced in the form of visions."[48]

[4.2.3] Abram Leon Sachar

In 1930, Abram Sachar published his classic work, *A History of the Jews*. At the time there was a new atmosphere about the study of Jesus, and many Jewish scholars were quite positive about him. There was also the undeniable fact of his influence. The life of Jesus, he wrote, "was destined to change

47. Jacobs et al., "Jesus of Nazareth," 172–73.
48. Kohler, "Saul of Tarsus," 81–82.

the history of the world more profoundly than that of any other single individual who ever lived."[49] Although twenty centuries of Christianity have "obscured his genius," and the New Testament documents themselves are "untrustworthy,"[50] Sachar produced a substantial biography. Jesus was first and foremost Jewish. In all that he did, "there seemed to be little in conflict with Jewish tradition as interpreted even by rigid Pharisees."[51] What distinguished Jesus was that he taught in his own name, rather than sighting previous tradition. From here, it was just a small step for him to come to believe that he was the Messiah. This was the reason for his famous trip to Jerusalem, to proclaim his Messiahship at the appropriate time and place.[52]

In Jerusalem, Jesus' teaching began a revolt that aroused Jewish leaders. The details of the trials that would follow are questionable. However, it is "incontrovertible" that Jesus affirmed his Messiahship to the Jewish leaders. This would ultimately lead him to Pilate and the cross.[53] After the crucifixion, the body was "deposited in a nearby tomb, and a stone was placed at the entrance."[54] But this was not the end of the story: "Then came a miraculous restoration of faith, inspired, according to all gospel accounts, by the resurrection and reappearance of Jesus."[55] Sachar mentions both the women finding the empty tomb, and the visions received by them and the disciples. These visions would become "the corner-stone of the new Christian religion."[56] Whatever they were, these visions were not the product of deliberate deceit. The disciples truly believed that Jesus was the Messiah. What then, might have caused such visions? Sachar continues: "Doubtless their imagination was set on fire when the body disappeared, and they sought no rational explanation."[57] The empty tomb, then, was the catalyst that inspired their visions of the resurrected Jesus. Sachar does not attempt to explain how it might have become empty in the first place. The visions that emerged, however, were quite real. The disciples saw Jesus "as vividly and as truly as Isaiah saw his heavenly visions, and as other sensitive spirits,

49. *Sachar, A History of the Jews*, 124.

50. Ibid., 125.

51. Ibid., 128.

52. Ibid., 130.

53. Ibid., 132.

54. Ibid., 133.

55. Ibid., 134.

56. Ibid.

57. Ibid.

in exalted religious moods, were certain of transcendental experiences."[58] These visions then "fortified" their convictions, and a movement was born.

As for Paul, he was a Hellenistic Jew who took part in the early disputes with the Nazarene sect, and was responsible for his share of persecutions against them. Sachar also believed that Paul was "sorely troubled by a sense of sin which no rationalizing and no amount of learning would still."[59] He, too, would undergo a dramatic change: "Then came a sudden vision to him, a tremendous psychological experience, which changed his whole balance. The prophet whose disciples were being persecuted suddenly appeared and opened a new way of life to Paul."[60] Sachar briefly attempts to find an alternative explanation for Paul's radical turnaround. Perhaps it was caused by Paul's failure to influence and win over the persecuted sect. Or, maybe Paul had no peace in Judaism and wanted something more.[61] Whatever the cause, Paul's own convictions grew and solidified. These beliefs were disseminated and then went on to change the world.

[4.2.4] Salo Wittmayer Baron

Originally published in 1937, Salo Wittmayer Baron's series, *A Social and Religious History of the Jews*, is the definitive single-author work in this field. It covers the entire history in sixteen volumes. Jesus' teaching, according to Baron, was quite common for his day, and he cites several examples of parallels from the Talmud. One distinction, "nourished by the ideas of Pharisaic Judaism," was his emphasis on the messianic hope, specifically his belief that it would be fulfilled in his own lifetime. This would have its effect on his listeners, who had already been "stirred by apocalyptic writers and preachers for many generations."[62] It would also help make sense of his death.

> Jesus' crucifixion at first stunned his disciples. Much as they may have cherished the literary recollections of Deutero-Isaiah's suffering Servant of the Lord and believed, with the author of Fourth Maccabees, that individual could through suffering atone for the sins of their fellow men, they like most other Palestinian Jews, could not quite divorce their vision of the advent of the messiah from that of a visible final triumph over all enemies.[63]

58. Ibid.
59. Ibid., 136.
60. Ibid., 136.
61. Ibid., 137.
62. Baron, *A Social and Religious History of the Jews*, 68.
63. Ibid., 71.

Here is an acknowledgment of a redeemer in Jewish thought whose suffering would atone for sin. This provided the theological justification. Although some of the disciples had lost faith, one occurrence would rally the group: "Not until they had the vision of Christ resurrected did the other apostles regain their composure and resume their mission."[64] The resurrection, along with the crucifixion and Last Supper, were combined to provide "an answer to the riddle of its founder's agonizing death."[65] This is the first of Baron's three stages of early Christianity. The second would take the movement a step away from its original geographical roots, only to make way for the third and decisive change: the Catholic Church. The transition from the first to the second stage is stated succinctly: "At this crucial moment Paul assumed the Leadership."[66] There is no mention of his life before he became a follower of Jesus, nor how he came to believe. His own contribution would come "not through a process of systematic thinking, but by lending expression to his high-strung emotions" and by seeking in creative fashion the reconciliation of his own Jewish and Hellenistic heritages. This included his views on "pagan mysteries of salvation."[67]

[4.2.5] Solomon Grayzel

In 1947, Grayzel published his own thorough study of Jewish history. He saw Joshua (as he called Jesus) as a disciple of John the Baptist. It was after John's death—and perhaps somewhat because of it—that Joshua began his own ministry. This was marked by calls to repent, preaching and healing the sick.[68] Grayzel believed that Jesus claimed to be the Messiah during the trial before the High Priest. This led to his meeting with Pilate, the crucifixion, and the burial. Joshua's friends "bribed the Romans to give his body to them."[69] They received the body, placed it in a cave and covered it with a rock. The plan was to return at a later time for a proper burial. The group scattered, but one among them returned to the cave and found it empty; "The body had mysteriously disappeared."[70] For those who expected a miraculous deliverance, and who had been taught that the coming Messiah

64. Ibid.

65. Ibid., 72

66. Ibid., 76.

67. Ibid.

68. Grayzel, *History of the Jews*, 131.

69. Ibid., 135.

70. Ibid.

meant the resurrection of the dead, Grayzel explains, "it was not impossible to see a miracle in the emptiness of the cave."[71]

A few years later, enter Paul. He was a devoted Jew who was "incensed" by the teachings of this new group. But then something intense happened to him as well. "In a flash" Paul had the idea that Judaism might be divided into two parts: law and ideals. The former would suit the Jews in Judea, and the latter would benefit the Gentiles.[72] Paul became convinced of this, and, "characteristically, became terribly earnest about convincing others."[73]

[4.2.6] Cecil Roth

Cecil Roth's 1961 book, *History of the Jews*, contains just a few pages about Jesus. His discussion of both the disciples and Paul's experience says nothing about the resurrection. The following facts are given as a backdrop for the discussion: "[I]n the year 33 C.E., a popular religious revivalist from Galilee named Joshua, who laid claim to Davidic descent, was crucified on Passover eve, after a summary trial, by the nervous administration."[74] Although others had claimed to be the Messiah, without success, the followers of Jesus would not abandon their faith. The crucifixion did not impede them as might be expected. For some reason the faith lived on. For this reason, Roth says, "his personal magnetism must have been amazingly great."[75] His followers continued to cherish his memory. Sometime later, the movement took a radical turn because of one specific event. Saul of Tarsus was on his way to Damascus and "suddenly became convinced of the Messianic claims of the dead leader, whose followers he had strenuously opposed before this."[76]

[4.2.7] Martin Goodman

The interaction between Jews in antiquity and the Roman Empire is an exciting and compelling story. It is the focus of Martin Goodman's popular book, *Rome and Jerusalem*. In the midst of the clash between these two great civilizations, another significant group would emerge. "It is a remarkable fact," he writes, "that one movement which began in Jerusalem in the first

---

71. Ibid.
72. Ibid., 151.
73. Ibid., 152.
74. Roth, *History of the Jews*, 101.
75. Ibid., 141.
76. Ibid.

century CE came by the fourth century to govern the world-view of those who held power in Rome."[77] Indeed, the origins of this movement need to be addressed.

Goodman is a professor at Oxford who specializes in Jewish history in the Roman world. He believes very little can be known about Jesus because of the "contradictions between the multifarious tales,"[78] referring to both the canonical Gospels and other sources. Yet, he does believe some things can be known. For example, Jesus was a Jew who probably came from Galilee, he was a teacher (although what he taught is debated), and he eventually died on a cross in Jerusalem under the governorship of Pontius Pilate.[79] His followers continued their faith even after the crucifixion, as Goodman explains: "What lead these Jews to affirm their faith in Jesus must have been mostly memories of his ethical teachings while he was alive and the eschatological fervour which had accompanied his preaching of the Kingdom of God."[80] Goodman does not mention the disciples' belief in the resurrection (nor does he deny it). He then briefly comments on what happened to Paul. The following is given without comment or explantion: "Shortly after the crucifixion of Jesus, he came into contact with some of the followers of the new movement and persecuted them in Jerusalem, but on the way to Damascus as an agent of the High Priest to arrest converts there, he was himself converted on the road by a vision of the risen Jesus and devoted the rest of his life to his work as "apostle of the gentiles.""[81]

[4.3] BIOGRAPHIES OF JESUS

It has been said that research about the life of Jesus tells us more about the researcher than about Jesus himself. There have been countless attempts to answer the question: *who is Jesus?* This section will survey the major attempts made by Jewish scholars.[82] It is perhaps the best representation of what was noticed by Galvin and Ben-Chorin regarding a general lack of interest in the resurrection of Jesus among Jewish scholars. This is the place, one might assume, where a discussion of the resurrection is appropriate.

---

77. Goodman, *Rome and Jerusalem*, 512.

78. Ibid., 517.

79. Ibid., 514–15.

80. Ibid., 516.

81. Ibid., 515.

82. Vermes would qualify in this category as well with his book, *Jesus the Jew*, but since he addressed the resurrection significantly elsewhere, he will be discussed below (4.5.2).

Of the nine scholars in this section, only one (Montefiore) significantly addressed the issue. The other scholars offered brief, often casual dismissals, of the event.

[4.3.1] Paul Goodman

Paul Goodman was a British Zionist leader and author. His book, *The Synagogue and the Church* seeks to offer a defense of Judaism, specifically by comparing it with Christianity. Like other scholars in the early twentieth-century he was positive about Jesus himself, while dismissing the religious system that would form around him. "The charm of his personality," he wrote, "has sent its rays all over the world, and infused countless human hearts with the Spirit of Love and self sacrifice."[83] He understands that there is a paradox. Gentiles around the world have embraced Jesus. But, why is it that his own people have not acknowledged him even though "the roots" of his life and thought "lie entirely in Jewish soil?"[84] Goodman sees the main problem as theological, objecting to the "fundamental Christian belief that Jesus Christ is God himself, the Lord and Savior of mankind."[85] He touches on other issues as well, including the resurrection: "Now, it is an unquestionable fact that the resurrection represents an event absolutely beyond our experience, and, if it really took place, it was contrary to all laws of nature."[86] Goodman questioned the way the four Gospel writers recorded the resurrection. He believed they "heard of the event more as of a current rumour turned into a tradition than as an actual occurrence of which they knew the real facts."[87] He specifically states "undeniable contradictions"[88] as the reason to dismiss their reliability. He then proposes his own interpretation of what really happened.

> From the significant concurrence of the evangelists, it would seem that the origin of the story came from Mary Magdalene, that weird figure among the followers of Jesus, who had been cured by him of a mental affliction by having "seven demons" cast out of her. Considering the nervous tension created in her excited mind by the death of Jesus, and her devoted attention to

83. Goodman, *The Synagogue and the Church*, 230.
84. Ibid.
85. Ibid., 223.
86. Ibid., 252.
87. Ibid., 253.
88. Ibid., 258.

his grave after the burial, it is possible that she may have imagined that she had seen angels, and even Jesus himself.[89]

By offering this construction, Goodman has acknowledged several things. These include that Jesus did perform a healing (albeit "mental" and not spiritual), that he was buried, and that his grave was commonly known. He also believed that the early Church was started by "the disciples he gathered around Him [sic] and those who believed in his mission as the Messiah promised by the prophets."[90]

[4.3.2] Claude G. Montefiore

Claude G. Montefiore was a scholar and leading figure of liberal Judaism in England at the turn of the twentieth century. In 1909, he wrote an exhaustive study on the synoptic Gospels. It consists of two volumes, each over 300 pages, including his translation of the texts. This was a pioneering and radical endeavor for a Jewish scholar at the time. It caused quite a stir in many circles. Daniel Langton summarized the reactions of Jewish scholars.

> Contemporaries such as Michael Friedlander, head of the Orthodox rabbinical training school, Jews College, maintained that Montefiore's writings revealed an "anti-Jewish tendency." The cultural Zionist Ahad Ha-Am agreed, detecting a "subservience of the Jewish thinker to the Christian doctrine," and argued that Montefiore's New Testament studies would only promote conversion. Chief Rabbi Joseph Hertz accused him of following the apostle Paul in abrogating Torah. Solomon Schechter argued that his teachings were not so much Liberal Judaism as Liberal Christianity.[91]

Montefiore saw the value in such a project, saying it is "of great importance for Jews to understand and appreciate aright the life and teaching of Jesus."[92] In this, he predated the *JANT* by one hundred and three years. Unlike the other authors in this category, he was not selective about what he addressed. He followed the texts, and approached them as a Jew, although a modern and enlightened Jew. Hence, miracles are questioned from the start. For those who do believe in miracles, he says, it would not

89. Ibid., 257

90. Ibid., 295.

91. Langton "Claude Montefiore and Christianity: Did the Founder of Anglo-Liberal Judaism Lean Too Far?," 98.

92. Montefiore, *The Synoptic Gospels*, xix.

be difficult to affirm the specific examples found in the New Testament. But, that is only one part of the argument. He continues: "If, on the other hand, like the writer of this book, we do not believe that the miracles happened then it seems tolerably certain that whatever substratum or residue of non-miraculous fact these stories may contain, they could not have been directly reported, in the form in which we now possess them, to the writer of the Gospel by actual eyewitnesses.[93]

Montefiore was well versed in the New Testament scholarship of his day, which was highly skeptical. In fact, he was often more sympathetic to the Gospels than some of the Christian scholars. Many of the events recorded in the Gospels are acknowledged as actual history. The crucifixion happened. Jesus died. Joseph of Arimathea, he believes, was a real person who provided the tomb where Jesus was placed. Arguments against the historicity of Joseph are dismissed. For example, Isaiah 53:9 ("being with a rich man in his grave") is sometimes assumed to be the antecedent for the creation of the Joseph story. But, this verse, he remarks, is not quoted in the Gospels. Also, he says, the burial is confirmed by Paul in 1 Corinthians 15:4. Montefiore believed Joseph's involvement was not necessarily because he was a disciple, since Mark originally says merely that he was waiting for the kingdom of God. This expression equally describes many Pharisees. Joseph was probably sympathetic, he writes, but his involvement with the burial is more likely related to his desire to carry out the law in Deuteronomy than anything else.[94]

He writes factually and addresses the historical questions, but Montefiore was also painfully aware of the horrors done against the Jews because of the death of Jesus. It is an ever-present reality. Yet, in spite of this, he believed that both the life and death of Jesus were "of immense benefit to the world." Because of Jesus, a large portion of Judaism's truth has been taught to the nations. All of these factors, for good and bad, he concludes, are part of God's calling upon the Jewish people.[95] He begins his discussion on the resurrection with a couple of explanations. First, the primary focus of his book is the life and teachings of Jesus. The narratives about his death have little importance for him, and those of the resurrection are "least important of all." Agreeing with other scholars, he saw the resurrection as more properly a discussion for Church history. Second, his book is not meant to be polemical, and therefore there was no reason to engage in all the details of the resurrection. That would entail a major examination of the evidence ranging

93. Ibid., xxiv.
94. Ibid., 378.
95. Ibid., 382.

from the internal inconsistencies in the texts, to the massive literature that argues against the empty tomb.[96] He says: "But the author of this book need not enter into these discussions. He writes frankly as a Jew, and therefore, as one who does not so "believe in" the resurrection as would logically compel him to change his creed. He is not concerned either to defend his own faith or attack the faith of others."[97]

After such a statement, the reader might expect him to skip over the resurrection entirely. But, he proceeds with the investigation and it is relatively detailed. He believes that it is most probable that "the disciples, or some of them, saw a vision of Jesus which they believed to be a vision of their risen Master." In this sense, he believes that the Gospels are historical. The disciples really had such experiences. For him, this is "more probable" than the popular counter theories of the day. These include that the stories were completely fabricated, that the disciples were lying, and that the story was based on legends that developed over time. Once the visions are accepted, there are two possibilities.

The first option is that the disciples actually saw Jesus in "some special supernatural manifestation." The other possibility is that what they saw was exclusively a "product of the mental condition of the seer." Montefiore assumes the latter. However, he goes on to say that belief in the former view, an actual supernatural experience, does not necessarily challenge the Jewishness of one who might hold such a view. For those who affirm the immortality of the soul, there is such a thing as a continued existence after death. A physical resurrection, ironically, is excluded as an acceptable Jewish view. While he does not believe in the immortality of the soul, he acknowledges that in the case of Jesus—or even Mohammed—such a supernatural existence is possible. In fact, he continues, it is easier to believe the great world religions that came from each of these men began with some type of "divine interventions" rather than subjective illusions.[98] He continues: "But, on the other hand, it is, for other reasons, our scientific duty to do without miracles when we can."[99] This is an appeal to a popular worldview in the name of reason, which is not the same as actually providing a rational alternative. A subjective experience is preferred, he says, because it adequately makes sense of the narrative, and it explains the events "with adequate psychological verisimilitude."[100] But for those who believe in immortality, he says, the

96. Ibid., 383.
97. Ibid.
98. Ibid., 384.
99. Ibid.
100. Ibid., 385.

resurrection of Jesus might have really happened. It is ultimately a matter of belief and preference. Thus, he states, "to those who have not grown up in, or who have not retained, the old Christian theology, the "resurrection" of Jesus has no central importance."[101]

One thing remains perplexing. He believes that Jesus did not rise from the dead. Yet, belief in the resurrection of Jesus created a movement that changed the world. As he says, "it is hard to be content that great religious results should have had not quite satisfactory causes." But, in the end, he reasons, there are many unresolved issues and mysteries in life. We cannot understand "the means which God allows" in His overall plan.[102] He next approaches the empty tomb. The women come to the tomb to anoint the body, although they did so after two days. This, for Montefiore, is "not likely to be historic." This is a minor detail, however, and ultimately he believed that the "narrative, in its essence, is historical."[103] The empty tomb account needs to be harmonized with the visions. For some, it is the empty tomb that caused the visions. Montefiore disagrees. He believes it came after the disciples' visions. He then surveys other views, including that Jewish authorities stole the body, Joseph buried the body temporarily and then reburied it, and that Mary Magdalene went to the tomb and had a vision that grew into the empty tomb story. All of these proposals are deemed "very doubtful." Explaining the origins of the empty tomb story is therefore "not quite easy."[104] For this reason, he offers a different solution: "It is better to assume that the body of Jesus remained where it was placed without disturbance or miracle."[105] This, however, is unsatisfactory based on his belief that both Joseph and the women knew where the tomb was.

[4.3.3] Hyman G. Enelow

Hyman G. Enelow was a leading figure in American Reform Judaism. He served as a rabbi and at one point he was the president of the Central Conference of American Rabbis. He was also instrumental in developing chairs of Jewish studies at both Harvard and Columbia. His book, *A Jewish View of Jesus,* appeared in 1920 and offered a very favorable portrait of Jesus. Enelow believed that Jews should be interested in Jesus for two reasons. The first concerns Jesus' influence on the world. "Whether we like it or not,"

101. Ibid.
102. Ibid.
103. Ibid., 387.
104. Ibid., 389.
105. Ibid.

he wrote, "Jesus has fascinated mankind."[106] The second reason was more personal. Quite simply, "Jesus was a Jew." Yet, he was unlike any other Jew who has ever lived: "He was a man of vision, a revealer, a spiritual perceiver and dreamer, a man who sought to point out the eternal things of life—the things that mean most in the universe."[107]

Enelow admired the life of Jesus, and was equally impressed by the way he died. Although his death would bring "endless agony to the Jew,"[108] Jews should nevertheless be proud that Jesus was ready and willing to die in a noble way. Jesus saw his own teaching as an expression of the "Jewish religious ideal."[109] He believed himself to be the one to usher in the Kingdom of God. If that in turn meant being the Messiah and God's son, Enelow reasons, then Jesus indeed thought of himself as the Messiah.[110] Enelow believed that the Gospels were written thirty to sixty years after the death of Jesus, and therefore it is doubtful that we have them in their original form.[111] For this reason, modern scholarship must step in to explain what really happened. He questions the accounts of the trial before the Sanhedrin, since they do not indicate whether it was the full Sanhedrin of seventy-one members, or the smaller Sanhedrin of twenty-three members. Enelow believed that Pilate himself orchestrated both the arrest and the trials.[112] The questioning of Pilate and the words Jesus spoke while on the cross—specifically his prayer to forgive others—are acknowledged as historical.[113] From here, legend takes the place of concrete facts.

Enelow believed that "Paul was the intellectual founder of the Christian religion."[114] However, he also acknowledged Paul's great training as a rabbi. Paul was originally hostile to the new movement and this was what first brought him in contact with the disciples. This interaction led him to "marvel at their devotion," think about Jesus for himself, and ultimately come to his own decision: "Paul's conclusion was that Jesus was the Messiah, that after the crucifixion he was resurrected, that his resurrection was a sign of his Messiahship, and that Jesus thus had become Savior of the world."[115]

106. Enelow, *A Jewish View of Jesus*, 5.

107. Ibid., 42.

108. Ibid., 61.

109. Ibid., 82.

110. Ibid., 130.

111. Ibid., 64.

112. Ibid., 146.

113. Ibid., 150.

114. Ibid., 158.

115. Ibid., 159.

[4.3.4] Joseph Klausner

Joseph Klausner originally wrote about Jesus in Hebrew. Born in Russia near the end of the nineteenth century, he went to Israel in 1920 and later served as professor at the newly opened Hebrew University. He is best known as a Zionist leader and biographer of Jesus (and later, Paul). Klausner's book, *Jesus of Nazareth*, appeared in English in 1925, just three years after it was originally published in Hebrew.[116] His approach to the New Testament was critical, yet more generous than many of his contemporaries. He specifically questioned the portions which either highlighted the supernatural or which he believed are antithetical to Judaism. Yet to him, Jesus was undeniably Jewish, fully in line with the "Pharisaic Judaism of his day."[117] His teaching promoted the highest moral standards and could—with modifications—be of value to Jews as well: "If ever the day should come and this ethical code be stripped of its wrappings of miracles and mysticism, the Book of the Ethics of Jesus will be one of the choicest treasures in the literature of Israel for all time."[118]

Klausner believed that Jesus did claim to be the Messiah. This is seen, for example, when he sent his disciples to find a colt for him to ride into Jerusalem. "The point is clear," Klausner writes about this incident, "Jesus was minded to enter Jerusalem as the Messiah."[119] But, Klausner did not believe that death and resurrection were part of Jesus' plan. Rather, he believed that upon entering Jerusalem, Jesus wanted to proclaim his messiahship and call people to "repentance and good works."[120] What actually did happen in Jerusalem was not expected. On the eve of Passover, Jesus was arrested and taken to the High Priest and then to Pilate. He was sentenced to death by crucifixion. Klausner comments: "Here ends the life of Jesus, and here begins the history of Christianity."[121] Since he does not accept "Christianity's" account of what happened after the crucifixion, he offers his own rendition.

After Jesus' death, Joseph of Arimathea asked Pilate for the body. Klausner says this was "probably at the request of the disciples."[122] After the burial, Joseph apparently had second thoughts about using his family's tomb. He "thought it unfitting that one who had been crucified should re-

---

116. ישו הנצרי : זמנו, חייו ותורתו

117. Klausner, *Jesus of Nazareth*, 363.

118. Ibid., 414.

119. Ibid., 309.

120. Ibid., 313.

121. Ibid., 355.

122. Ibid.

main in his ancestral tomb." Because of this, he "secretly removed the body at the close of Sabbath and buried it in an unknown grave."[123] The women and the disciples arrive and discover the empty tomb. At some point after this—and perhaps because of this—they all have visions of Jesus. At first, he does not wish to entirely dismiss the visions. He believes that they were definitely real, but that they were "spiritual and not material" in nature.[124] There must have been something real, he reasons, since the faith of millions lasting for nineteen hundred years "is not found in deception."[125] This part of the story is also discussed in his next book, *From Jesus to Paul*, although here he is less sympathetic. The disciples, he now writes, had visions because they were "enthusiastic to the point of madness and credulous to the point of blindness."[126]

His view of Paul is important because he saw him as quite Jewish, long before this view was prominent among scholars. He acknowledges that Paul was, in fact, a student of Gamaliel.[127] He was highly educated, unlike the fishermen who originally followed Jesus. Paul's encounter with the risen Jesus (as recorded in the New Testament) must likewise be reinterpreted. Many scholars have offered psychological explanations for Paul's transformation. But, Klausner's attempt is once again distinct. He first asks whether or not Paul could have known Jesus prior to the crucifixion. It is possible, he says, that Paul could have at least seen Jesus during his lifetime. Klausner's imagination perseveres, and he suggests that Paul could have even been a witness at the crucifixion. This possibility, combined with Paul's memories of the stoning of Stephen, might have had a revolutionary impact on his life: "These two fearful events [the crucifixion and the stoning of Stephen] haunted him, and in conjunction with an involved psychological process brought about the vision on the Damascus Road."[128]

[4.3.5] E R Trattner

Ernest Trattner was a Reform rabbi and scholar. His 1931 book, *As a Jew Sees Jesus*, was passionate about the Jewishness of Jesus. He begins with the following.

---

123. Ibid., 357.
124. Ibid., 359.
125. Ibid.
126. Ibid., 256.
127. Ibid., 307.
128. Ibid., 316.

For Jesus was born a Jew; he lived on the ancestral soil of Palestine, never once setting foot on alien territory; he taught a small group of disciples all of whom were as Jewish as he; the language he spoke dripped with Jewish tradition and lore; the little children he loved were Jewish children; the sinners he associated with were Jewish sinners; he healed Jewish bodies, fed Jewish hunger, poured out wine at a Jewish wedding, and when he died he quoted a passage from the Hebrew book of Psalms. Such a Jew![129]

After introducing this pedigree, Trattner asks why Jesus has remained a stranger to the Jewish world. The answer, of course, is because of the centuries-old persecution done in his name. It is only Christianity's recent "rediscovery of its oriental Master"[130] that has enabled Jewish people to begin a new discussion. The search for the historical Jesus has invariably uncovered a Jewish Jesus. Therefore, the historical Jesus must be "rescued" from church dogma. Trattner then surveys the literature of the previous decades to cite examples of both positive and negative views of the Jewishness of Jesus. "Even at this late date," he writes, "few people really know that the language of Galilee was Aramaic."[131]

Trattner addresses Jesus' own belief in his messiahship. He is at first agnostic, saying that "one cannot penetrate the mind of the Nazarene deeply enough to find exactly what he thought of himself."[132] Two pages later he reveals that, "it is more probable than not that Jesus regarded himself in some sense as the Messiah."[133] Finally, when the High Priest asks Jesus if he is the Messiah, Trattner accepts that Jesus responded in the affirmative.[134] Ultimately, Jesus was not identified as strictly a Pharisee, Sadducee or an Essene. Like all men of "lonely greatness," he was "outside of every party label."[135] Trattner believed that the Gospels were originally oral traditions that were later passed down in different forms. This means that we do not have a "clear portrait" of his life, but only a "fragmentary impression."[136] Trattner acknowledges that Jesus was handed over to Pilate and that the crucifixion happened. After this, "the Christian oral tradition began to take

---

129. Trattner, *As a Jew Sees Jesus*, 1.

130. Ibid., 11.

131. Ibid., 28.

132. Ibid., 66.

133. Ibid., 68.

134. Ibid., 133.

135. Ibid., 102.

136. Ibid., 114.

shape."[137] The apostle Paul now becomes the chief architect of these new traditions.

Trattner does not deny Paul's Jewishness, but believed that his "experience within Judaism does not seem to have been a natural or healthy one."[138] Paul is then charged with borrowing the concept of a resurrected god from pagan Roman religions. This was how and why the early church came to believe in the resurrection of Jesus. Because of this, Trattner and others of his day could embrace the Jewishness of Jesus, but reject many of the issues in the New Testament deemed un-Jewish (pagan). He writes no specific comments about the resurrection, but offers the following general conclusion: "The supernatural Jesus of the gospels is a dated figure. He is the product of the first century A.D., when the pagan world believed in savior-gods, virgin births, incarnations, healing miracles and the atoning effect of sacrificial blood."[139]

[4.3.6] Yehezkel Kaufmann

Yehezkel Kaufman was born in Russia and received his PhD from the University of Berlin in the field of Bible Research and Semitic Languages. After coming to Israel in 1929, he served as professor at Hebrew University.[140] In 1929–1930 he wrote *Exile and Estrangement* in Hebrew. Three chapters of this work were translated in English and published in 1988 as *Christianity and Judaism: Two Covenants*. The second chapter, which will be addressed here, is called "Origins of the Christian Church."

Kaufman saw Jesus as a Pharisaic Jew who did not intend to break with Jewish practice. However, "opposition to Judaism is implicit in his teaching even though he was unconscious of that."[141] Jesus was a teacher of the law, he came to fulfill the law, and he also "held himself to be a unique being," namely the Son of God.[142] His disciples, too, believed that there was "a divine element in Jesus' nature," although he himself was not divine. This belief ordained Jesus to forgive sins and cast out evil spirits. For Kaufmann, notions that Jesus was merely a "preacher and teacher" only "falter and fail."[143] He was more than that. Jesus claimed to be the Messiah, but his claim was

137. Ibid., 134.
138. Ibid., 142.
139. Ibid., 156
140. Patai, *Encyclopedia of Zionism and Israel*, 657.
141. Ibid., 51.
142. Ibid., 52.
143. Ibid., 72.

considerably different from others in his day, as well as others who would appear in later history. His mission was to proclaim the kingdom of God. But, he was more than a herald, he was also to be the reigning king. His vision was that of the "apocalyptic redeemer-messiah." This was based on an amalgamation of Jewish eschatological beliefs that emerged in the late Second Temple period.[144] The kingdom of Heaven was not a "religious-moral-psychological concept" but rather "an apocalyptic kingdom, which was destined to come at the time appointed, at the "end" which had been fixed from the beginning." The "foundation stone" for these beliefs, Kaufmann believed, was the resurrection of the dead.[145] Along with these eschatological views was another that made Jesus unique. He required belief in himself. No other teacher or prophet spoke in such a manner. The miracles he performed were to point others to his power. "To Jesus, therefore, the lack of faith in him and his mission to destroy the kingdom of Satan and the demons who cause men to sin and afflict them in body and soul was a mortal sin which beset the whole generation. He did not distinguish between faith in God and belief in his own "power.""[146]

Jesus went to Jerusalem on Passover to inaugurate his kingdom, specifically to establish the "monarchy of David." Kaufmann rejects the traditional view, which claims that Jesus went to suffer and die and bring atonement. This was not part of Jesus' eschatological beliefs.[147] The details of the arrest are not given, but he does believe that the trial before the Sanhedrin really happened and that Jesus did affirm that he is the Messiah. The New Testament's description of these events, he says, is "inexact."[148] Jewish scholars, Kaufmann writes, have often tried to shift the full blame to the Romans. He admits that the crucifixion was a Roman punishment, and that the Romans were certainly involved. But, he also believed that "according to Jewish law, Jesus was liable to the death sentence."[149] He cites Deuteronomy 18:20-22, where a prophet is to be examined by demonstrating a sign to exonerate himself. This is what happened at the trial (Mt 26:63-64). Jesus' "refusal" to offer a sign was seen as evidence that he was "a false prophet, which meant that Jesus was guilty of blasphemy."[150] Jesus never wavered in his belief of being the Messiah. Even at the cross, he expected to be rescued.

144. Ibid., 74–79.
145. Ibid., 89.
146. Ibid., 102–3.
147. Ibid., 108–9.
148. Ibid., 121.
149. Ibid., 123.
150. Ibid., 125.

His disciples, on the other hand, lost hope in their Master and fled. The "sudden catastrophe" of the crucifixion negated all hopes and "seemingly put an end to the movement."[151] This would not last.

> But on the third day after the crucifixion, there occurred the event which would determine the course of development of Christianity: The body of Jesus vanished from the grave. Just how this happened is unknown, but the disappearance of the corpse was certainly the occasion of the renewal of the messianic movement.[152]

Kaufmann credits the empty tomb for the original belief in the resurrection of Jesus. Other scholars maintain that the visions of Jesus were responsible for establishing their faith. Kaufmann disagrees, since the event was considered a miracle and it "brought renewal of faith after the disappointment of Golgotha."[153] The appearance of a mere spirit or ghost, he says, could not have had such an effect. He briefly attempts to explain why the grave was empty. Perhaps it was "like thousands of instances of "rebirth" of the dead" which have occurred throughout history. Maybe Jesus did not die on the cross but merely lost consciousness, "and then revived and rose from his grave and fell in some other place."[154] Whatever the reasons, the "legend of the resurrection" brought a renewed hope and many "beheld" Jesus. This new movement constituted a sect within Israel, only to later be broadened and disseminated to the gentiles by Paul.

[4.3.7] Schalom Ben-Chorin

Schalom Ben-Chorin was born in Germany and moved to Israel in the 1930s. He then lived in Jerusalem for the next six decades, and was a philosopher and free thinker. In 1967 he published the original (German) version of *Brother Jesus*,[155] but the English translation (which will be discussed here) did not appear until 2001. The title is an allusion to Martin Buber's famous words and similarly conveys Ben-Chorin's empathy and admiration of Jesus. This book was an attempt to interact with "the rabbi from Nazareth" and not the "Christ of the Church."[156] Following the lead of Leo Baeck,

---

151. Ibid., 133.
152. Ibid.
153. Ibid.
154. Ibid.
155. Ben-Chorin, *Bruder Jesus: der Nazarener in jüdischer Sicht.*
156. Ben-Chorin, *Brother Jesus*, vii.

he believed that the New Testament must be seen as "a document of the history of the Jewish people."[157] He admits that by studying the Gospels his own "path in life" has led him closer to Jesus. Although to do so, he believed, one must make an effort to "recover Jesus' picture from the Christian over-painting." Specifically, he did not believe that Jesus thought of himself as the Messiah.[158] Ben-Chorin does however regard the teachings of Jesus quite seriously. For him, they represent a Jewish voice that has not been heard by his own people. His words should be given a place next to other great sages of the period. "I see in Jesus of Nazareth a third authority," he wrote, "whose views are to be placed alongside Hillel and Shammai."[159] Along with his teachings, his very life should be seen as both an example *for* the Jewish people, and *of* the Jewish people.

> Is not the suffering Jesus, the Jesus scorned as he hangs dying on the cross, a likeness for his entire people who, tortured and bloodied, have been hanged time and time again on the cross of anti-Semitism? And is the Easter message of the resurrection not a parable for postwar Israel, which has risen out of the abasement and disgrace of the darkest twelve years in its history to a new incarnation?[160]

The basic story of the life of Jesus is acknowledged as historical. However, Ben-Chorin discards the supernatural, as well as events that point to Jesus being the Messiah. His reconstructions, like many critical attempts, are sometimes fanciful. They include, in the words of Amy-Jill Levine's review of this book, "highly conjectural historiography."[161] For example, he believes that Jesus' entry into Jerusalem happened at the Feast of Tabernacles,[162] although the trials and crucifixion did occur during Passover. After the crucifixion, Joseph of Arimathea—along with Nicodemus—received the body from Pilate and performed the burial. The women came to the tomb on Sunday and found it empty. At this point, echoing Klausner, he states: "Here ends the story of Jesus. Here begins the story of Christ."[163] The empty tomb is seen as the pivotal evidence that caused the disciples to

---

157. Ibid., 4.

158. Ibid., 7.

159. Ibid., 10.

160. Ibid., 19.

161. Levine, Review of *Brother Jesus: The Nazarene through Jewish Eyes*, 223.

162. Ben-Chorin, *Brother Jesus*, 113.

163. Ibid., 187.

believe in the resurrection. They "construed the disappearance of the body of Jesus as a resurrection."[164]

Ben-Chorin takes a brief moment to mention others who have attempted to explain away the empty tomb. These include the *Toledot Yeshu*, Herman Samuel Reimarus, Hugh Schonfield and Werner Hegeman.[165] He did not want to give too much attention to these, since "speculation contends faith."[166] The empty tomb remains an enigma. He acknowledges that skeptics cannot explain it away, but neither is it enough for him personally to believe in the resurrection. He concludes with the following: "The resurrection of Jesus cannot be apprehended as a historical phenomenon. Even in the gospels its documentation is insufficient to merit factual status: ultimately we know nothing about what happened after the burial of Jesus."[167] Ben-Chorin already admitted that there (at least probably) was an empty tomb, and that this caused the disciples to believe in the resurrection. To then say we know "nothing" about what happened after the burial is, at best, an overstatement. He continues with another theory that explains the origin of the belief in the resurrection. As was popular, and convenient in his day, he blamed Paul: "The actual historical resurrection of Christ took place only later in Damascus, with Paul's "Damascus Road" conversion, an experience rooted deeply in the subjectivity of this contradictory and controversial personality."[168] Nevertheless, Ben-Chorin's final thoughts are optimistic. Although he denies the physical, bodily resurrection of Jesus, he nevertheless believed that "he has risen time and time again in the souls of men and women who have encountered him."[169]

[4.3.8] David Flusser

In the first half of the twentieth century, it was still somewhat of a novelty for Jewish scholars to write about Jesus. David Flusser was one of the first to write a life of Jesus without specifically stating his own Jewish standpoint. On the other hand, the fact that he taught at Hebrew University in Jerusalem might have been a clue. His book, *Jesus,* appeared first in German in 1968 and was translated into English a year later.[170] In the midst of a

164. Ibid.
165. Ibid.
166. Ibid.
167. Ibid., 188.
168. Ibid., 187–88.
169. Ibid., 188.
170. Flusser, *Jesus: mit Selbstzeugnissen und Bilddokumenten.*

cynical climate of New Testament scholarship, Flusser wrote this book "to show that it is possible to write the story of Jesus' life."[171] The early Christian accounts of Jesus, he wrote, "are not as untrustworthy as people think."[172] For example, the fact that there are limited corroborative accounts should not be a reason to abandon the study. "He shares his fate with Moses, Buddha, and Mohammed, who likewise received no mention in the reports of non-believers."[173] Flusser saw Jesus as "a miracle worker and preacher," and he was largely concerned with placing him in his own Jewish context. In his view, Jesus was "faithful to the Law."[174] Departing from most scholars, he believed that much of the material in the Gospels have a Hebrew (not Aramaic) source.[175] Jesus preached not only that we are on the threshold of the kingdom of God, but also that "the new age of salvation had already begun."[176] In all areas, Jesus was nothing if not a Jew: "He was perfectly at home both in Holy Scripture, and in oral tradition, and knew how to apply this scholarly heritage."[177]

Many of the events of Jesus' final days in Jerusalem are acknowledged as historical, while some are not addressed at all. He was arrested and taken to the High Priest, although not to the Sanhedrin.[178] After the crucifixion, Joseph of Arimathea (who was a member of the "city council") asked Pilate for the body. He and Nicodemus arranged the burial. For Flusser, "the fact that two Jerusalem councilors performed the final act of charity to Jesus proves that it would be false to think that the supreme authorities in Jewry had delivered Jesus up to the Romans."[179]

Jesus was then sent to the cross to be executed. Many scholars view this as the end of the "real" history, and what follows after is the stuff of legend. As Flusser wrote earlier in the book, he wanted to separate "the historical Jesus" from the "kerygmatic Christ."[180] But apparently, whatever happened after the burial was not worth discussing. There is no mention of an empty tomb, nor the disciples' belief that they had seen the risen Jesus. After a

---

171. Flusser, *Jesus*, 7 (English translation).
172. Ibid., 8.
173. Ibid., 7.
174. Ibid., 46.
175. Ibid., 12.
176. Ibid., 90.
177. Ibid., 18.
178. Ibid., 119.
179. Ibid., 120.
180. Ibid., 9.

brief discussion about the crucifixion, Flusser concludes the book with the following three words: "and Jesus died."[181]

This topic is somewhat addressed in a later collection of essays about the beginnings of Christianity. The resurrection, he says, is couched in mythological (although purely Jewish) terms. This leads him to conclude that the event itself must also be mythological. He writes, "The fact that passages from the Old Testament, speaking of victory over death and reflecting pre-biblical mythology, are used in the New Testament as an expression of the belief in Jesus' death and resurrection shows the mythic aspect of this metaphysical drama of Christ."[182]

Flusser gives one hint as to when belief in the resurrection began. It comes in the midst of a discussion on the evolving view of Christology. "We can therefore imagine that during the period between Jesus' death and Paul's conversion some Jewish believers, whose Judaism was already strongly re-mythologized, reinterpreted Jesus' self awareness, the Cross and the belief in his resurrection in the light of their own understanding of the faith."[183]

[4.3.9] Paula Fredriksen

Paula Fredriksen teaches religion and history at Boston University and Hebrew University. She has written two complete books on the life of Jesus. The first book, *From Jesus to Christ*, appeared in 1988. Like Flusser, there is no mention of a specific Jewish approach. She was writing as a historian attempting to reconstruct the life of Jesus. The Gospels, in her view, are "a self conscious Christian tradition that deliberately distanced itself from the historical Jewish context in which Jesus had lived and died."[184] This book dealt more with theological issues. About a dozen years later she wrote *Jesus of Nazareth, king of the Jews*. This follow-up work focused on the historical Jesus. While there is much overlap between the two books, there are also some differences. For example, she acknowledges that her belief in why Jesus died had changed. In the years between these two books, she writes, "my contemplation of this anomaly has steadily eroded my conviction in my previous conclusions."[185] This is the mark of an honest scholar, willing to go where the evidence points. It also underscores how challenging New Testament scholarship can be.

181. Ibid., 132.
182. Ibid., 619.
183. Ibid., 623.
184. Fredricksen, *From Jesus to Christ*, xii.
185. Fredricksen, *Jesus of Nazareth, King of the Jews*, 9.

Fredriksen's Jesus is "a prophet who preached the coming apocalyptic Kingdom of God."[186] This had social and political ramifications and would result in his death. Finding the truth is not easy, since one must sift through the layers of tradition and editing. Few events are considered absolutely historical. The most "solid fact" in her view is his death by crucifixion under Pontius Polite.[187] Following that, "the disciple's conviction that they had seen the Risen Christ," is to her a non-negotiable. She calls it "historical bedrock."[188] Another important fact, for the purpose of this study, concerns the spread of the new Jesus movement. Some scholars have questioned the extent and origin of the young church. But, Fredriksen accepts the general account recorded in Acts. She acknowledges that the movement went quickly beyond Jerusalem, and that "evidence abounds" for the new movements "rapid dissemination."[189] The first question that needs to be addressed is, "why would the disciples believe that they saw him alive after he had clearly died?" At first, she is agnostic on the issue, believing that "what these disciples actually saw or experienced is now impossible to say."[190] At another point, she offers a suggestion:

> And finally, the traditions about the resurrection appearances that grew in the wake of this black moment display the power of his closest followers' commitment to Jesus' message that the Kingdom really was at hand. That Passover in Jerusalem, they were expecting an eschatological event, the arrival of God's kingdom. What they got instead was the crucifixion. But then, an unexpected eschatological event occurred: God, they became convinced, had raised Jesus from the dead. Two of the prime promises of the messianic age—the resurrection of the dead and the vindication of the righteous—these men believed they now saw realized in the person of their executed leader.[191]

She does not employ the language of psychology, but it seems to be implied. The disciples "became convinced" that a supernatural event had occurred based on "their commitment" to Jesus' teachings about the Kingdom of God. This raises a number of questions. What exactly did Jesus teach? Why was the disciples' commitment to their leader stronger than that of all the other groups who abandoned their leader after his death?

186. Ibid., 266.
187. Ibid., 8.
188. Ibid., 264.
189. Ibid., 236.
190. Ibid., 261.
191. Ibid., 252.

Why did the earliest proclamation of their belief take the form that had no precedence? Did they create a new paradigm? If so, why did other Jews who were not among his original followers come to believe it as well? A more complete study would also address the origin of the empty tomb story and Paul's dramatic turnaround (especially since he never had a "commitment" to Jesus' teaching).

Fredricksen addressed the disciples' belief in another article as well, where she reviewed Jon Dominic Crossan's theory that the body of Jesus was ravaged by wild dogs. This idea is worthy of discussion for her as it is a non-supernatural alternative. An actual resurrection is beyond discussion since, as noted earlier, she believes that all miraculous claims should be excluded from the historical investigation.[192] But, while the wild dogs are worth pondering, Fredricksen more strongly disagreed with Crossan over another point. He suggested that the disciples did not believe in the resurrection. This is not an option for her. She is adamant that the disciples really believed it happened, and is careful to clarify that she does not.

> But, the resurrection is something else. The movement stands or falls with it, and I cannot imagine so many people in the first generation changing their lives so radically without taking them at their word. They were convinced that Jesus had risen from the dead. If they just thought that he had died but his truth went marching on, they could have said that. But, they didn't; they spoke of resurrection. Please read me correctly: I am not saying that Jesus really rose from the dead because his disciples said that he did. I am saying that they really thought he had.[193]

[4.4] ARTICLES

The section is made up of three scholars who do not quite fit easily into any of the other categories. They each wrote either an article or a chapter in a book that touches on the resurrection in different ways. They wrote at different stages of the twentieth century, which reveals different presuppositions. Cohn-Sherbok's article is especially relevant as it represents the first post-Lapide attempt at seriously studying the resurrection.

192. See above, 3.3.3.
193. Fredricksen, "What You See is What You Get: Context and Content in Current Research on the Historical Jesus," 85.

[4.4.1] Elias Bickerman

Elias Bickerman was a distinguished Jewish scholar of the early and middle twentieth century. Originally from Russia, he taught at Jewish Theological seminary and Columbia University. A recent reprint of his writings includes an article called "The Empty Tomb," which offers a unique approach to the subject. His main argument is the distinction between the concepts of rapture and resurrection in ancient literature. The former refers to a disappearance of a body (like Enoch), while the latter refers to a translation to heaven that may be accompanied by visions of the one who was resurrected. The combination of the two in the gospels is therefore incongruent: "The empty tomb is proof of rapture; but a resurrection is never characterized or demonstrated by the disappearance of the corpse, but only by the apparition of the one who has been restored to life."[194] Bickerman interacts with a wide body of literature to make his case. Unfortunately, he does not distinguish between Jewish and pagan texts and lumps them all together as examples of ancient literature. There is no understanding of the unique perspective of Second Temple Judaism. Discussing Mark, he says that it is "perfectly appropriate to situate his narrative in the literary tradition which begins roughly with the story of Aristeus in the sixth century BCE and continues for twelve centuries, until the novel about Simeon."[195] The resurrection of Jesus not only disagrees with this vast literature it goes against Jewish theology. He writes: "But the figure of a messiah raised from the dead was wholly foreign to Judaism."[196]

For Bickerman, the resurrection does not meet literary or theological criteria. He did not interact with what did, or what might have, actually happened. His working assumption was that Mark reported earlier traditions, while adapting the "framework of the Hellenistic theology."[197] It is the apparitions that are suspect and assumed to be later embellishments. The story of the tomb, however, points to a "probably older stage of faith in Christ."[198]

[4.4.2] Eugene Borowitz

Eugene Borowitz was a Reform Rabbi who taught at Hebrew Union College—Jewish Institute of Religion for over fifty years. He also founded the

194. Bickerman, "The Empty Tomb," 717.
195. Ibid..
196. Ibid., 722.
197. Ibid., 721.
198. Ibid..

journal *Sh'ma*. In 1980 he wrote *Contemporary Christologies*, a book that interacted with modern Christian theologians and their differing perspectives on Jesus. He felt it was important for the furthering of Jewish-Christian relations for Jews to be aware of the Christian doctrine of Christ, not just the historical Jesus.[199] To discuss only the historical issues would be incomplete. Such an approach too easily "allows the Jewish historian to reject the major assertion of Christian faith without ever having to raise the troublesome question of their own beliefs."[200]

In a chapter called "Berkouwer, Barth and Pannenberg: Modern Claims for the Traditional Christ," he compares these three famous theologians. The main difference between them, as discussed by Borowitz, is the way in which one comes to believe in Christ. For Berkouwer and Barth it was a question of faith, based entirely on God's grace. Pannenberg's approach centers on the historicity of the resurrection. He believed this event may be weighed objectively and is available for discussion even amongst non-believers. Berkouwer and Barth, by contrast, believed the resurrection was a "divine mystery, one whose truth can only be gained by faith in the Christ which is a gift from God."[201] Borowitz first questions the resurrection because of the lack of Jewish documentation.

> Jews have felt there was no good reason to believe Jesus was resurrected. Had he died and then been given life in some eschatological fashion, they do not think their forefathers would have utterly ignored such an event. Yet rabbinic literature is silent on the subject. While most of our sources were compiled decades later than Jesus, some echo of so extraordinary an event should still sound in them. So much else, of so heterodox a character, is found there that Jews find this absence of contemporary corroboration telling.[202]

Yet, Pannenberg's belief that the resurrection was a historical event "makes it possible to discuss our differences," Borowitz says. The theological dogmatism of Barth and Berkouwer, by contrast, make dialogue extremely one-sided. With such an approach, "all hope of finding common ground with non-Christians is shattered."[203] Pannenberg's views of the resurrection are then discussed. He was a conservative scholar who had liberal tendencies in some of his opinions about scripture. First, the historicity of the res-

199. Borowitz, *Contemporary Christologies*, 3.

200. Ibid., 4.

201. Ibid., 30.

202. Ibid., 31.

203. Ibid., 35.

urrection hinges on Paul's report in 1 Corinthians 15:1–11, with the Gospel accounts being too "legendary" for certainty. Paul's words are to be trusted because of their close proximity to the event in question, and because he appealed to a "formulated tradition" which reached back to "the first five years after Jesus' death." Because of this, Pannenberg does not take seriously counter theories of dying and rising saviors from other traditions. Nor is he impressed with anti-supernatural arguments or psychological theories. Also, an invented account of the resurrection in light of the reality of Jesus' death does not correspond to Jewish apocalyptical beliefs of the time. Finally, Paul's claim of the appearance to the five hundred cannot be a "secondary construction." This is because Paul says that "most of them" (the five hundred) are still alive, an apparent reference to the possibility of checking this fact.[204]

Overall, Borowitz liked this approach (although he will negate the specific arguments). Historical evidence puts the matter on equal footing. It might be evaluated by both Jews and Christians, he says, "excepting those liberals who are dogmatically antiresurrectionist (*sic*)."[205] This brings the discussion beyond the traditional boundaries of the Jewish-Christian debate. "There is no distinctive Jewish response to Pannenberg's argument. There does not need to be, for the question raised is a neutral one: does the evidence Pannenberg presented justify the historical conclusion he reached?"[206]

Borowitz then offers responses to Pannenberg's assertions. First, the fact that the resurrection tradition goes back to just a few years after Jesus' death does not make it true. This tells us "only what the Church had come to believe about that death."[207] Likewise, Paul's testimony about people who are still alive tells us only that the traditions were still alive at that point. It "does not tell us much about their historical reliability." Pannenberg was also too quick to dismiss religious or psychological phenomena such as the "will-to-believe." Also, regarding the nature of this type of an eschatological event, it was not unthinkable in the light of passages about Enoch and Elijah. Indeed, Borowitz argues, these Biblical events "were associated with the anticipated messianic resurrection" in rabbinic tradition.[208] Borowitz knew that neither Pannenberg's work nor his own would be the final word on the subject. A

---

204. Ibid., 35–36.
205. Ibid., 37.
206. Ibid.
207. Ibid.
208. Ibid., 38.

good deal more, he said, "might yet be fruitfully learned" by continuing such discourse.

[4.4.3] Dan Cohn-Sherbok

Just a few years before the dawn of our current century, British theologian Gavin D'Costa brought together scholars from a variety of religious backgrounds to discuss the resurrection of Jesus. The resulting book was called *Resurrection Reconsidered*. Dan Cohn-Sherbok is a Reform Rabbi and professor of Judaism who has published several dozen books. He begins his article by explaining a conversation he had with his wife about the Apostles Creed. He enthusiastically acknowledges his belief in God. After that, he was able to affirm about half of the Creed. "At the heart of my rejection of these Christian beliefs," he says, "is my inability to accept the claim that Jesus rose from the dead. Traditionally this has been the linchpin of the entire Christian theological edifice."[209]

After this introduction, he surveys the general belief in resurrection throughout Jewish history, concluding that by the early rabbinic period it became a "central principle of faith."[210] But, Jewish opinion for the last two thousand years has clearly rejected Jesus as the Messiah, and this includes his resurrection from the dead. Cohn-Sherbok then mentions Pinchas Lapide as an exception to this long-standing tradition. He sees no "logical" inconsistency between Judaism's belief in a general resurrection and Lapide's belief that Jesus was personally resurrected.

Examining the issue more closely, Cohn-Sherbok then puts forth an alternative to both traditional Judaism and Pinchas Lapide. He acknowledges that liberal Judaism has questioned the notion of resurrection on modern, philosophical grounds. This has led some to prefer the belief in the immortality of the soul, rather than a resurrection from the dead. Cohn-Sherbok agrees, and sees traditional Judaism's view of resurrection as "implausible." The resurrection of Jesus, however, is not dismissed on theological or philosophical grounds, and he does acknowledge some events in the life of the historical Jesus. He believes that Jesus existed, that he was crucified under Pontius Pilate, and that he died and was buried.[211] He also believes that a movement sprang up which proclaimed his resurrection and has continued to exist throughout history. He also has reasons for doubting the resurrection. The first comes from the New Testament itself. He specifically cites

209. Cohn-Sherbok, "The Resurrection of Jesus: A Jewish View." 185.

210. Ibid., 190.

211. Ibid., 185.

the "conflicting records of the gospel writers." Biblical scholars in the last hundred years, he says, have cast doubt on these records and there is "no universality of agreement." On top of this, the New Testament is "religious propaganda" without corroborative evidence.[212] He then asks what evidence exists in history, and he explores the faith of the first disciples.

> And, even if we could substantiate (which we cannot) that Jesus' disciples really had some experience of the living Jesus after his death, this would not provide conclusive proof that he had been raised from the dead. It is after all possible, indeed likely, that those who encountered Jesus after his crucifixion had nothing more than a subjective psychological experience.[213]

He next addresses the "personal religious experience" of Christians throughout history. This too is discarded immediately as inconclusive evidence. "Arguably," he says, these experiences are "of a similar character to those subjective experiences of the early Christian community." This type of evidence, he says, is "not sufficiently conclusive." What he wants is "objective data."[214] He is not against believing it, he just wishes there was stronger evidence: "As a Jew and a rabbi, I could be convinced of Jesus' resurrection, but I would set very high standards of what is required. It would not be enough to have a subjective experience of Jesus. If I heard voices or had a visionary experience of Jesus, this would not be enough."[215]

He then gives some details describing what he would need in order to believe. They include a "host of angels trailing clouds of glory and announcing his Messiahship for all to see." It would also have to be public, "televised on CNN and other forms of the world's media."[216] It must be "concrete, objective, observable evidence."[217] This type of request is actually purely *subjective* even as it claims to demand objective evidence (see the discussion above, 3.3.1). It also marginalizes the evidence that does exist. For example, he mentions Lapide's book, but does not interact with Lapide's arguments for the resurrection, nor does he interact with the empty tomb or Paul's belief. Nevertheless, while he is "not persuaded" that Jesus rose from the dead, he concludes the article with the following words: "But I am capable of being persuaded. I wait for the evidence."[218]

212. Ibid., 197.
213. Ibid.
214. Ibid.
215. Ibid., 198.
216. Ibid.
217. Ibid., 199.
218. Ibid., 200.

[4.5] FOCUS ON THE RESURRECTION

There are three Jewish scholars who have written seriously and exhaustively on the resurrection of Jesus. They have already been quoted extensively above. Lapide and Vermes each wrote an entire book on the subject. Segal wrote even more than each of them, mostly from chapters in his book on the afterlife. They are all critical scholars, but they did not settle for simplistic dismissals. Their conclusions were remarkably positive regarding the evidence, although less positive about how it should be interpreted. Even Segal, who argued that it is impossible to make a case for the resurrection, nevertheless provides insight in favor of the historical evidence. These works have set the standard for the Jewish discussion of the resurrection of Jesus.

There are, in fact, a few other books by Jewish scholars that have addressed the resurrection. These works (by Schonfield, Sigal, and Alter) have a different agenda. They are not concerned with deciphering what may have happened after the crucifixion. Their interest is solely in debunking the canonical narrative. These views need to be mentioned as well and they are discussed in the section immediately below.

[4.5.1] Pinchas Lapide

Pinchas Lapide was born in Germany in 1922 and immigrated to Jerusalem in 1938. For many years he served as a diplomat in the Israeli foreign office, and later was the director of the Government Press Office in Jerusalem. His education included a BA and MA from Hebrew University and a PhD from the Martin Buber Institute for Judaic Studies at Cologne University.[219] He wrote numerous books, mostly in German. One of his main contributions was in the field of Jewish-Christian dialogue, often teaming up with Catholic scholar Hans Kuhn (see bibliography). In 1975, Kuhn and Lapide met in Germany for a radio dialogue (it appeared in print two years later). The event was characterized by mutual respect, and yet each participant was forthright in stating his own beliefs and areas of disagreement. Lapide's view of Jesus was positive: "My Judaism is 'catholic' enough, in the original sense of the word, to find a place for both Spinoza and Jesus, for Philo and Flavius Josephus. I do not see why I should renounce a luminary of Judaism such as the Rabbi from Nazareth merely because some of the Christian images

---

219. Küng and Lapide, "Jesus a Bond or a Barrier?," 466. See also Galarneau, "A Feminist Interpretation of Pinchas Lapide's Jewish Theology of Christianity as a Model for Christian Self-Understanding".

of Christ mean nothing to me."[220] On the question of Christology, Lapide admits that the ideas of *kenosis* and incarnation were not foreign to Judaism, and that they "entered later Christianity not from Hellenism, but in fact from certain Jewish circles." But, this does not mean he was ready to accept the whole package, or even some of it.

> With the utmost seriousness, as an Orthodox Jew, I must say that I cannot accept what you call resurrection, kenosis, and *apokatostis*, since this is not suggested by our Jewish experience of God. But, neither can I deny it, for who am I as a devout Jew to define *a priori* God's saving action? To *define* means to assign limits, and this, from a Jewish standpoint, would be blasphemous.[221]

Just a couple of years later, he addressed the question more comprehensively in his book, *The Resurrection of Jesus*. His conclusion, to the surprise of many, was that the best explanation of the evidence is that the resurrection was an actual historical event. In the introduction, Carl Braaten said such a thing was "without precedent" and called it an "ecumenical miracle."[222] Many scholars reviewed the book, including Philip Sigal, a Reform rabbi who held a PhD in New Testament. Sigal was not convinced that Lapide believed in the resurrection to the extent that many of the reviewers were claiming: "After 124 pages we really cannot conclude what Lapide believes explicitly about the resurrection of Jesus. He says in passing, almost contradicting Braaten's introduction, that the resurrection event "is still controversial, cannot be conceived historically.""[223]

Lapide's argument throughout the book, however, is that there is enough evidence to make a case for the resurrection, and that in his opinion the explanation that fits best is that it actually happened. He is aware that it cannot be proved historically and that there will be differing points of view. As he says in the prologue: "For that which happened on the "third day" in Jerusalem is in the last analysis an experience of God which enters into the realm of things which cannot be proved, just as God himself is unprovable; it can be grasped only by faith."[224]

In the first full chapter, called "But if Christ has not been raised . . .," Lapide sets the tone by explaining the importance of the crucifixion and the resurrection for New Testament faith. The former is considered "historically

220. Ibid., 467.

221. Ibid., 481.

222. Ibid., 5.

223. Sigal, "Review of the Resurrection of Jesus, a Jewish Perspective," 26.

224. Lapide, *The Resurrection of Jesus*, 31.

certain," while the latter is controversial. It has "led from the beginning to doubt, discord, and dissention."[225] Yet, it is ultimately the more important of the two events; "Without the experience of the resurrection, the crucifixion of Jesus would most likely have remained without consequences and forgotten, just as were the innumerable crucifixions of pious Jews which the Romans carried out before Jesus."[226]

Lapide begins with the negative case. Both Jews and Gentiles are skeptical of the New Testament's description of the event and surrounding circumstances: "No wonder, in no other area of the New Testament narrative are the contradictions so glaring. Nowhere else are the opposites so obvious and the contrasting descriptions so questionable as in the realm of the resurrection of Jesus."[227] Lapide then quotes several New Testament scholars to confirm this point. He also surveys some of the common reasons for disbelief both in the ancient world and today. These include Paul's lack of knowledge of an empty tomb, the disbelief of the disciples themselves, the "elaborations" made by each evangelist, and the parallels with pagan deities who were said to also die and rise again.[228] It is in spite of these arguments that Lapide will make his case. He was well-aware of the negative theories which potentially undermined the historicity of the resurrection.

His own view of the New Testament was quite similar to most of the other writers in this study. He believed the Gospels contain a core element of historical truth with layers of later embellishments. Most liberal scholars admit that at least some things can be adduced as historical fact. Lapide argues that the resurrection is one of these things. Many commentators miss this, he says, because they are not taking into consideration the Jewish context of such a study: "It is a lack of empathy with the Jewish locus of that original Easter faith whose eyewitnesses and first testifiers were without exception sons and daughters of Israel."[229]

The crucifixion seemed like the end of the story. Many followers must have lost confidence and hope. Others may have chosen to flee, perhaps seeing themselves as victims of another false messiah. Still others might have chosen to honor the memory of their great teacher even after his death, much as was done with Rabbi Akiva a century later. All of this would influence the disciples' understanding, as Lapide states in the chapter called "The Must of the Resurrection." As he explains, he is not using the term "must" to

225. Ibid., 32.
226. Ibid., 33.
227. Ibid., 34–35.
228. Ibid., 35–42.
229. Ibid., 43.

mean "illusory wishful thinking." Rather, he was referring to God's character and His interaction with His people throughout history. He then surveys
passages from the Tanakh which allude to the "third day" (Gen 22:4, 42:18;
Ex 19:16, Jonah 1:17, Ezra 5:1, Hos 6:2). This phrase refers to "God's mercy
and grace which is revealed after two days of affliction and death by way of
redemption." It is here that Lapide makes his most definitive statement.

> Thus, according to my opinion, the resurrection belongs to the
> category of the truly real and effective occurrences, for without
> a fact of history there is no act of true faith . . . In other words:
> Without the Sinai experience—no Judaism; without the Easter
> experience—no Christianity. Both were Jewish faith experi-
> ences whose radiating power, in a different way, was meant for
> the world of nations.[230]

The following chapter is called "Traces of a Jewish faith experience."
Lapide again asserts that the New Testament contains "embellishments" and
"the fiction of later generations."[231] But, Jewish scholars of the New Testament, he says, must search for the traces of truth underlying the documents.
He then proceeds to explain which events should be considered authentic
history. He begins with a discussion about the women who found the empty
tomb. They are mentioned in all four Gospels and figure prominently. A
fictitious report would not have invented such detail, given the status of
women at the time.[232] These women also went to the tomb to anoint the
body, illustrating that a resurrection was not expected. Another factor concerns the silence of detail regarding the actual resurrection. No human eye
saw it, and no one was even present. It would have been quite easy, and
perhaps tempting, for later generations to "supplement" information with
embellishments. But, that was not done. This, he believes, is further evidence of the New Testament's authenticity.

Moving to Paul's writings, Lapide focuses on 1 Corinthians 15:3–7.
This is the oldest statement concerning the resurrection in the New Testament. Along with other scholars, Lapide believes that what Paul "received"
and then "delivers" is best understood as "a statement of eyewitnesses for
whom the experience of the resurrection became the turning point of their
lives."[233] He gives eight reasons to validate this passage's pre-Pauline origins
(listed above, 3.1.1). The New Testament also does not promote the resurrection with the fanfare and hyperbole that is common in apocryphal litera-

230. Ibid., 92.
231. Ibid., 94.
232. Ibid., 95.
233. Ibid., 99.

ture. This too lends to its credibility. The evangelists are telling the ordinary circumstances surrounding an extraordinary occurrence. In fact, the Gospels seem to go out of their way to make the resurrection a non-spectacular event. This, he says, is in keeping with Jewish tradition. Lapide takes several pages to illustrate the difference between the Tanakh's frequent brevity and the wordier expounding by later commentators. As he explains, "Often does "a whole mountain of interpretations hang on a hair" (*Hagigah* 10a) of a brief scripture passage, as it is the case with the creation of Adam."[234]

In the chapter called "The Pedagogy of God" he focuses on two counterarguments to the resurrection. The first is the "nonpublic" manner of the event. In other words, why were there not more witnesses? This objection was first voiced by Celsus in the second century, and was also employed by Herman Samuel Reimarus in the eighteenth century.[235] Lapide sees the limited witnesses to the resurrection as "proof of its genuineness" rather than a reason to deny its authenticity. Throughout history, God often revealed Himself supernaturally to just one person or a limited few. The relatively small audience of the resurrection is in keeping with the Biblical record.[236] The next objection advanced in this chapter concerns the "unoriginality" of the event, specifically in the light of pagan mystery religions. For this, he turns to Maimonides. God, Maimonides wrote, used the pagan practices of the ancient world (such as sacrifices) as a teaching device for Israel. God was bringing forth something new, but used existing forms and experiences to guide and explain. So too, Lapide argues, God could use the pagan beliefs in resurrection as preparation for "the true resurrection" that would carry the knowledge of God to the ends of the earth.[237]

Lapide's final analysis may be grouped into three possibilities, as he does in the chapter called "The "Lesser of Two Evils."" The first option is that it is an actual event in history. This would then raise the question of whether or not such an event may be recognized underneath the "layers of legends." The second option is that it is a myth with no historical support. The final possibility is that the visions of the resurrected Jesus were actually subjective experiences, unable to be confirmed objectively. Such examples exist in the Talmud and throughout history. But, Lapide cannot embrace this third possibility on the grounds that these other examples did not result in changed lives. It is different with the New Testament.

234. Ibid., 103.
235. Ibid., 116.
236. Ibid., 120.
237. Ibid., 125.

Despite all the legendary embellishments, in the oldest records there remains a recognizable historical kernel which cannot simply be demythologized. When this scarred, frightened band of the apostles which was just about to throw away everything in order to flee in despair to Galilee; when these peasants, shepherds, and fisherman, who betrayed and denied their master and then failed him miserably, suddenly could be changed overnight into a confident mission society, convinced of salvation and unable to work with much more success after Easter than before Easter, then no vision or hallucination is sufficient to explain such a revolutionary transformation.[238]

Based on this, Lapide holds that an actual resurrection is the "lesser of two evils" for those who are seeking a rational explanation "of the worldwide consequences of that Easter faith."[239] Suggestions of deception—including theft of the body, a trance or counterfeit miracles—are likewise unable to account for the early faith. Something historical must have happened since the results were historical, he concludes.[240] At the end of the following chapter, he quotes several Jewish scholars who have commented on the resurrection. Rabbi Samuel Hirsch believed that God created in the disciples the belief in the resurrection, so that "Jesus' power of hope and greatness of soul should not end with his death." Leo Baeck said his followers believed in him after his death so that it became for them an "existential certainty" that he had actually risen. Samuel Sandmel thought Jesus must have been a special Jew to "have been accorded a special resurrection." Philosopher Samuel Bergman said it is "unfounded" that the belief in an individual resurrection be excluded from Jewish thought.[241] These scholars (beginning with Hirsch in 1842) represent some of the dominant Jewish views of the resurrection. They were each attempting to find a place for Jesus if not in Judaism then at least as a good Jew. Lapide's book has taken the reclamation of Jesus to a whole new level. Yet, his ultimate conclusion about Jesus (for Jews) was quite traditional: "He was a "paver of the way for the King Messiah," as Maimonides calls him, but this does not mean that his resurrection makes him the Messiah of Israel for Jewish people."[242] And finally, "I therefore can

---

238. Ibid.
239. Ibid., 126.
240. Ibid., 128.
241. Ibid., 137–39.
242. Ibid., 152.

accept neither the messiahship of Jesus for the people of Israel nor the Pauline interpretation of the resurrection of Jesus."[243]

[4.5.2] Geza Vermes

Geza Vermes was born in Hungary to nominal Jewish parents (who died in the Holocaust) and yet was baptized a Catholic at a young age. He became a priest, and wrote the first ever dissertation on the Dead Sea Scrolls. In the late 1950s he left the priesthood and reclaimed his Jewish identity. He then spent several decades as professor of Jewish studies at Oxford, where he also edited the *Journal of Jewish Studies*. He has written numerous books about Jesus from a Jewish point of view, beginning with *Jesus the Jew: A Historian's Reading of the Gospels*, in 1973. His view of Jesus can be summed up as follows: "The representation of Jesus in the gospels as a man whose supernatural abilities derived, not from secret powers, but from immediate contact with God, proves him to be a genuine charismatic, the true heir of an age-old prophetic religious line."[244] He spent several pages on the resurrection in this earlier book.

Thirty-five years later, he wrote *The Resurrection: History and Myth*. This remains the only full-treatment of the subject on a scholarly level apart from Lapide's book. He too includes a discussion about resurrection in Judaism. Like many modern scholars, Vermes believes that it was relatively obscure in the Tanakh, only to be given more prominence by the later rabbis. He spends the early chapters surveying the Tanakh, apocryphal literature, Philo, Josephus, early rabbinic and even Roman writings. He concludes that there is no specific unified belief about resurrection that influenced the New Testament, although what the Gospels present is unique. Vermes begins his study of the resurrection of Jesus with a survey of discrepancies he finds in the Gospels. Some of the stories contain elements not found in the other Gospels, he says, while others "attest details that are irreconcilable."[245] These include the number and identity of the women who visited the tomb, the number of persons seen by the women, the number and location of the apparitions and the place where the apostolic mission was conferred.[246] He also concludes that the predictions of his death and resurrections are

---

243. Ibid., 153.
244. Vermes, *Jesus the Jew*, 69.
245. Ibid., 107, and see above 3.1.2.
246. Ibid., 109–10.

"inauthentic."[247] Before his own investigation, he acknowledges that there are different ways to evaluate the evidence.

> To quote the two extremes, N.T. Wright, the learned twenty-first-century Bishop of Durham, author of a disquisition of over 800 pages, concludes that the resurrection of Jesus was a historical event. By contrast, the more succinct David Friedrich Strauss, one of the creators of the historical-critical approach to the Gospels in the nineteenth century, declares that "rarely has an incredible fact been worse attested, and never has a badly attested fact been intrinsically less credible."[248]

Vermes then surveys the evidence in the Gospels and the rest of the New Testament. Regarding the kerygma in Paul's first letter to the Corinthians, he says it was "inherited from his seniors,"[249] but did not otherwise comment on the dating of this hymn. Vermes mentions Paul's admission of his own vision of Jesus (1 Cor 15:8), and remarks: "no doubt his mystical experience outside of Damascus (Acts 9:3–4)."[250] Nowhere does he comment on why Paul would have had such a vision, but by acknowledging Damascus he was presumably admitting that Paul was once a persecutor of the early followers of Jesus. The transformation of a former skeptic is important evidence, but it is not part of Vermes' discussion.

Vermes sees two main pieces of "circumstantial evidence" for the historicity of the resurrection. The first is the women who found the empty tomb. They arrived and were told that Jesus was resurrected. The second is the appearances of the risen Jesus to different disciples. In each case, Vermes (along with most critical scholars) sees inconsistencies between the accounts of the four different authors. On the other hand, he also recognizes that there is an element of authenticity in both the testimony of the women as well as the accounts of the appearances.

The evidence furnished by female witnesses "had no standing in a male-dominated Jewish society." The differing number of witnesses is a problem, but it is "clearly an early tradition." If it were fabricated, he reasoned, the accounts would have included reliable witnesses and uniform details. Despite these acknowledgements, the various reports make it difficult for him to believe. Even a "credulous non-believer" would likely not be convinced. His says the same about the visions: "none of them satisfies

247. Ibid., 86.
248. Ibid., 104–5.
249. Ibid., 122.
250. Ibid.

the minimum requirements of a legal or scientific inquiry."[251] At this point, an alternative theory is needed to explain what may have happened. The section that immediately follows is called, "Six theories to explain the resurrection of Jesus." There were actually eight, he tells us, but he discarded the two extremes—"the blind faith of the fundamentalist believer" and the "out of hand rejection of the inveterate skeptic." The six theories, in his words, are as follows: 1. The body was removed by someone unconnected with Jesus, 2.The body was stolen by his disciples, 3. The empty tomb was not the tomb of Jesus, 4. Buried alive, Jesus later left the tomb, 5. The Migrant Jesus (similar to #4, but then Jesus goes to India), 6. Do the appearances suggest spiritual, not bodily, resurrection?[252]

His discussion of these negative theories also yields some of his own positive beliefs. In discussing a possible stolen body, he acknowledges that Joseph and Nicodemus performed the "funeral duties." Because these two were well known, he reasons, they could have easily been asked to supply the body. This "strongly mitigates against" the stolen body theory.[253] Arguing against the second theory, he continues with this theme. If they disciples went to the wrong tomb, they surely would have checked with Joseph, "who was apparently the owner of the tomb."[254] He also touches on the suggestion that the appearances were spiritual and not bodily. He first says that the visions were no different from the visions "of mystics through the centuries" and concludes the following: "No doubt the New Testament characters believed in the reality of their visions of Jesus." There is no discussion (yet) on how their visions should be interpreted. That will come later in the book. After discussing each of the alternative options, he concludes that, "all in all, none of the six suggested theories stand up to stringent scrutiny."[255] Therefore, neither the New Testament's account nor the alternative theories can be definitively argued. Vermes presents one final bit of evidence at the close of the book. He does not choose one option over the other, but he changes the question.

After the resurrection, and specifically after Pentecost (fifty days later), the disciples became bold in their faith. There was a radical transformation in their lives as they "underwent a powerful mystical experience." These once fearful men became "ecstatic spiritual warriors."[256] Vermes credits the

---

251. Ibid., 142.

252. Ibid., 143.

253. Ibid., 144.

254. Ibid., 146.

255. Ibid., 149.

256. Ibid., 150.

"tale" of the empty tomb and the appearances as part of the reason for their hope.[257] These two points were acknowledged earlier, although somewhat halfheartedly. Now, they are not in doubt and they become the cause of a dramatic chain of events. The disciples not only "proclaimed openly the message of the gospel," but did so with the "charismatic potency" imparted to them by Jesus. It was a dramatic transformation: "The formerly terrified fugitives courageously spoke up in the presence of the authorities and healed the sick in public, at the gate of the Temple itself."[258]

The reality of this change, he continues, "opened the apostles' eyes to the mystery of the resurrection."[259] Given this, Vermes attempts to bring the whole picture into focus. The empty tomb and the visions "momentarily illumined their dark despair with a ray of hope." There were doubts, but their self-confidence was revived "under the influence of the Spirit" and they became increasingly sure that Jesus was with them.[260] In the end, "the helping hand that gave them strength to carry on with their task was the proof that Jesus had risen from the dead." Finally,

> The conviction in the spiritual presence of the living Jesus accounts for the resurgence of the Jesus movement after the crucifixion. However, it was the supreme doctrinal and organizational skill of St Paul that allowed nascent Christianity to grow into a viable and powerful resurrection-centered world religion.[261]

Vermes' argument is somewhat circular. The empty tomb and the visions combined to cause a belief in the resurrection. This belief caused them to experience the presence of Jesus. In the midst of doubts, the presence of Jesus reminded them that the evidence was true, and then confirmed their belief in the resurrection. What first needs to be explained is the reason for the disciples' "powerful mystical experience." In spite of this, the empty tomb and the visions are dismissed as not meeting the "minimum requirements" of inquiry. But, Vermes fully acknowledges these two points and admits that alternative accounts fail. While the amount of evidence *for* the resurrection may be limited, the evidence for the counter position is, according to Vermes, non-existent.

What would cause such a dramatic turnaround, in such a short period of time, especially to an entire group of people? The reason for such a

257. Ibid., 151.
258. Ibid., 150.
259. Ibid.
260. Ibid., 151.
261. Ibid., 152.

change, according to Vermes, was the disciples' conviction of "the spiritual presence of the living Jesus."[262] But, what does this actually mean? If Jesus was still dead, what type of "spiritual presence" could have been imparted to the disciples? And why did they go from despondency after the crucifixion to elation just days later? Vermes does not answer these questions, but he concludes the book with an alternative option. He advocates "resurrection in the hearts of men," which he believes is something available to all people. In words similar to the conclusion of Ben-Chorin, he writes: "Whether or not they adhere to a formal creed, a good many men and women of the twenty-first century may be moved and inspired by the mesmerizing presence of the teaching and example of the real Jesus alive in their mind."[263]

Vermes was a rare Jewish scholar who allowed for the possibility that all people (not just Gentiles) may benefit spiritually from Jesus. But, on what basis is this possible? The New Testament credits the resurrection for bringing about changed lives. If the supernatural element—and specifically the resurrection—is removed, in what way can Jesus be a "mesmerizing presence?" Also, if critical scholarship declares that most of the events of his life probably did not happen (or that we cannot know for certain), in what way can Jesus be an example for us?

Geza Vermes' belief about Jesus is complex. He dismisses much of the New Testament as myth, yet he strongly believes that some things can be known about Jesus. But, where does he stand on the resurrection? Officially he is agnostic, or better yet non-committal. But he does acknowledge the following: 1. Jesus died on the cross and was placed in a tomb owned by Joseph of Arimathea, 2. There is evidence for the empty tomb and none against it, 3. The disciples' belief in the resurrection goes back to an early source (even if discrepancies prevent us from knowing the precise details), 4. Alternative attempts to explain away the resurrection are lacking in credibility, 5. The disciples became radically transformed people who boldly proclaimed "the gospel," 6. Paul had some type of mystical experience outside of Damascus (which may allude to the acknowledgement that Paul was a persecutor turned believer), and 7. In some way, Jesus' life and teaching can bring inspiration even today.

The title of his book (*History and myth*) refers to Vermes' understanding of the New Testament documents. He believes they are a mixture of facts and legendary material. Other scholars use this assumption to automatically discredit the authenticity of the New Testament, and therefore assume that the resurrection could not be historical. But, Vermes was attempting to

262. Ibid.
263. Ibid.

look more closely. Although his own position was non-committal, he has nevertheless written a remarkably positive case in favor of the resurrection.

[4.5.3] Alan F. Segal

Alan Segal has already been discussed and quoted quite a bit in this study. He taught at Columbia University/Barnard College, and wrote extensively on the afterlife and Second Temple Judaism. In one article, as part of a symposium on the resurrection of Jesus, he addressed the historicity of the event. The symposium was built around a discussion between N.T. Wright and Jon Dominic Crossan. His main argument in this article is that "bodily resurrection in the New Testament means different things to different writers in the New Testament."[264] This was an argument he made more exhaustively in a chapter from his book, *Life after Death*, and which was summarized above.[265] In that chapter he offered elaborate theories based on Paul's own experiences and comparisons with contemporary literature. He acknowledged that these arguments could not ultimately be affirmed. His overall conclusion hinged on two verses from 1 Corinthians 15, namely verses 44 and 50. But, as seen above,[266] he did not exegete these verses in their contexts nor did he interact with the prevailing scholarship.

In this present article, he again rests his case on these passages: "Paul explicitly denies that flesh and blood can be resurrected (1 Cor 15:44, 50, 53–54). We should take this statement completely seriously. There is no reason to suppose that he means anything else than what he says: 'Flesh and blood cannot inherit the kingdom of God, nor does the perishable inherit the imperishable" (1 Cor 15:50).'[267] He does not question these verses, but takes his own interpretation as a given. The article then goes in a different direction, as he provides another novel attempt at answering the question. He begins by saying that Paul believed that the resurrected body of Christ is somehow similar to the resurrected bodies of "believers." All would agree on this point. He then employs three passages from Philippians. Philippians 2:6 says that Jesus shares "the form of God," and commenting on Philippians 3:10, he says that "the believer shares something of his identity with Christ."[268] Further, Philippians 3:20–21 says that the believer's body will be

---

264. Segal, "The Resurrection: Faith or History," 122.
265. See above, 4.4.3.
266. Ibid.
267. Segal, "The Resurrection: Faith or History," 122.
268. Ibid., 127.

transformed into (Jesus') "glorious body."[269] He never actually ties this all together to make an argument. What seems to be implied is that since Jesus' body was like God (who has no body), then the believer's body will therefore not be physical. The closest he comes to making this argument is as follows:

> The implication of the term morphe, "form," is that Christ has the form of a divine body identical with the kavod, the glory, and equivalent also with the eikon (Greek for "image"), for in Greek in Genesis 1:26 man is made after the eikon of God and thus has the divine morphe (Greek for "shape" or, in Hebrew, Demuth).[270]

This is another example of an elaborate explanation when a simple one would have sufficed. If he wanted to comment on the meaning of the word *morphe* in Philippians 2:6, he should have looked to the very next verse which is the only other place in the New Testament where the word is used. After writing that Jesus was in the "form" of God (verse 6), he then took the "form" of a slave (verse 7). Had Segal evaluated each usage of the word in relation to each other he almost certainly would have come to a different conclusion. But, this argument is used to make the case that Paul and the Gospels had a different view of the nature of the resurrection of Jesus. He says the differences are much like the differences between mystical literature and apocryphal literature. The former describes things as visionary while the latter describes the same things as factual and prophetic.[271] His ultimate point is that the Gospels cannot be trusted. Segal was certainly correct that some of Paul's words are confusing. The exact nature of the type of body he was describing defies both Greek and Jewish categories. This should not be surprising considering his belief that this event represents the start of something new, a new era. Paul does use different language than the Gospels. But this does not mean that Paul was speaking about something non-physical.

Segal ends the article with thoughts about whether or not the resurrection can even be studied historically. This too was discussed above (4.3.1). Many if not most of the participants at that seminar (for which the article was written) were not only committed Christians, but were convinced that the resurrection can be demonstrated historically. Segal was right to respond that it cannot be proven (a claim that does sometimes appear among Christian apologists). But, he overstates his case to the point of negating any discussion. Clearly there is evidence and there is a discussion. He himself

269. Ibid., 125–27.

270. Ibid., 126.

271. Ibid., 134.

interacted with several key issues which we will go to now. Most of the following comes from his book, *Life After Death*.

Segal acknowledges at least a few facts about the disciples, including that they believed Jesus rose from the dead. In fact, this belief began soon after the crucifixion. Citing Lüdemann, he says that "the original experience of the risen Christ must have been visionary appearances after death and that they must have started, as tradition has it, on the first day after the Sabbath, Easter Sunday."[272] This leads to the question of what actually happened to cause such a belief. In an earlier book, *Rebecca's Children*, he explains that such a belief would not have been out of the ordinary.

> It is understandable that several of Jesus' followers came to feel that Jesus was resurrected and had ascended to a new order of being. Since ascension and enthronement were common motifs of resurrection stories at the time, especially of stories dealing with martyrdom, it was entirely appropriate to identify Jesus with the enthroned figure about whom he had preached.[273]

His endnote cites 4 Maccabees as an example. Eighteen years later, returning to his book, *Life After Death*, he had a different take on this. In his survey of contemporary literature he again mentions 4 Maccabees but now rules out the likelihood of this being an influence on the disciples, at least on its own. The text does equate suffering and the afterlife. But, the comparison is limited. He concludes: "there is still a clear relationship between martyrdom and immortality, but the immortality is not resurrection."[274] The basis of the disciples' belief, then, must have had a variety of sources. He writes, "Since Jesus died as a martyr, expectations of his resurrection would have been normal in some Jewish sects. But the idea of a crucified messiah was unique. In such a situation, the Christians only did what other believing Jews did in similar circumstances: They turned to Biblical prophecy for elucidation."[275] The "Christian innovation,"[276] as he calls it, was to combine popular teachings of the day—including an angelic or divine figure who brought judgment (the Son of Man from Daniel 7:13), and one who could be called "Lord"—with Jesus as the messiah. On the basis of Daniel 7:9–14 and Daniel 12, together with Psalms 8 and 110, the Christian community "found the scriptural support" that clarified what God had in mind for the

272. Segal, *Life after Death*, 448.
273. Segal, *Rebecca's Children*, 87.
274. Segal, *Life after Death*, 387.
275. Ibid., 427
276. Ibid.

end of history.[277] These passages and the fact that Jesus died as a martyr, "produced the kerygma of the early church."[278]

This is an elaborate theory. In order for this to work, it needs to be demonstrated that the disciples knew of the relevant literature and the contemporary commentaries. It also assumes that Galilean fisherman would have had the sophistication to create their own midrashic commentary while they were grieving over the unexpected tragedy of the loss of their leader. Segal himself calls their new belief "absolutely novel." But, what really needs to be explained is why the disciples needed to find scriptures to validate their belief. In other words, what caused them to believe in a resurrection in the first place if it was such a novel idea? Segal offers several responses to this question in various places throughout his book. One was an appeal to eschatological visions. Just as Paul's visions were interpreted as "the actual presence of Christ and anticipatory of the end-times," he writes, "I suspect the visions of Peter and even James and the others were similar: They convinced Jesus' followers that he not only survived in a new spiritual state but that that state was as the manlike figure in heaven, "the Son of Man," whose reign inaugurated the millennium."[279] Comparing the disciples' visions with those of Paul is curious considering Segal went to great lengths to explain that Paul's experiences were the result of his unique background and temperament (see immediately below). But, the question remains: why a resurrection (of one individual messiah) when there were other options regarding the afterlife which would have fit much more naturally?

Segal often appeals to psychological jargon, specifically "religiously altered states of consciousness."[280] Yet, he also acknowledges that Jesus clearly had a unique influence on people. This is noticed in contrast to John the Baptist and his followers. Something no doubt happened to Jesus and to the disciples, as evidenced by their response. Martyrdom was an important part of the belief (based on the texts mentioned above), but he admits that there must have been something more to cause their original belief in the resurrection. He writes,

> What changes the portrait is not Jesus' martyrdom alone, as John was also martyred. It is Jesus' followers' interpretation of the Easter event. After the Easter events and Jesus' presumed resurrection, the Jesus movement began experiencing his presence in their midst. Apparently, people anticipated that John the

277. Ibid.
278. Ibid., 428.
279. Ibid., 448.
280. Ibid., 392.

Baptist might come back, but no one actually experienced it.
But, Jesus' disciples experienced his resurrection.[281]

This sounds like something more than mere visions, and it also needs to be asked why Jesus succeeded while John the Baptist failed. The original "Easter event," as he calls it, still needs to be explained. What actually happened? By Segal's own admission, it was something more than a combination of expectations and creative use of scripture, as much as he believes that these factors influenced their belief. In one other place he makes a remarkable statement about the event. The death and resurrection of the enthroned figure, he says, is "not inevitable" in the biblical narrative. Therefore, the faith of the disciples must have had an additional catalyst: "It must have come from the historical experience of the events of Jesus' life, not the other way around. The early Christian community, after they experienced these events, found the Scriptures that explained the meaning of the events."[282] Segal then jumps into an explanation of the hermeneutics that produced the early church's theology. But, the experience alluded to here is not further clarified. The statement is left hanging. Segal is referring to an event, something that actually happened, as he says: the "events of Jesus' life." The event of "Easter Sunday" that caused the disciples to believe in the resurrection of Jesus remains unexplained.

Segal also briefly commented on the origin of Paul's belief. His book, *Paul the Convert*, offers a wealth of information from history and the social sciences about converts. Most of the discussion is about what happens after conversion and there was very little, almost nothing, about why Paul went from one form of Judaism to a different form of Judaism (as Segal sees it). There is one definitive statement: "Paul is not converted by Jesus' teachings, but rather by an experience, a revelation of Christ, which radically reorients his life. Initially a religious persecutor of Christians, he became a principle Christian evangelist."[283] Exactly what did happen, according to Segal, is difficult to say. Luke's telling of the story is suspect since he has a theological agenda.[284] Paul's own testimony (passages such as 1 Cor 9:1, 15:8–10; Gal 1:13–17 and Phil 3:4–11) can also not be taken at face value. Using the contemporary research of religious conversion, Segal explains that "converts" find the meaning of their conversion and visions in the context of their new communities. In short, as he says in one footnote: "Paul's recollection of

---

281. Ibid., 393.

282. Ibid., 428.

283. Segal, *Paul the Convert*, 3.

284. Ibid., 4.

these events was influenced by his communal experience."[285] He later states: "Paul may have decided to become a Christian for the reasons that Luke suggests, or the experience itself may be lost forever since Paul himself does not tell us how it took place."[286] If his recollection was influenced by his new community to some extent (which is certainly possible), this does not negate the basic points that Segal affirms. The historical kernel regarding Paul, according to Segal, is that he was once hostile to a movement that he later joined. The cause of his new belief was based on some type of encounter which Paul actually had, and which he believed was an encounter with the risen Jesus.

Finally, Segal has a few words about the empty tomb as well. If the empty tomb tradition was unknown to Paul, as Segal asserts, there needs to be an explanation as to why it entered the Gospel documents at a later time. The Gospel of Mark, the shorter ending, is the focus here as it is the first source that mentions the empty tomb. He begins with the burial narrative and says that early tradition is "solid about the experiences of the women on the Easter morning, less solid on the antiquity of the empty tomb."[287] This is an odd dichotomy. It is not clear how the story of the women at the tomb could be early, and yet the emptiness of the tomb could be a later invention.

The empty tomb tradition might have existed earlier, he continues, and Paul might have neglected it simply because he was unaware of it. On the other hand, the narrative of the burial is "so manifestly polemical" as to question its credibility. But, finally, he writes, "Jesus' burial is a stable part of Gospel tradition and Paul explicitly said that Jesus was buried."[288] He does not provide a definitive conclusion on the tomb, apart from his overriding belief of Paul's view of a non-physical resurrection.

As to why an empty tomb story may have been invented, he gives several possibilities. First, the account of the empty tomb is both "good story telling"[289] and a "missionary strategy."[290] It serves to both flesh-out (quite literally) the account of what happened, and also present the message in a form that will help in its promotion. He later says that such an account "objectifies the issue of confirmation."[291] This argument explains how a belief in a physical resurrection might have been confirmed or promoted, but it does

285. Ibid., 310n17.
286. Ibid., 38.
287. Segal, *Life after Death*, 447.
288. Ibid.
289. Ibid., 444.
290. Ibid., 448.
291. Ibid., 450.

not explain how such a belief originated, especially in light of Segal's view that the disciples originally believed in a non-physical resurrection.

Second, the account of the empty tomb might have been a corrective. There were no eye witnesses to the actual resurrection. Segal believes this was a "critical difficulty" for the early Church and says: "The empty tomb itself becomes the vehicle for alleviating that dearth of testimonial for the resurrection, as well as the demonstration that the post-resurrection appearances were not hallucinations."[292] There is no evidence however, apart from Segal's assertion, that the lack of an eyewitness was ever considered a problem. If it was, the empty tomb story would be an obscure attempt to alleviate the problem. Why not just add an eyewitness account? The later Gospels, according to Segal, added numerous embellishments to Mark's work. But, they as well did not see the need to provide some type of correction to this alleged problem. In a footnote, however, he uses the lack of eyewitness as evidence of the historical Jesus. "No one would have made up a story of a Savior who was resurrected and then neglected to narrate it."[293] This could be used as an argument *for* the historicity of the resurrection. As Lapide argued, the narrative does not read as one trying to impress or convince anyone. It is a simple story of what was actually known. Nevertheless Segal continues: "On the other hand, it does nothing for the historicity of the resurrection itself."[294]

Third, the empty tomb story denies the idea that Jesus rose from the dead merely as a spirit. This brings the discussion back to 1 Corinthians 15:44, and Paul's use of the term "spiritual body." Segal's view is that it was a unique spiritual event, yet it was not physical. Mark's audience, Segal argues, may have misunderstood this subtle distinction and lead people to interpret it as a "disembodied soul," which would have denied the uniqueness of Jesus.[295] Segal is proposing a solution for something that has never before been considered a problem. But, if Mark was so worried about his audience getting Paul's original message wrong, why would he supply a story that itself (according to Segal) went completely counter to Paul's message? Segal has not accounted for the origins of the empty tomb story. It remains a mystery and he seems to be aware of this.

> The empty tomb has considerable narrative value, even though it does not present us with an indubitable historical truth, like the lack of witness to the resurrection itself. It is always conceivable

292. Ibid., 448–49.

293. Ibid., 762n8.

294. Ibid.

295. Segal, *Life after Death*, 451.

that, against our best logic, it actually happened. But, even if it did, the story of the empty tomb is not a particularly strong affirmation of the central events of Christianity, especially in comparison to the dramatic and life-changing personal visions of Paul.[296]

This is a curious admission. The empty tomb is compared with Paul's radical transformation as being of lesser evidential value. But, the two are not in competition. This is like a defense attorney saying that exhibit A is not as strong as exhibit B. If there is no contradiction, they each remain in evidence and the combination of the two makes the case that much stronger. To this should be added Segal's conclusion that the disciples' belief in the resurrection cannot simply be explained by psychological factors. In the end, Segal is correct in saying that the resurrection cannot be proven, at least not scientifically. Yet, even his masterful interaction with ancient sources was not able to navigate around the reality that there is historical evidence pointing to the resurrection and no cogent arguments against it.

4.6 ALTERNATIVE SUGGESTIONS

Many books have been written about the life of Jesus, perhaps more than any other topic in history. Most have been positive or at least respectful. But, there have also been many challenges along the way. These may be divided into two basic groups. The first is the flamboyant, over the top, spectacle that is intending to be provocative.[297] The most recent example of this is Dan Brown's book, *The Davinci Code*. Jacob Neusner noticed this phenomenon.

> People can make a great name for themselves by saying whatever they want about "the historical Jesus," making the front page of the *New York Times* (if that is what they wish to manufacture for themselves) if what they say is sufficiently scandalous, and therefore newsworthy. Announce that Jesus is precisely what the Gospels say he was—and still is—And even in churches some will yawn.[298]

Jewish scholars have been creative and provocative as well. This section includes two versions of the "swoon" theory, the idea that Paul was not born Jewish, and a belief that the works of Josephus provide a better source for Jesus than the New Testament. The scholarship of the second group in

296. Segal, *Life after Death*, 450.
297. For a survey of some of the recent examples, see Evans, *Fabricating Jesus*.
298. Neusner, "Who Needs the Historical Jesus?," 115.

this category is much more sober. This may include alternative explanations for the resurrection specifically, or theories that more generally call into question the entire New Testament. Many of the scholars from the above categories provided alternative explanations. The difference is that these authors are more adamant and more focused on doing so. The fact that there are new theories every year is itself evidence that no previous counter theory has gained a consensus even among critical scholars. Collectively, as a genre if we may call it that, these books are helpful to the overall discussion of the historicity of the resurrection. They demonstrate that simple attempts at alternatives to the canonical narrative are not adequate, and that elaborate or extreme theories are necessary. They also demonstrate that creative and elaborate reconstructions (at least so far) do not ultimately work either.

[4.6.1] Isaac M. Wise

Isaac M. Wise almost singlehandedly brought Reform Judaism to the United States. In 1874, he wrote *The Martyrdom of Jesus of Nazareth*. His stated purpose was to examine the New Testament from the "standpoint of reason." He claimed complete objectivity, and declared that he "wears no sectarian shackles, stands under no local bias, and obeys no mandates of any particular school."[299] His critical assumptions were typical of the day. None of the Gospels, he believed, were written in the first century, and he assigns to Mark the date of 135–138.[300] The historicity of the Gospels cannot be trusted: "Simple facts were skillfully wrought up into a divine drama, after the pattern of the Pagan mysteries, in defiance of the plain resultants of reason and the simple teachings of the Bible."[301]

Wise ultimately wanted to demonstrate two things. First, that the Jews did not kill Jesus. Therefore, he denies both the trials before Jewish leaders (where the sentencing would have taken place), and the crucifixion itself (where the death would have taken place). The first of these would occupy the minds of a number of scholars in later years. But the denial of crucifixion itself is a unique position. The second thing he wanted to counter was the theological meaning behind the crucifixion. The New Testament says that Jesus died for the sins of the whole world. As a product of the Enlightenment, Wise believed the concept of one dying in the place of another was "immoral."[302] He discredits the trials before the Jewish leaders by pointing

299. Wise, *The Martyrdom of Jesus of Nazareth*, 5.

300. Ibid., 13.

301. Ibid., 152.

302. Ibid., 12.

to discrepancies in the texts. Specifically, he argues, the four writers of the Gospels gave incomplete accounts of the arrest and trials. This is enough to question their reliability.

> Circumstantial evidence is insufficient. If for instance one has seen a man lying in wait, another has seen him load a pistol, a third has heard the noise of a shot coming from the tree where the man laid in wait, and a fourth sees the victim shot dead; their testimony would not convict the murderer to subject him to the sentence of death. Each witness must have seen the whole deed.[303]

Wise then offers his own explanation of what really happened. Jesus was "captured at night as quietly as possible," brought to an unknown place which was "secluded from the eyes of the populace" and brought to Pilate early in the morning.[304] This would explain how the Jewish trials were avoided. After this, he gives several reasons to prove that the crucifixion never happened. For example, the Talmud refers to Jesus as the "hanged one" not the "crucified one."[305] In the Book of Acts, Peter says that he was hanged on "a tree" (Acts 5:30, 39, 13:29), not a cross. The Roman historian Tacitus does say that Jesus suffered under Pontius Pilate, "but he says not what."[306]

As to why the crucifixion story was needed (and therefore "invented"), "It is well known that the cross was the symbol of life and eternity long before the Christian story transpired." To support this he offers two examples. The first is a fanciful interpretation of Ezekiel 9:4 and 6, and the second is an appeal to pagan sources.[307] Wise's story ends with Jesus being led to Pilate. What happens next is not known. From here, popular theories were advanced. "Some said he was crucified; others thought he was hung on a tree; and others again said he did not die at all."[308] The crucifixion story is then credited to Paul. He would be the one to embellish the story and mix it with pagan ideas. Because he strongly emphasized the crucifixion (1 Cor 17:23), Wise sees this as "proof that the crucifixion was denied by other teachers of the gospel."[309] In other words, Paul made a point of emphasizing it specifically to counter previous teachers who were not mentioning it.

303. Ibid., 71.
304. Ibid., 125.
305. Ibid., 100.
306. Ibid.
307. Ibid.
308. Ibid., 126.
309. Ibid., 100.

But, if these other "teachers of the Gospel" did not believe in the crucifix-ion, what exactly was the message they were proclaiming? Wise explains: "The spiritual resurrection of Jesus, which the original apostles taught, was transferred into a bodily resurrection for the benefit of heathens with gross conceptions of Spirit and God."[310] This view may serve as an object lesson for today. While the scholarly presuppositions are out of date, the general approach is quite similar to some of the modern attempts at explaining away the resurrection. Perhaps it is easier to recognize the problems when what is being argued is less controversial.

[4.6.2] Hugh Schonfield

The all-time bestselling book about the resurrection of Jesus was written by Hugh Schonfield in 1965. He was a raised in a Jewish home, came to believe in Jesus as Messiah, and then later abandoned his faith completely.[311] He wrote several books, but none would be as well-known as the *Passover Plot*. This work is described by the author as "an imaginative reconstruction of the personality, aims and activities of Jesus."[312] It is far-fetched, outrageous and controversial. And yet, in many ways it is not that different from many of the other reconstructions offered by critical scholars. In Schonfield's view, Jesus believed himself to be the Messiah. This is something he can support, as long as this belief is divorced from the "pagan doctrine of the incarna-tion of the Godhead." This, he believed, would be antithetical to "Jewish monotheism."[313] Jesus was aware of prophecies that said that the Messiah must die and rise again. This was the catalyst for the plan—the plot—that was set in motion. He would go to Jerusalem and arrange for all that was needed. The plan was kept a secret, even to his closest friends: "The destined road for Jesus led to torture at Jerusalem on a Roman cross, to be followed by resurrection. But these things had to come about in the manner pre-dicted by the Scriptures and after preliminaries entailing the most careful scheming and plotting to produce them."[314]

Schonfield then comments on such a scheme. He called it a "nightmar-ish conception of the frightening logic of a sick mind, or of a genius."[315] Jesus did his part, and along the way others would become involved as well. Judas

---

310. Ibid., 127.

311. Harvey, "Don't Pass over the Plot," 2002.

312. Schonfield, *The Passover Plot*.

313. Ibid., 21.

314. Ibid., 132.

315. Ibid.

realized that his role was to act as the betrayer, and he obediently did what was expected.[316] The trials before the Jewish leaders and then Pilate also went as planned. At some time prior to this, Jesus had divulged the plan to Joseph of Arimathea. He too would play a vital role in staging the resurrection: "Two things, however, were indispensable to the success of a rescue operation. The first was to administer a drug to Jesus on the cross to give the impression of premature death, and the second was to obtain the speedy delivery of the body to Joseph."[317]

This was the essence of the plan. A drug would be used to give the appearance that Jesus had died, although he would merely be in a coma. The Gospels themselves are used to support this theory. For example, the sponge with the vinegar given to Jesus while he was on the cross was said to have the special drug. Also, Joseph went to Pilate to ask for the body. Schonfield points out that in Mark 15:43 and 45 Joseph asks for the body (*soma*), whereas Pilate refers to it as a corpse (*ptoma*). The differing Greek words are cited as evidence that Joseph did not believe that the body was in fact dead.[318] Jesus was placed on a cross and remained there for three hours before being taken down. Schonfield mentions a passage in Josephus that tells of a man who was taken down from a cross and eventually lived.[319] However, Jesus was then placed in a tomb for over twenty-four hours. What "seems probable" is that on Saturday night, "Jesus was brought out of the tomb by those concerned in the plan" and that he "regained consciousness temporarily but finally succumbed."[320] It was in those last moments of consciousness, with his final breaths, that Jesus told his disciples that he would rise again.

The next morning, Mary Magdalene and others would find an empty tomb. They would also experience visions of the risen Jesus. Schonfield believes that they must have seen a real person and not merely a series of subjective visions. He accounts for this by saying that it must have been someone other than Jesus that they all mistook for Jesus. He then offers another possibility. He suggests that the man in question was a medium. And it was through this man that Jesus—now in the afterlife—spoke with his own voice. That is why the disciples would have recognized him as Jesus.[321] Schonfield's version of the story is certainly one of the most imaginative. The belief that Jesus even had such a plan is, of course, pure speculation. And

316. Ibid., 136.
317. Ibid., 66.
318. Ibid., 168.
319. Ibid., 162.
320. Ibid., 172.
321. Ibid., 179.

being in a tomb would be an impossible place to heal after the torture of crucifixion. Some critics categorically deny the supernatural, and therefore look for alternative options. But, Schonfield actually used the supernatural (the medium) to explain away the risen Jesus. He was not against the supernatural, nor Jesus being the Messiah. He was merely trying, like many others have done, to fit Jesus into his own acceptable mold.

One of the astonishing things about the *Passover Plot* is how optimistic Schonfield is about the whole thing. He sees it as a success. Jesus did the right thing by playing the role of the Messiah. Although he did not actually rise from the dead, he sincerely tried. For this, he serves as an example: "Wherever mankind strives to bring in the rule of justice, righteousness and peace, the deathless presence of Jesus the Messiah is with them."[322] If nothing else, Schonfield's reconstruction serves as a reminder of how difficult it is to explain away the resurrection without resorting to contrived speculation.

[4.6.3] Max Dimont

Max Dimont became famous for writing the bestselling book, *The Jews, God and History*. It is in a smaller, later work that he addresses the resurrection. In *Appointment in Jerusalem*, he sees four basic possibilities to explain what actually happened. The first is that it was an actual historical event. The second, following Reimarus, is that the disciples stole the body and then spread the news of the resurrection. The next view is that Jesus did not die on the cross, and later revealed himself. The final view states that there was no plot or deception, but that the events were written to conform to the new faith.[323] At first, Dimont does not take sides, saying that the resurrection is ultimately "an enigma embedded in faith."[324] He does, however, have sympathy for the fourth view stated above, and makes an argument that the Gospels themselves provide evidence of this. He begins with Mark. This Gospel ends abruptly. Since the empty tomb is mentioned but without comments, he deduces that this issue "held little or no significance" for Mark.[325] This led to questions among potential converts who would hear or read the story: "The orchestration of doubt began to sweep Christian communities in the decades following Mark's Gospel. Pagans considering conversion

---

322. Ibid., 81.
323. Ibid., 115.
324. Ibid., 123.
325. Ibid., 118.

to Christianity were puzzled by Mark's abrupt ending. They wanted more proof of a resurrection."[326]

This chain of events—offered by Dimont without verification—leads to a new generation that did not know whether the resurrection was real. This is where Matthew and Luke come in. Matthew's main contribution was to address the "persistent rumors" that the disciples stole the body. Specifically, he "executed a brilliant checkmate" by "shifting the suspicion from the disciples to the Jews."[327] Luke added that Jesus told the disciples to examine his hands, thus demonstrating that Jesus was alive after having been crucified. But even after the three synoptic Gospels were written, other questions arose. Specifically, how can it be known for sure whether or not Jesus actually died after being on the cross? Dimont sees this as an appropriate question, since "one did not usually die on the cross in only six hours."[328] To account for this, the Gospel of John adds that the Roman soldiers also stabbed Jesus with a spear. The message was now complete and finalized: "Jesus became a messiah by popular demand, and the concept of a resurrection was born in faith and handed down by tradition."[329]

[4.6.4] Gaalyahu Cornfeld

Gaalyahu Cornfeld was an archaeologist and writer who lived in Jerusalem and wrote several books. In 1982 he published *The Historical Jesus: A Scholarly View of the Man and his World*. It contains a number of brief articles by his friend, David Flusser, which are interspersed throughout the book. It also includes a wealth of pictures of ancient sites and artifacts that make it an engaging introductory work on the subject. For most of the book, Cornfeld is more concerned with archaeological issues surrounding the life of Jesus. He has a very low view of how much of the life of Jesus should be considered historical. For him, the "sole incontestable fact in the life of Jesus" is the crucifixion.[330] Similar to Vermes, he sees Jesus as a "charismatic Jewish *tsaddik*."[331] Since the crucifixion definitely happened, the origin of the belief in resurrection needs to be explained.

Cornfeld uses rabbinic *halacha* to shed light on the burial of Jesus. Quoting from Mishnah *Semahot*, he explains an ancient custom dictating

326. Ibid.
327. Ibid., 119.
328. Ibid., 120.
329. Ibid., 123.
330. Cornfeld, *The Historical Jesus*, 8.
331. Ibid., 13.

that cemeteries should be visited within three days. According to this source, "it once happened that a (buried) man was visited and went to live another twenty-five years." Indeed, he continues, "experience had taught caution and the necessity for making sure that someone taken for dead was not actually in a coma, or a deep swoon."[332] This tradition explains why the women went to visit the grave of Jesus. But, by the time they arrived the body was gone.

> It had been removed to preserve the life of a man crippled, but possibly not bereft of life by crucifixion. Hence the urgency. This was a case of survival, so strange that it really was miraculous and lent the crucified Jesus an aura of indestructible holiness, even immortality. His followers prefer the latter description.[333]

To advance his theory, Cornfeld—like Schonfield—refers to a passage in Josephus that speaks of a man who was taken down from a cross and survived. This, he says, "lends credence to the "swoon" theory advanced in past years to explain the disappearance of the body from the tomb."[334] But, before continuing in this direction, Cornfeld wanted to summarize other theories that have attempted to explain away the resurrection. To do so, he employs an extended series of passages—some eight pages—from Paul L Maier's book, *The First Easter*. Maier is a conservative scholar who believes in the resurrection.

Cornfeld summarizes Maier's work, explaining alternative theories that have been employed in the past. These include the stolen body theory, the wrong tomb theory, and a curious one called the "lettuce theory" (this refers to the gardener who did not want people trampling on his lettuce on the way to visit Jesus, and therefore removed the body). Other efforts include psychological and/or hallucination theories. Also, the "twin brother" theory has been used to claim that people actually saw Jesus' look-alike twin brother after the crucifixion. Maier responds to these and then offers positive evidence for the resurrection, including the changed lives of the original followers.[335] After this interlude, Cornfeld returns to his own narrative. Maier's arguments helped Cornfeld dismiss many of the standard alternative theories. In spite of this, it is remarkable that he spends no time pondering the possibility that Maier's own view (that of an actual resurrection) might have happened. He is left with one option, the one alluded to above: "Namely, that the women who came to inspect the tomb, as ordained in

332. Ibid., 176.
333. Ibid.
334. Ibid., 177.
335. Ibid., 179–86.

the *Halakhah*, found to their consternation not a body, but an empty tomb. The physical survival of the wretched body of Jesus led to the enthusiastic retroactive effect of the "resurrection."[336]

[4.6.5] Hyam Maccoby

Hyam Maccoby was librarian at Leo Baeck College and later lecturer at the University of Leeds. He wrote several books on New Testament themes, and many of his views are quite extreme. In 1973 he wrote *Revolution in Judea*. It includes a wealth of background information on both Jewish and Roman sects of the time, but he begins with a familiar question. "How does it come about," he asks, "that a religion which borrows so heavily from Judaism has, for the major part of its history, regarded the Jew as pariahs and outcasts?"[337] This book seeks to examine the question from a Jewish point of view.

He begins with a discussion about Barabbas, the man whom the Gospels say was crucified alongside Jesus. This figure, Maccoby believes, is crucial to understanding the entire story of Jesus. Ultimately, he believes that later editors invented the Barabbas account as a device to blame the Jews for the crucifixion of Jesus. For most of the rest of the book he deconstructs the life and times of Jesus. At the end he returns to Barabbas to explain, as the title of chapter nine states, "what really happened." Maccoby sees Jesus as a political figure: "From the moment that he began to preach the advent of the "kingdom of God" he was a marked man, and when he claimed the Messiahship he was in head-on collision with Rome."[338] Maccoby believed that Jesus was a Pharisee and that anti-Pharisee expressions found in the Gospels are all inventions. He was not only a Pharisee, "he remained a Pharisee all his life."[339] In fact, Jesus should be counted among the great Jewish teachers in history. Both Jesus and Rabbi Akiva, he says, "were Jewish heroes whose significance lies in their lives, not their deaths."[340]

Maccoby's story takes a unique turn as he approaches the final days of Jesus' life. He believed that Jesus was arrested (as a political revolutionary) at the end of the Fall festival of Tabernacles. He then spent the next six months in jail.[341] At Passover, he was brought before Pilate. Maccoby believed that the Sanhedrin trial never happened, and that the story of Judas was likewise

---

336. Ibid., 187.
337. Maccoby, *Revolution in Judea*, 12.
338. Ibid., 101.
339. Ibid., 106.
340. Ibid., 103.
341. Ibid., 167.

invented purely to blame the Jews.[342] The account of Pilate asking the crowd who should be set free, and their choice of Barabbas, is likewise "invented" to further induce Jewish guilt. At the same time, this scenario poses a problem, for which Maccoby needs a solution. Throughout the Gospels Jesus is portrayed as popular, admired and applauded by the Jewish crowds. But how can it be, Maccoby wonders, that the very crowd that hailed him as king during his triumphal entry shouted "crucify him!" less than a week later? The answer pivots on the person of Barabbas, whose first name was also Jesus: "The Jewish crowd did in fact call to Pilate to release "Jesus Barabbas," but that was because "Jesus Barabbas" was the name of the man also known as Jesus of Nazareth."[343] According to Maccoby, the Jewish crowd that hailed Jesus as he entered Jerusalem really did shout for his release before Pilate. The later editors of the New Testament, however, in their attempt to cast blame, deliberately (and falsely) portrayed them as calling for the release of Barabbas. It was therefore Pilate's decision—and not that of the Jewish crowd—to send Jesus to his death.

With his main thesis accomplished, Maccoby had little interest in discussing the resurrection and adds but a few brief comments. Maccoby believed Jesus was crucified in the year 30 CE.[344] After his death, Joseph of Arimathea, "a Pharisee member of the Sanhedrin," asked Pilate for the body and buried it.[345] At some point after this, "Jesus' immediate supporters, the Twelve and a small band of followers, after an initial period of dismay, came to believe that Jesus was still alive. He had been brought back to life, like Elijah, and would soon return to lead a new attack on the Romans which this time would be successful."[346] In *The Mythmaker*, discussed above (3.5.1), Maccoby explains Paul's dramatic experience. His "conversion" was based on the conflict between his pagan background and his disappointment over his own failure at not being a successful Pharisee. From this, something new was created which would profoundly impact the entire world. Paul's vision

---

342. This thesis about Judas is continued and expanded upon in Maccoby's book called, *Judas Iscariot and the Myth of Jewish Evil.* Levenson's review found the scholarship lacking. Specifically, he said Maccoby's speculations, "though always suggestive, sometimes come to resemble a veritable house of cards." In the end, Levenson wrote, his theory about Judas is "as unconvincing as it is bold" Levenson, "The Sacred Executioner," 56, 58.

343. Ibid., 165.

344. Ibid., 169.

345. Ibid., 167.

346. Ibid., 168.

of Jesus was "the epiphany or divine appearance which initiated Christianity, just as the appearance of God in the burning bush initiated Judaism."[347]

[4.6.6] Ellis Rivkin

For many, the crucifixion immediately raises the issue of blame. Who is responsible for the death of Jesus? But, this is perhaps the wrong starting point. Ellis Rivkin reframed the question, and offered an answer, in his book *What killed Jesus?* His entire approach to the study of Jesus is unique. Rather than begin with the New Testament and then decide which parts are credible, he takes a completely different route. Rivkin, who taught for fifty years at Hebrew Union College in Cincinnati, begins his study by rejecting the New Testament altogether. This is because it is "penned with faith, written with passion, and bristling with hostility and resentment."[348] A better place to start, he says, is in the works of Josephus. In this he follows the writings of his mentor, Solomon Zeitlin. Both writers favor Josephus because they believe his writings are more historically accurate than either the New Testament itself or any other extra-biblical literature.

Josephus specifically wrote about the High Priest Annus, John the Baptist, and "James the brother of Jesus." Some scholars have questioned the reference to James and Jesus, saying it may not actually be referring to the famous Jesus of Nazareth. But Rivkin is convinced that it does. "Clearly," he wrote, "no further explanation was necessary, since every cultured Greek and Roman who might read Josephus' *Antiquities* would have known about the Christians."[349]

Rivkin sees in John the Baptist a remarkable charismatic figure. But after John's death, no one continued to follow him or proclaim his merits. He then ponders what type of person would be able to sustain a following even after his death. It is this question, combined with the historical background provided by Josephus, which enables him to construct an idealized person whom he calls the "charismatic of charismatics." Such a man "must have fused within himself the wonder working charisma of an Elijah, the visionary power of an Isaiah, and the didactive persuasion of a Pharisaic sage." He continues the description as follows: "To outlive death itself, he would have had to feel the sufferings of the poor, experience the humiliation of the degraded, sense the loneliness of the outcast, taste the despair of the sinner,

---

347. Ibid., 104.
348. Rivkin, *What Killed Jesus*, 16.
349. Ibid., 66.

and envelop all who came within his shadow, his graciousness, compassion, and undemanding love.[350]"

The "charismatic of charismatics" would also have been seen as the embodiment of such biblical concepts as the "son of man," as well as that of a healer and even the Messiah. This amazing figure would also have preached that "the souls of the righteous soar up to God the Father, where they await the day of resurrection."[351] Finally, the "charismatic of charismatics" would have been sentenced to death on a cross. His disciples would have remembered his teaching about resurrection, and this ultimately would have brought them to a new faith: "Stunned, bewildered, disoriented, disbelieving the sight of their beloved Teacher crucified, would not the eyes of the faithful see what the eyes of the faithless could not—that their Master, their Teacher, their Lord was as alive as he ever had been when he had preached among them."[352]

Rivkin has devised an extremely detailed history of someone ("the charismatic of charismatics") based on very general information. This history is then compared with the life of Jesus as portrayed in the Gospels. Rivkin discovers that the two stories actually have quite a bit in common. For this reason, the Gospels may now be vindicated. Because the Gospels agree so much with his own construction, he then refers to them as "precious sources for our knowledge both of the historical Jesus and of the risen Christ."[353] One of the only points of disagreement between his view and the Gospels is the resurrection itself. And this is a no small thing.

> We thus face an unbridgeable chasm—a chasm separating the charismatic of charismatics drawn by a non-Christian historian from the writings of Josephus, and the Jesus who proved himself to be the Christ through his resurrection—a resurrection attested to by his disciples but neither attested to nor believed by any known Scribe-Pharisee other than Paul.[354]

Some readers might balk at Rivkin's approach, seeing it as implausible to the point of absurdity. Others might see it as a literary device to help him make his point. Yet, for all of his machinations, Rivkin still arrives at virtually the same place as most other critical scholars. The basic plot line of the Gospels is accepted. The crucifixion, however, is blamed on the Roman political system as a whole, thus answering the question posed by the book's

350. Ibid., 72.
351. Ibid., 88.
352. Ibid., 89.
353. Ibid., 109.
354. Ibid., 108.

title. While many other details are questioned, Rivkin believed that "whatever the findings of critical scholarship, a triad of facts—trial, crucifixion, attested resurrection—undergird Christianity."[355]

Rivkin also commented on the early beliefs of the movement in two separate articles. Both are found in books of ecumenical conversations. In each case, he shows that faith in Jesus seemed to be against all odds. For example, in the first article he writes about the disciples' belief in him as Messiah. While others made that claim and were not successful, only Jesus had success: "he did so after the very crucifixion which should have refuted his claims decisively." He continues,

> But it was not Jesus' life which proved beyond question that he was the Messiah, the Christ. It was his resurrection. It was only when his disciples were convinced that Jesus had indeed risen from the dead that they were stunned into awareness that Jesus was the Christ. It was not by virtue of any signs that attended his earthly ministry, but by his resurrection.[356]

In the second article, Rivkin addresses Paul's belief. Although he originally persecuted the Church, he too would be dramatically changed. This would happen, Rivkin says, in spite of himself: "He came to Christ because he saw Jesus Christ risen from the dead, not because he wanted to see him risen, but because he could not help seeing him resurrected and alive. What Paul had thought was a blasphemous claim had been transformed for him into an undeniable fact."[357]

[4.6.7] Michael J. Cook

Hebrew Union College is a seminary of Reform Judaism which trains rabbis and scholars, and it is the only Jewish institution in the world that requires its students to study the New Testament. Heading up this department for several decades now is Michael J. Cook. He stands in a different place than the others in this category as he is a trained New Testament scholar. But, some of his views about Jesus are no less creative. His book, *Modern Jews Engage the New Testament*, was written in 2008. He recognized that most Jews do not know enough about the New Testament to adequately respond to questions about Jesus. This, he writes, is the exact opposite way that Jews normally approach a problem. Usually, they choose to "amass—not

---

355. Ibid., 116.
356. Rivkin, "Meaning of the Messiah in Jewish Thought," 62.
357. Rivkin, "A Jewish View of the New Testament," 92.

shun—knowledge."[358] But, because of Jewish aversion to reading the New Testament, they feel bad about rejecting it in ignorance. This book seeks to help, and this is apparently the meaning behind the book's subtitle, *Enhancing Jewish well-being in a Christian environment.* The focus of his book is "not for readers to learn the New Testament's *content.*" Rather, it is to help them "discern the *dynamics*—the problem solving techniques—that underlie the content."[359]

His view of the Gospel narratives is as follows: "the early Christian communities refined their conceptualizations, especially of Jesus himself, to address problems of *their* later day, not his."[360] For this reason, he advocates looking for "Gospel dynamics," which he defines as "those skillful techniques—evinced in the Gospels—by which early Christians molded their traditions to address their needs decades after Jesus died."[361] He begins by explaining two models to help understand early Christianity. The first one, called "Configuration A," refers to the original Jewish followers of Jesus. This movement arose in Israel and would eventually die out. "Configuration B" refers to the movement that began in the Diaspora. This movement combined the early beliefs of the original followers with "Greco Roman religious currents" and eventually attracted Paul. He, in turn, would add elements of his own Judaism along with further ideas from paganism. This Paul movement, he says, "became the nucleus of a Christianity that endured."[362] The Gospels, since they were written after Paul's writings, present Jesus through the lens of "Configuration B" Christianity. The accounts of the crucifixion are questioned, but Cook does acknowledge that Jesus died in approximately 30 C.E.[363] In his summary of "Configuration A" Christianity, he gives a few bare facts that are perhaps all we can know about the original Jesus movement. It was

> an outgrowth of a small number of Jews remaining impacted by, and committed to, teachings of Jesus, to their companionship, interactions, and exchanges with him, and to their consequent belief that he was the Messiah. They admitted that he did not conform to the then political expectations for this figure, and at first were demoralized by his crucifixion. But they rebounded

358. Cook, *Modern Jews Engage the New Testament*, xiii.
359. Ibid.
360. Ibid., 83.
361. Ibid.
362. Ibid., 35.
363. Ibid., 34.

through faith that he rose from the dead and would imminently return to complete his mission.[364]

Cook affirms that belief in the resurrection began with the original disciples. They were "demoralized" by the crucifixion, and yet for some reason were dramatically changed because of their belief in the resurrection. Cook does not spend much time on this issue, and says it is "beyond historical reconstruction."[365] However, in an endnote, he offers the following suggestion by way of a rhetorical question.

> Did belief in Jesus' resurrection arise among his followers from their struggle with cognitive dissonance: that Jesus died without accomplishing his messianic mission? Then, to address this dis-confirmation, did they come to believe that Jesus' presence still (so to speak) "abode among them" *spiritually?* Then, when circulated, was this misconcretized [sic] into word of physical appearances—first to those worthy (as the kerygma specifies)?[366]

Cook dedicates a whole chapter to the empty tomb and there are several points of discussion. First, he says that Paul "betrays no awareness of the empty tomb story."[367] Along with Segal, Cook states that Paul's language (specifically in 1 Cor 15, verses 44 and 50) speaks of a non-physical resurrection. He does not elaborate on this (see the discussion above, 3.4.3). In addition, he says that Paul does not specifically mention the empty tomb. The word used for "buried" in 1 Cor 15:4 is *etaphe*, which does not specify the place of burial. He therefore concludes that it is "compatible with burial in a grave, pit or trench, or buried alone or alongside others or in a common grave for criminals, or in a tomb."[368] This point has been the subject of much debate.[369] It usually rides on the assumption that Paul *would have* included a specific mention of the tomb if there really was one. But, there was no reason for that. Paul's words in 1 Cor 15:3–7 are a concise declaration of what happened to Jesus, it does not include any additional descriptions of subsequent events.

Second, he wonders about the women finding the tomb. Why were they not included in the kerygma? A traditional answer, he states, is that only men qualified as witnesses. Paul might have deleted mention of the

364. Ibid., 35.

365. Ibid., 158.

366. Ibid., 324; emphasis in the original.

367. Ibid., 155.

368. Ibid., 156.

369. See Licona, *The Resurrection of Jesus*, 333–39.

women based on current prejudices. But, this answer assumes there really was an empty tomb. Cook sees it differently. Employing his "Gospel Dynamics," he writes, "I prefer a different explanation, which is that only when Mark himself (ca. 72 CE) introduced the motif that the men ran away did he thereby leave women as the only ones of Jesus' followers in the vicinity to whom the resurrected Jesus could appear—an editorial matter about which those formulating the kerygma, decades earlier, would have known nothing."[370]

In other words, Paul did not include the story of the women at the tomb because it had not yet been invented, and Mark (or someone around the time of Mark) was responsible for creating it. This theory needs to be evaluated in light of Cook's own thesis. For him, many of the characters and events in Mark's Gospel are complete fabrications. Just a few pages earlier he wrote: "We should not overlook that Mark serves as the sole source (or creator) of half a dozen or so bit players like Joseph."[371] Given this assumption, it seems much more likely that Mark would have simply created one or more male characters to find the tomb as opposed to being constrained to fabricate a story of less than ideal witnesses.

Third, Cook offers an explanation as to how the empty tomb story might have first been conceived. He writes: "If Jesus, after death, was reported sighted, then whatever the place where his corpse had been lain [sic] became presumed *vacant.*"[372] This too needs to be evaluated based on Cook's presuppositions along with the historical context. He believes that the Jewish arm of the movement disbanded early, and that the notion of an empty tomb arose later, around the time of the writing of Mark. So, it must have been a pagan in Cook's hypothetical suggestion. But, first-century pagan beliefs about the afterlife did not normally include a physical aspect. As Segal remarked, "A person might survive death through the immortality of the soul in Greek thought but a bodily resurrection was never any significant part in Greek thinking."[373]

Fourth, he needs to explain the burial story and Joseph of Arimathea. If it is not historical, why was it created? He provides an elaborate example of his "Gospel Dynamics." While acknowledging that Joseph of Arimathea might have been a real person,[374] he believes that the burial story is entirely fictitious. Mark's reason for creating this account, Cook argues, may have

---

370. Cook, *Modern Jews Engage the New Testament*, 156–57.

371. Ibid., 152.

372. Ibid., 157; emphasis in the original.

373. Segal, *Life after Death*, 425.

374. Cook, *Modern Jews Engage the New Testament*, 160.

been misunderstood by the other Gospel writers who borrowed Mark's story and added additional material. For example, Mark said that Joseph was
"seeking the kingdom of God." This may have led Matthew (and possibly
John) to see Joseph as a disciple of Jesus. But, this does not necessarily mean
that Joseph was a disciple, Cook argues, since (as Montefiore also suggested)
Pharisees were also seeking the Kingdom of God. Therefore, Matthew's des-
ignation of Joseph as a "disciple" may be an example of how and why he
added additional, erroneous information.[375] He continues,

> But some inferences could be plainly wrong if Mark's intent
> was to present Joseph as Jesus' *opponent*. As unexpected as
> this sounds, Mark expressly has "all" those trying Jesus (this
> would have to include Joseph) condemn him as deserving death
> (14:64)—and this in a Sanhedrin scene that Mark himself in-
> vented (so we must presume Mark planned this out as a consis-
> tent piece).[376]

To summarize, Mark's original reason for creating the Joseph story was
to portray him as an opponent of Jesus, not a disciple. This was misunderstood by the other evangelists. Ultimately, his intent was to show how "even
Joseph, someone who condemned Jesus, behaved as a true disciple *should*
have behaved; he was on the scene to do that for which Jesus' official des-
ignees—his runaway disciples—had made themselves unavailable."[377] This
was in keeping with Mark's overall strategy to acknowledge the Jewish roots
of the movement, yet condemn the Jews in the eyes of his intended Gentile
audience.[378]

This suggestion is highly nuanced and indeed brilliant. But it is not
without its problems. The first is the overriding assumption that the evangelists not only completely fabricated their Gospels, but that an anti-Jewish
agenda was one of their main motivations. As discussed above, this line of
thinking is out of date particularly among Jewish scholars (see above, 3.2).
The bigger problem for this scenario is the selective use of texts. He makes
the point that the Sanhedrin members were "*unanimously* arrayed against
Jesus,"[379] based on the fact that Mark 14:64 says "all" condemned him. This
must be read in context. The pericope begins in Mark 14:53, which says
that the chief priests and the elders and the scribes came together. As Cook

---

375. Ibid., 151.

376. Ibid., 152; emphasis in the original.

377. Ibid., 154.

378. This is further explained later in the same book (ibid., 176–91) and was discussed above (3.2.1) from an earlier article by Cook.

379. Ibid., 153; emphasis in the original.

rightly explains, Mark 14:63 does say that "all" of them (the three groups just mentioned) condemned Jesus. But, the narrative does not end there. The first verse of the next chapter (Mark 15:1) refers to the same three groups mentioned above—chief priests, elders and scribes. It goes on to say that these groups met with "the whole counsel." This seems to imply that the pivotal word "all" in Mark 14:64 was a select group and not the whole Sanhedrin, and there is therefore no reason to suggest that Joseph was among those who condemned Jesus.

Cook also discusses Paul. The Book of Acts is dismissed as a complete fabrication, and Paul's letters are critically examined. He does affirm that Paul persecuted the "Christian missionaries."[380] On one hand, Cook says, Paul was an "ecstatic visionary."[381] Perhaps, he says about Paul's revelation, Paul "might have "received" it from the very Damascus Christians whom he persecuted (and then joined)."[382] As he learned of their beliefs, he also might have credited God for what he was receiving.[383] Cook further suggests that the followers of Jesus in Damascus were already heavily influenced by paganism. This is what he refers to as "Configuration B" Christianity. He continues, "This configuration attracted Paul. He deepened it by incorporating motifs derivative from his Judaism (especially atoning sacrifice, or atonement through sacrifice), and sacramental benefits akin to this promised by Mystery cults of dying and rising savior deities."[384]

Cook also explains why Paul might have been attracted to such teachings. He prefers the terms "reversion" or "extension" to "conversion," since Paul ultimately switched from one form of Judaism to another.[385] Cook suggests that Paul was dissatisfied with Pharisaism based on Romans 7:14. The Pharisees, Cook says, saw repentance itself as effective, while Paul argues that something more and beyond him was needed to deal with sin. This, combined with Paul's upbringing in Tarsus –where Mithraism and other cults spoke of redemption—caused Paul's ultimate struggle. It was a battle between the religions he grew up with, "which he may have long suppressed," and his Jewish identity. This brought Paul to "a higher rung on the same ladder that his fellow Jews had always occupied with him—but one that most of them could not bring themselves to join him now in ascending

380. Ibid., 58.
381. Ibid., 66.
382. Ibid., 67.
383. Ibid., 68.
384. Ibid., 35.
385. Ibid., 69.

further."[386] Cook acknowledges some link between Paul and Judaism, but for the most part places his thought in the world of paganism. As discussed above (3.5.1), Jewish scholarship has been steadily drifting away from this position as well.

[4.6.8] Gerald Sigal

The Karaite author, Isaac Troki, wrote a famous book in the sixteenth century called *Faith Strengthened*. It is a classic polemical work designed to refute the claims of Christianity. Many of his arguments and his general approach would surface anew in the late twentieth century as "anti-missionaries" were needed to respond to the phenomenon of Messianic Jews. In the initial stages of this literature[387] the resurrection was not part of the discussion. But, in the last decade or so this issue has become a topic of concern.[388] The first complete book on the resurrection in this genre is by Gerald Sigal, who wrote *The Resurrection Fantasy, Reinventing Jesus* in 2012. Sigal's understanding of the New Testament is hyper-critical. Some of his views parallel the typical presuppositions found within scholarly circles, while others are taken to an extreme. His view of the Gospels is as follows:

> Each Gospel author interprets the pre-Gospel stories he received from his own later perspective. In their final redaction, the Gospels are not objective records but merely record what some early Christians claimed as *truth*, not necessarily what was reality. This is not objective historicity. Even when the Gospel narrative is assumed to be based on an historical fact, it has often been so thoroughly changed and adapted in the course of preaching and writing that the end product is no longer historical, but rather a work of fiction.[389]

He illustrates this position in an accompanying footnote. "For example," he writes, "the four evangelists record three separate statements as being Jesus' last words from the cross." He then cites Matthew 27:46, Mark 15:34, Luke 23:46 and John 19:30 and asks: "Did Jesus make all three statements from the cross, only one, or none of them? Only one statement could be Jesus' last words before dying. Undoubtedly, different strands of tradition

---

386. Ibid., 70.

387. See Wyschogrod and Berger, *Jews and Jewish Christianity*; Sigal, *The Jew and the Christian Missionary*; Kaplan, *The Real Messiah?*

388. Singer, *Let's Get Biblical*, 327–40. And see immediately below, 4.6.9.

389. Sigal, *The Resurrection Fantasy, Reinventing Jesus*, 42.

are reflected here, each one with its own decided theological bent."[390] Most conservative scholars would agree that there were different traditions handed down and even that each author had their own unique agenda. But none of the documents specifically claim to be recording his "last words" so any such discrepancy is imaginary rather than actual.

Sigal questions virtually every event recorded in the Gospels, even some which are usually accepted by the most critical scholars. Regarding the crucifixion he wrote: "The Gospels themselves leave the reader in doubt as to whether Jesus was actually crucified by the way they present the supposed events surrounding this episode."[391] He then compares Mark 15:20–22 (which says that Simon of Cyrene carried the cross) with John 19:17 (which says that Jesus carried the cross). Other claims surrounding the crucifixion are questioned as well. These include the darkness that covered the land in the synoptics (Matthew 27:45; Mark 15:33; Luke 23:44) and the saints who were raised from the dead which is recorded only in Matthew (27:51–53). Sigal is not alone in challenging some of these events. But, to question the historicity of the crucifixion itself is something that most critical scholars are not willing to do. Sigal elsewhere assumes the crucifixion as part of his counter argument. This is a common occurrence in his book—questioning the historicity of an event in one chapter, yet affirming it in another chapter (and, as will be seen below, this ambiguity sometimes appears within the same sentence).

There is a whole chapter about the burial of Jesus. The reason why Joseph buried the body is not because he was a disciple of Jesus, but simply out of religious duty. Jewish law required a burial prior to sundown on the Sabbath, and Joseph may have been the "agent of the Sanhedrin" assigned the task of burying the body.[392] He writes: "Joseph complied with the Torah's requirement even though he had no personal reason to honor the crucified individual."[393] According to tradition (he cites *Semahot* 13:5 and *Semahot* 10:8[394]), such burials would have been temporary until a permanent tomb was found after the Sabbath. He both affirms and questions this in the same sentence: "That someone assigned by the Sanhedrin did the burial (if it occurred) is very probable, considering Christian animosity toward the Jewish

390. Ibid., 95.
391. Ibid., 228.
392. Ibid., 185.
393. Ibid., 186.
394. Ibid., 197.

authorities; a fictional Christian creation *ex nihilo* of a member of the San-hedrin who does what is right is highly unlikely."[395]

Determining what happened to the body is also difficult, since "legend, distortion and censorship burden the sparse New Testament information."[396] Sigal's theory is that Jesus was placed in the temporary tomb, only to be moved shortly afterwards. This provides a preliminary explanation for why the tomb was empty. But, what actually happened? Joseph and Nicodemus provide the key to Sigal's argument, although this argument is equally am-biguous: "In all likelihood, immediately after the Sabbath these two men (presuming their existence), accompanied by servants hastily removed the body from the temporary burial place that had been quickly chosen because of the approaching Sabbath (John 19:41–42)."[397]

In another place he writes: "Except for those who moved the body, Je-sus' disciples and the early Christian community simply did not really know what happened to the remains of their crucified leader."[398] These quotes seem to indicate that he believes there was an empty tomb. But, earlier in the book he says that it is "impossible to know"[399] whether or not the tomb was empty, or if the story of the empty tomb was a creation made by those who thought Jesus appeared to them. As an example of the latter, he suggests that Mary Magdalene thought the tomb was empty and although the oth-ers did not originally believe her, they "realized that such a tale could give consolation"[400] to the faithful. But, apart from this brief suggestion, Sigal's working hypothesis throughout the book presumes an empty tomb as the catalyst for the new movement. For example: "With the corpse missing, the followers of Jesus were mentally primed for what occurred next. Following upon the news that Jesus' tomb was empty the disoriented depressed dis-ciples, overwhelmed by grief and disappointment, were ripe for psychologi-cally induced suggestion."[401]

He acknowledges that it is not possible to "pinpoint the exact mecha-nism" that caused the claims of appearances to the disciples.[402] He offers two possibilities although without details. These include planned deception

395. Ibid., 193.
396. Ibid., 239.
397. Ibid.
398. Ibid., 204.
399. Ibid., 39.
400. Ibid., 44.
401. Ibid., 45.
402. Ibid., 84.

and hallucination.[403] His discussion on Paul is equally brief and highly speculative. Sigal says Paul was "a troubled individual and in his weakened mental and physical state he came under the influence of Ananias and other followers of Jesus."[404] He also writes: "One may speculate that Paul's compulsive preoccupation with the problems engendered by Jesus ironically caused him to have a visionary experience in which he imagined hearing Jesus speak to him during his seizure."[405] Sigal challenges everything and concedes nothing, although many of his responses presume the very events that he attempts to refute. His conclusion is nevertheless dogmatic: "Based on a thorough investigation of the improbable and inconsistent evidence provided by the New Testament the refutation is emphatically *no*, it never happened."[406]

[4.6.9] Michael J. Alter

The final case study in this chapter is that of Michael J. Alter, an educator and author who wrote *The Resurrection, A Critical Inquiry* in 2015. It is in many ways an impressive book. Spanning over 850 pages, it includes numerous charts and an extensive bibliography. Commendably, he interacts with scholarship and popular works from diverse perspectives. These include conservative and liberal scholars as well as those who are more dogmatically against the idea of the resurrection. However, the bibliography includes no works from Pinchas Lapide (who should perhaps get an honorable mention as the first Jewish scholar to write a whole book on the resurrection) or Alan Segal.

Alter was originally challenged by Anthony Buzzard to investigate the resurrection. Buzzard believes that Jesus rose from the dead although he does not believe in the trinity. Alter's main help in producing this book was Rabbi Moshe Shulman, who has been active in "countering missionaries and teaching Torah and Chassidus for over twenty years." Shulman also leads an organization called Messiah Truth, whose goal is to "combat the deceptive missionary techniques of evangelical Christian denominations and the Messianic Movement."[407] Some of Alter's personal beliefs are stated at the beginning: God exists, the Hebrew Bible is God's revealed word, and

403. Ibid., 85.
404. Ibid., 92.
405. Ibid., 89.
406. Ibid., 279; emphasis in the original.
407. Ibid., xlix.

supernatural events can occur.[408] His purpose in this volume is to respond to the claims of "evangelical and Christian apologetic writings" regarding the resurrection of Jesus. His working hypothesis is that "sufficient issues are refuted adequately for Christians and any others to rethink the truth of Jesus' claimed resurrection, post-resurrection appearances, and ascension."[409] The book's primary focus is on the narrative sections of the Gospels, although it briefly touches on Paul and other issues as well. It is divided into 113 issues, which are broken down into "120 contradictions" and "217 speculations."[410] The contradictions refer to the different ways the events are recorded in the New Testament. The speculations refer to various claims made either in the New Testament itself or by Christian authors. There are far too many issues to adequately summarize here. But a few overall comments about his approach may be helpful.

First, most of the textual issues that Alter raises are not new. Critical scholars have been addressing these things for over three centuries. Alter makes no reference to the fact that the same types of discrepancies he finds in this study have been widely cited in critical studies of the Tanakh as well,[411] not to mention the Talmud. These include questions of dating, authorship, anachronisms, historicity of main characters and events, use of scriptural citation, contradictions between sources, verisimilitude, etc. Michael Brown has documented this in an article called "Unequal Weights and Measures."[412] An acknowledgement that these challenges are not exclusive to the New Testament would have provided Alter's intended audience with a much more objective approach to the discussion.

Second, New Testament scholarship in the last few decades has been greatly enhanced by the study of genre. Alter acknowledges that there has been much discussion and speculation in this area and alludes to a number of relevant sources. Various genres have been suggested for the Gospels over the last century. One of the dominant trends in recent decades has been to recognize the Gospels as a form of Roman biographies, or *bios*. Some of the authors Alter cites[413] have convincingly argued in this direction. This has shed important light on the question of literary license in the New Testament.[414]

---

408. Ibid., 3.

409. Alter, *The Resurrection of Jesus, A Critical Inquiry*, xlvii.

410. Ibid., xliii.

411. See, Gigniliat, *A Brief History of Old Testament Criticism: From Benedict Spinoza to Brevard Childs*.

412. Brown, *Answering Jewish Objections to Jesus*, 5:269–77.

413. Burridge, *What Are the Gospels?*; Aune, *The New Testament in Its Literary Environment*.

414. More recently, see Licona, *Why Are There Differences in the Gospels? What We*

Alter's own interaction with this topic is brief. Because the Gospels have a theological and evangelistic purpose he says that "it is the position of this text that the Gospels are not a biography, and they are not written to record history in a modern sense."[415] It would be interesting to know which ancient sources Alter would accept as meeting modern standards of historicity. The historian's job is to evaluate both the content and the form of ancient texts. Poetry, for example, is not interpreted the same way as narrative and the specific type of narrative literature needs to be identified as well. Scholars will certainly have a variety of opinions on these issues. But, to categorically dismiss the veracity of the Gospels because they do not conform to modern standards of history is a systemic problem throughout Alter's book.

Third, as discussed above (3.1.2), discrepancies in the texts do not automatically negate historicity. This is as true for the resurrection narratives as it is for the crucifixion narratives. Alter's case, however, is based almost entirely on textual issues and he sees things in black and white. After discussing the women who went to the tomb and the post resurrection appearances, he writes: "These conflicting accounts, along with those discussed throughout this text, prove that the Christian scriptures are unreliable."[416]

Nevertheless, Alter does acknowledge the historicity of some of the events in the life of Jesus. In fact, the list he gives at the beginning of the book is relatively generous. These include the following: Jesus definitely existed and lived in the first century, he spoke Aramaic and Hebrew, he was a Galilean who preached and healed, he selected disciples who are referred to as the twelve, his activity was in Israel, he engaged in controversy about the Temple, he was crucified outside of Jerusalem during the rule of Pontius Pilate, after his death his followers continued as an "identifiable movement," and there were some Jews who resisted parts of the new movement and persecuted both the original followers and Paul.[417] The acknowledgement of these issues immediately raises a number of questions for the historian. *Why did the movement continue at all after the horror and disappointment of the crucifixion? What form did it take? Why were the disciples "persecuted?" Who was Paul and how and why did he come to believe the message as well?* These questions are directly relevant to the resurrection regardless of one's view of discrepancies in the texts. Unfortunately, after initially affirming these truths, he never interacts with them or their consequences in the remainder of the book.

Can Learn from Ancient Biography.

415. Alter, *The Resurrection of Jesus, A Critical Inquiry*, 4.

416. Ibid., 457.

417. Ibid., 3.

At the end, Alter says that he is working on a second volume. This one will directly respond to Christian apologists regarding the belief that Jesus physically rose from the dead. This will include the works of William Lane Craig, Norman Geisler, Gary Habermas, Michael Licona, Gerald O'Collins, and N. T. Wright. It will hopefully also address the historical issues that he himself raised, and this will likely be much more relevant to the discussion of this present study.

CHAPTER FIVE
CONCLUSIONS

[5.1] WHAT DOES JEWISH SCHOLARSHIP TELL US ABOUT THE RESURRECTION OF JESUS?

The resurrection of Jesus has been an integral part of the quest(s) for the historical Jesus, and several scholars have documented this research.[1] Gary Habermas has studied 2,000 books and articles published between the years 1975 and 2000 that have commented on the resurrection. These works were written in English, German, and French. He observes that about three quarters of these authors would fall into the category of "conservative," which he defines broadly as those who believe "that Jesus was actually raised from the dead in some manner."[2] This includes beliefs about both bodily and spiritual types of resurrection, and it implies that something actually happened to Jesus, as opposed to there being only subjective experiences of the disciples. The disciples' belief, along with the empty tomb and Paul's own testimony are the main points of discussion. The differences between Habermas's study and this present one are clear. The most obvious is volume. This refers to both the number of scholars discussed in this present work, and the fact that most of them had extremely little to say about the resurrection.

Another difference concerns the worldview of the participants. Many of those discussed by Habermas were committed Christians who already believed in the resurrection by faith. Others may have been less committed to all of the details but were nevertheless sympathetic. This affects the

---

1. Ryder, "The Recent Literature upon the Resurrection of Christ"; Salvoni, "Modern Studies on the Resurrection of Jesus."

2. Habermas, "Resurrection Research from 1975 to the Present: What Are Critical Scholars Saying?," 135–36.

scholarship. The fact that most of them affirm, for example, that there was an empty tomb might mean nothing more than many of them already had a faith commitment. This is an issue for New Testament scholarship on the whole. Jeremy Cohen alluded to this when discussing Raymond Brown's work on the crucifixion. He noticed that Brown begins with the premise that the Gospels are historically accurate. "His commentary therefore affords an illuminating example of how thoroughly prior assumptions concerning the historical accuracy of the Crucifixion story—precisely because it is Holy Scripture—have dominated both popular and scholarly opinion."[3] The same has been said about the resurrection. It is sometimes stated that there is a consensus (or near consensus) of scholars who acknowledge certain points. Neusner referred to this as "constructive theology masquerading as history."[4] Alan Segal said that "this only underlines the obvious fact that there exists a group of scholars who are hostile to any other conclusion than that of literal resurrection. Under the circumstances, it is difficult to demonstrate that scholarly disinterestedness has been maintained."[5]

The scholars surveyed in this book are, by definition, in a different category. They represent a variety of beliefs regarding the possibility of the miraculous and/or the way ancient texts should be interpreted. But, none of them had a predisposition to affirm the historicity of the resurrection and many had a predisposition leaning in the opposite direction. This is the very thing that makes this research valuable. Their views of a few key events will be listed below. Virtually all of the scholars above commented on at least one of these events.

Before looking at the data, a few caveats are in order: 1. Many of these comments were made without a study of the larger context. They were peripheral comments; 2. The historical time frame of the scholars is between the mid nineteenth century and the contemporary period. The former did not have the Dead Sea Scrolls (among other discoveries) and there was a very different climate for Jewish-Christian relations; 3. It is not always easy to differentiate between what should be taken as serious scholarship and that which is fanciful. The authors in the section on historical fiction (4.1) will not be included here. Schonfield's theory may easily be recognized as unrealistic, yet Kaufmann was a serious Bible scholar who also suggested the swoon theory. Klausner is another example of someone who produced serious scholarship, but offered highly speculative suggestions when it came to the resurrection. These factors, along with the reality that this is a very

---

3. Cohen, "*Christ Killers*," 22.

4. Neusner, "Who Needs the Historical Jesus?," 121.

5. Segal, "The Resurrection: Faith or History?," 135.

small pool, make it difficult to produce a definitive picture of the Jewish view of the resurrection of Jesus. The following information may nevertheless be useful in determining which events are the building blocks for a proper discussion of the historicity of the resurrection. There may be a variety of suggestions about why the disciples believed they encountered Jesus, for example, but whether or not they themselves believed this is virtually beyond dispute. Other issues have various degrees of unanimity. The quotes in this section are taken from content that appears above, where citations may be found.

[5.1.1] The Crucifixion

Virtually all of the scholars affirmed the historicity of the crucifixion, or at least did not deny it. The exception that proves the rule was Isaac Wise, who wrote in 1874. His reasons for denying it were not historical but theological. It was both a response to the charge that Jews killed Jesus, and also his own enlightenment rationalism that found the idea of a vicarious atonement distasteful. Gerald Sigal questioned the historicity of the crucifixion and pointed out discrepancies between the four Gospels. He nevertheless assumed the crucifixion in his various responses to the canonical narrative and did not ultimately argue against it. Michael Cook also questioned the accounts of the crucifixion, but elsewhere affirmed that Jesus died in 30 CE.

That Jesus died on a Roman cross in Jerusalem is perhaps the one truth with virtual unanimity in this study (along with his existence and the fact that he was a Jew). The crucifixion is important for the discussion of the resurrection. On one hand, the only prerequisite for a resurrection is death. The manner of death is not necessarily important. But the crucifixion establishes both the fact of his death and the general timeframe. All would agree that crucifixion leads unmistakably to death. The swoon theory was employed by three of the authors in various ways (Schonfield, Cornfield, and Kaufmann), but even each of them acknowledged that Jesus died soon after being taken down from the cross. This establishes the time of death (give or take a couple of years). The dating in this study ranged from 29 to 33 CE, with a number of scholars simply rounding it off to 30 CE. The importance of the date rests in its relationship to other known events and documents. Most notably, three of the scholars (Levenson, Segal, Lapide) addressed Paul's hymn in 1 Cor 15:3–7 and deduced that it appeared early, within just a few years of the crucifixion. This establishes that the claim of the resurrection itself, along with the appearances to both his followers and at least one skeptic, were documented almost immediately by ancient standards.

[5.1.2] The Burial

Joseph of Arimathea is a curious character who appears in all four Gospels. A number of the scholars above acknowledged not only his existence, but also his role in providing a burial tomb for Jesus. Montefiore said he did so not necessarily because he was a disciple, since the fact that he was "waiting for the Kingdom of God" (as the Gospel of Mark has it) could have just as well meant he was a Pharisee. Rather, Joseph's involvement in the burial was likely related to his desire to carry out the law in Deuteronomy which says there is a curse on the land if a body is left hanging. Klausner specifically said that Joseph asked Pilate for the body, and that this was at the request of the disciples. At least three of the scholars (Ben-Chorin, Flusser, and Vermes) said that Nicodemus helped Joseph with the burial. For Flusser, the fact that "two Jerusalem councilors" did this is evidence against the assertion that the Jewish leaders delivered Jesus to the Romans.

Two authors specifically questioned the burial account. Segal's comment was concise: the narrative of the burial is "so manifestly polemical" as to question its credibility. However, he also immediately acknowledged that the burial tradition is a "stable part" of Gospel tradition, and Paul did say that Jesus was buried. Michael Cook's argument was more elaborate. He acknowledged that Joseph may have been a real person, but argued that the burial account is a creation based on Mark's theological agenda. He suggested that Mark's intent was to demonstrate that Joseph, who was not really a disciple of Jesus, acted more like a true disciple than the real disciples. This was to demonstrate to Mark's (Gentile) readers that the message of Jesus has Jewish roots, yet they should not feel they are in any way inferior to the original Jewish disciples. His argument revolves around the word "all" in Mark 14:64, suggesting that all of the council (including Joseph) condemned Jesus. However, the narrative continues in the following chapter. Mark 15:1 mentions the same groups that had just been described as "all" (namely, the chief priests, elders and scribes) and then adds the following words: "and the whole council," implying that the previous groups did not constitute a "unanimous" decision as Cook argued. This seems to counter Cook's main argument that Joseph must have condemned Jesus and was therefore not a disciple, undermining his main claim that the Joseph story was a complete fabrication.

Segal's charge that the story is polemical went without explanation, whereas Cook's explanation demonstrates both how elaborate a theory is needed as well as how difficult it is to provide a credible alternative. Finally, Jodi Magness explained that archaeology is helpful to the discussion. She does not comment on the historicity of Joseph, but nevertheless affirms the narratives' claims as being in sync with what is known about whether or not people who had been crucified would be eligible for such a burial, and what kind of person would have owned such a tomb. This understanding, she says, "removes at least some of the grounds for arguments that Joseph of Arimathea was *not* a follower of Jesus, or that he was a completely fictional character."

[5.1.3] The Disciples' Belief

All of the scholars acknowledged that the disciples continued to believe in Jesus after the crucifixion. Martin Goodman said that the reason for this was a combination of his ethical teachings and eschatological fervor about the Kingdom of God. Roth said that they continued their faith because Jesus' "personal magnetism must have been great." Neither of these two specifically mentioned the resurrection as a reason for the disciples' belief, but neither did they deny it. Virtually all of the other scholars acknowledged that the disciples' belief was in some way related to the resurrection. Paul Goodman suggested Mary Magdalene first believed in the resurrection because of her "nervous tension." At least two of the authors implied that the disciples looked to the scriptures for an explanation. Graetz suggested that after the "shameful death" of crucifixion the disciples found Isaiah 53 and "made the events fit the prophecy." Similarly, Baron alluded to their use of the suffering servant passage and, in conjunction with Fourth Maccabees, deduced that Jesus' death could atone for sins. These explain how they theologically justified their new belief, not why they believed in the resurrection in the first place.

The most common response was a psychological explanation of one type or another. Sachar said that the empty tomb caused their visions, which were as real to them as Isaiah's vision in the Temple. Montefiore wrote slightly more than most of the others on this topic and he considered more than one possibility. Either they really saw something, he argued, or it was a product of the "mental state" of the seer. A subjective experience is preferred, he concluded, since it is our "scientific duty" to go without the supernatural when we can. Nevertheless, Montefiore still believed in God. Klausner was more dogmatic, saying that the disciples "were enthusiastic to the point of madness and credulous to the point of blindness." For Fredricksen, the fact that the disciples believed in the resurrection is "historical bedrock." Her explanation did not use the language of psychology, but said their belief was based on "their commitment" to his eschatological message. This is nevertheless a psychological explanation, as she is saying they ultimately believed something that did not actually happen. Dan Cohn-Sherbok was less clear on whether or not the disciples actually had some type of experience of Jesus after the crucifixion. But if it did happen, it was "likely" that they had nothing more than a "subjective psychological experience."

Lapide pondered the idea that they had visions or hallucinations. He also looked at the big picture. The disciples, he wrote, denied and failed their master but became something quite different after the cross. He concluded that "no vision or hallucination is sufficient to explain such a revolutionary transformation." Vermes' view is somewhere in between Lapide and the scholars just mentioned. Like Montefiore, he weighed the options. At first he said that the visions were basically the same as any other mystical visions recorded throughout the centuries. On the other hand he noticed that the results of this belief were not ordinary. The disciples underwent a "powerful mystical experience" and became "ecstatic spiritual warriors." It was their conviction of the "actual presence of Jesus" that explains the resurgence of the Jesus movement after the crucifixion.

Cook acknowledged that the disciples believed in the resurrection soon after his death. This is perhaps the only event that he does not challenge or attempt to explain away by use of his "Gospel Dynamics" theory. He briefly suggested that it was "cognitive dissonance" that addressed the disconfirmation of Jesus not accomplishing his messianic mission. This theory (cognitive dissonance) was perhaps the only psychological diagnosis that had any type of substance to it. The other appeals to psychological factors were convenient, but usually based on little more than wanting a naturalistic explanation. But, as shown above, cognitive dissonance theory does not adequately include all of the relevant data. A full discussion of this would need to include the antecedent and contemporary literature of the first century, a review of modern social and psychological literature, and a reconstruction of the disciples' original message. Dein comprehensively surveyed the modern literature on sociology, psychology, and the Chabad movement, but said nothing about the historical context of the disciples. The belief that arose after the crucifixion was complex, unexpected, and unprecedented. The only scholar in this study who attempted to weigh all of the relevant factors was Alan Segal. He argued, at first, that the disciples' belief was in some way a combination of psychological factors and scriptural antecedents. But, in the end, he conceded that there must have been something more. The disciples' new and "novel" belief cannot be explained by these factors alone. Something must have happened, and specifically he said that this something must have happened on the Sunday immediately following the crucifixion. There is certainly room for other interpretations, and perhaps in the future more definitive explanations will emerge. What is not debated, however, is that the disciples went from being despondent after the crucifixion to being reinvigorated based on their belief that they had encountered the risen Jesus.

[5.1.4] The Empty Tomb

Authors who addressed the empty tomb showed a lot of creativity. Grayzel said that the disciples bribed the guards to retrieve the body. They then hid the body and when they returned to the place where they hid it they found that it was gone. Klausner said that Joseph buried the body but then felt guilty about using his family's tomb. He then removed the body and reburied it in a different location. Montefiore briefly mentioned theories for the empty tomb and did not find them convincing. These include the following: that Jewish authorities stole the body, that Joseph buried the body temporarily and then reburied it, and that Mary Magdalene went to the tomb and had a vision that grew into the empty tomb story. All of these proposals are deemed "very doubtful." He therefore concluded that Jesus remained in the tomb "undisturbed." However, he also believed that both Mary Magdalene and Joseph knew the whereabouts of this tomb, making the theory of an unchecked tomb untenable (unless a further scenario is created as to why neither of them or their acquaintances went to check it). Ben-Chorin simply said that the women came to the tomb and found it empty. Lapide said that a fictitious report would not have included women, and the fact that the women were going to anoint the body is evidence that a resurrection was not expected. Vermes agreed that it was not likely that a story would be invented with women as the chief witnesses. He also said that the discrepancies in the Gospel accounts of the tomb make it more likely that it was a real event and not an invention.

Segal, Cook, and Fredricksen all said that Paul did not believe in a physical resurrection, based mainly on two verses from 1 Corinthians 15 (verses 44 and 50). Segal spent a lot of time on this, Cook and Fredricksen mentioned it in passing. Several of the other scholars (Lander, Levenson, Vermes, and Setzer) offered evidence against this position. These verses, along with the fact that Paul does not specifically mention an empty tomb are the basis for denying the empty tomb story. It still needs to be explained, however, how and why the story appeared in Mark. Segal gives three possible explanations. First, it might have been "good missionary strategy" to "objectify" confirmation of the event. Second, the empty tomb may be a "corrective" to the problem that there were no eyewitnesses. Third, an empty tomb might have been an attempt to clarify Paul's meaning about the type of body that is resurrected. In the end, Segal acknowledged that these explanations were only makeshift and did not offer legitimate answers. He did not quite concede that there was an empty tomb, but seemed to admit that he had not been able to provide a satisfactory alternative.

Cook also offered several suggestions. If there was a sighting of the risen Jesus, someone may have assumed that the place where he was put was now empty. This is problematic, however, since in pagan thought (Cook believes the empty tomb story began at the time when Jews were no longer involved) there was no context for a belief in bodily resurrection. As for why women were used in the story, Cook said that Mark was forced by the narrative to create the story of the women. Yet, Cook's entire thesis revolves around the belief that Mark (and the other evangelists) fabricated virtually all of the characters and events in their stories. Finally, Claudia Setzer did not comment on the historicity of the empty tomb, but she argues from the texts of the Gospels that the women's presence at the tomb was both early (prior to Mark) and a source of embarrassment for the movement.

[5.1.5] Paul's Experience

The Apostle Paul is perhaps the most psychoanalyzed individual in history. This is partly because we have first person testimony of his own experiences and feelings, something that we do not have with the disciples. Most of the comments here are based on the older, more negative view of Paul. The association with paganism makes it easier to not only dismiss Paul from the Jewish world, but it also provides convenient ammunition which may be used in discussing his transformation. All of the theories rely heavily on speculation. According to Graetz, Paul was "excitable and vehement." He persecuted the disciples because they broke with the teaching of the Pharisees. Paul then learned that many heathens were attracted to Judaism. This might have caused him to wonder if the time had come for God's plan to be taken to the Gentiles, which in turn may have caused him to think that Jesus "made himself manifest." But how was this possible, if Jesus had died? The answer is that he must have been resurrected.

The *Jewish Encyclopedia* suggested that Paul may have previously thought about the concept of the Son of God, which may have resulted in "a mental paroxysm experienced in the form of visions." Sachar said that Paul was troubled by his own sin and had a "tremendous psychological experience" which caused him to believe in the resurrection. He offers two possible options. Maybe it was based on Paul's failure to win over the disciples, or maybe he simply had no peace in Judaism. Whatever it was, Sachar concludes, Paul's own convictions grew. Grayzel said that Paul was "incensed" with the new movement. But, then he got the idea that Judaism might be divided into two parts, one for Jews and one for everyone else. His specific belief in the resurrection of Jesus is not further explained. Enelow said that Paul's hostility toward the disciples brought him in contact with them. This caused him to "marvel at their devotion" and eventually come to their beliefs. Roth says only that Paul "suddenly became convinced."

Klausner imagined that two events triggered Paul's turnaround, one is canonical the other is speculative. He suggested that on the way to Damascus he was reminded first of the stoning of Stephen. Klausner also suggests the possibility that Paul witnessed the crucifixion. It may have been the combination of these two events, along with an "involved psychological process," which brought about Paul's experience. Maccoby perhaps wins the prize for being the most creative, although he certainly had competition. He said that Paul was not even born Jewish and that his conversion is "psychologically and socially understandable" when it is understood that his yearnings to be a proper Pharisee were never realized. Ben-Chorin does not explain what happened, other than saying Paul had an experience "rooted deeply in the subjectivity of this contradictory and controversial personality." Cook suggested that Paul was attracted to the Christians in Damascus who were already mixing the original (Jewish) message of Jesus with paganism and specifically the idea of dying and rising saviors. This combined with the tension between his Jewish upbringing in a pagan environment might have stirred up something "which he may have long suppressed."

The above comments are a mix of psychoanalysis, historical speculation, and negative assumptions about Paul. Scholars advocating the newer view of Paul, however, place him in the context of Judaism and not paganism. These scholars are perhaps less likely to comment on Paul's experience, preferring to focus on his theology. Alan Segal wrote a whole book about the consequences and meaning of Paul's "conversion," yet had virtually nothing to say about what actually happened to him. He says simply that whatever it was is probably lost to us, since converts often retell their stories in the language of their new beliefs. Hopefully more research will be done on this as well from those affirming the newer paradigm. For now, the "historical bedrock" is that Paul was against the followers of Jesus to the point of persecuting them, and that he came to believe in the resurrection of Jesus, and that according to his own testimony the reason he came to believe was that he had encountered the risen Jesus.

[5.1.6] Furthering the discussion

The evidence for the resurrection of Jesus goes beyond the historical details mentioned above. Unlike other ancient teachers or miracle workers whose influence is relegated to history books, the influence of Jesus is noticeably different. Martin Goodman said that it is a "remarkable fact" that a movement which began in Jerusalem would come to overtake Rome in just three centuries. To take Goodman's words a step further, it was not just a movement that began in Jerusalem. It is the story of a Galilean Jew who was not a military leader or a political leader, who never wrote anything (as far as we know), who died on a cross in—or just outside of—Jerusalem, and who is remembered most of all for the claim that he rose from the dead. Today the whole world marks history as having happened either before or since his coming. This does not prove that he rose from the dead, but neither should it be dismissed as irrelevant. However skeptics choose to respond to this, it is another piece of the puzzle. A comprehensive examination of the resurrection of Jesus will go beyond these issues as well and enter the realms of metaphysics, epistemology, and even (as will be discussed in a moment) cultural boundaries. But, it all begins with the historical question and where the historical evidence leads.

The Jewish study of the resurrection of Jesus is in some ways quite different than the wider field of scholarship, and yet in some ways quite similar. Many non-Jewish scholars already have a faith commitment to Jesus. This does not mean that their scholarship should summarily be discarded as biased. It should be evaluated on its own merit. Nevertheless, the reality is that presuppositions are influential. Jewish scholars begin with a different set of presuppositions. But, what is interesting to note is that the main historical events that make up this discussion are virtually the same for both groups: crucifixion, burial, disciples' belief, empty tomb, and Paul's dramatic turnaround. Again, the question is not whether these things can be proven scientifically. The question is: what hypothesis fits the evidence best? Not all of these points have the same level of acceptance, but those that may have less agreement (for example, the burial) still need to be explained. If it is not historical, an explanation needs to be given as to why it was created. In the discussions above, there were no viable alternatives presented to these points individually or collectively.

This study has addressed one small group of scholars, a microcosm of the total scholarship on the resurrection. No definitive comment can be made here about the state of resurrection research in the wider field. Then again, it could be argued that Jewish scholars would be aware of a plausible alternative if one existed. But, no theory has yet received a modicum of popularity even among skeptics. A survey of the Jewish scholarship on the resurrection yields a couple of simple truths: 1. There *is* historical evidence pointing to the resurrection of Jesus, and, 2. This evidence cannot be explained away easily. The study has only just begun. The works of Lapide, Vermes, and Segal have opened the door and the definitive Jewish work on the resurrection has yet to be written.

[5.2] WHAT DOES THE RESURRECTION OF JESUS TELL US ABOUT JEWISH SCHOLARSHIP?

The Jewish study of Jesus has always been concerned with two distinct boundary markers, although there is certainly overlap. Theological boundary markers comment on the historical Jesus, while cultural boundary markers determine which beliefs are acceptable within the Jewish community today. Both categories are somewhat fluid and have changed considerably over the years. For most of the last two thousand years Jesus and the New Testament were considered the epitome of that which is non-Jewish. The twentieth century saw big changes, including the reclamation of Jesus as a Jew (a work that is still in progress). What was dangerous for Jews to say about Jesus a century ago is now commonly acknowledged. The Jewishness of Jesus is no longer debated. This has produced a new wave of Jewish scholarship in about the last two decades which has taken the discussion to a whole new level. As seen above in chapter 3, a number of theological and historical positions are being re-evaluated. These include the Jewishness of the Apostle Paul, the growing recognition that the New Testament is not anti-Jewish, and new understandings of what constitutes the role of the Messiah. Even the incarnation, which has traditionally been the most defining theological boundary marker, has been acknowledged as Jewish by several mainstream Jewish scholars. These issues have not been reclaimed to the extent that Jesus has, but they do represent a trend.

The study of the historicity of the resurrection of Jesus falls within this contemporary wave. Ben-Chorin noticed that Jewish scholars stay away from this issue because it is not of interest to them personally, nor does it appear to be relevant to Judaism as a whole. That was about four decades ago. More recently, there has been a slight interest in addressing the question.

This may or may not be the result of more personal interest in this issue, but it is certainly part of the current trend of Jewish scholarship which is confronting all relevant New Testament issues. Yet, the resurrection of Jesus is not like the other theological claims. This was noticed by Vermes. "Unlike the crucifixion," he wrote, "it is an unparalleled phenomenon in history. Two types of extreme reaction are possible: faith or disbelief."[6] This quote is somewhat ironic given Vermes' non-committal stance on the subject. But, he is nevertheless correct that the resurrection potentially moves the discussion from the historical/theological to the personal.

A belief in the historicity of the resurrection does not necessarily lead to personal faith (as demonstrated by Lapide, Kogan, Goldberg, Zass, and perhaps Levenson). The implications of the event need to be addressed as well. The resurrection brings the possibility of faith to the forefront in a way that other theological issues do not. Historians can debate whether a certain belief existed during the Second Temple period. But, whether that belief is acceptable for Jews today is a very different question. There are unique consequences for Jews who embrace the traditional implications of the resurrection. This is explained by Fydra Shapiro, an Orthodox Jewish author who lives in Israel.

> It is the particular historical relationship of Judaism and Christianity, and their particular compositions that refuses Jesus-belief but permits atheism, Buddhism, and goddess worship as nonthreatening "wrong beliefs" that a Jew can embrace while still calling himself a Jew. But while these beliefs are unacceptable by any known religious or doctrinal Jewish standard, they do not place a Jew who embraces them outside the community in the way that Jesus-belief does.[7]

This view is not exclusive to Orthodox Jews. Dis-belief in Jesus is not only a given for most Jews, in some circles it has virtually become a defining tenet of Judaism. Steven L. Jacobs is a Reform Rabbi and professor of Judaism at the University of Alabama. He stated the following.

> That is to say, truthfully, there is only *one* Jewish theological affirmation that unites *all* streams of religious Judaism, namely, that Jesus is *not* the Messiah for the Jewish people, regardless of how he is perceived, understood, and affirmed by others. Thus, at the moment at which a Jewish person *chooses* to embrace/welcome/accept this Christ, that person—born of Jewish parents, inheritor of both the Jewish religious and historical traditions—is no

6. Vermes, *The Resurrection*, 2.
7. Shapiro, "Jesus for Jews, the Unique Problem of Messianic Judaism," 14.

longer a Jew but a Christian and must be understood as such,
even while acknowledging with sadness the failure of that which
I hold most sacred to meet that person's religious and spiritual
needs.[8]

The stance taken by Jacobs remains strong and perhaps even dominant
in the Jewish world today. Theological scholarship alone will not challenge
this position. This will perhaps be a future phase of the Jewish reclamation
of Jesus—not only recognizing that Jesus himself was a Jew, or rethinking
theological concepts, but pondering the possibility that modern Jews may
embrace Jesus as he is presented in the New Testament. For many, this notion is nothing short of scandalous. It is every bit as scandalous as was the
idea of a Jewish Jesus a century ago. However, there are a few hints that argue
for the possibility of this future phase. At the turn of this present century,
four Jewish authors wrote books about Messianic Jews with unprecedented
objectivity.[9] In 2013, a Pew Research Center poll of American Jews revealed
that 34 percent said that it *is* possible for a Jewish person to believe in Jesus
and remain a Jew.[10] The very inclusion of this question on the survey is
perhaps as relevant as the percentage. It is also interesting to note that both
Orthodox Jews[11] and Conservative Jews[12] are sometimes more 'liberal' than
Reform Jews in acknowledging the Jewish identity of Jews who profess faith
in Jesus, even while strongly disagreeing with that belief. Along with the
theological barriers, the cultural boundaries—and specifically the fear of
assimilation—are a constant concern. This too has been challenged. Shapiro made the following observation about Jewish believers in Jesus: "The
movement has also proved itself over time, there are now many second and
even third-generation Messianic Jews coming of age in those communities.
This is also the case in Israel, where Messianic Jewish congregations have

8. Jacobs, "Two Takes on Christianity: Furthering the Dialogue," 513; emphasis in
the original.

9. Ariel, *Evangelizing the Chosen People*; Cohn-Sherbok, *Messianic Judaism*; Feher,
Passing Oover Easter: Constructing the Boundaries of Messianic Judaism; Harris-Shapiro,
Messianic Judaism: A Rabbi's Journey through Religious Change in America;

10. Goodstein, "Poll Shows Major Shift in Identity of U.S. Jews."

11. Wyschogrod wrote: "According to authentic Jewish teaching as I understand
it, a Jew remains a Jew no matter what religion he adopts and this basic truth cannot be changed for political or prudential reasons." Wyschogrod, "A Letter to Cardinal
Lustiger," 207.

12. Novak wrote: "The important thing to remember when dealing with the issue of
the Jewish Christians is that according to normative Judaism, they are still Jews. Jewish
status is defined by the divine election of Israel and his descendant." (Novak, "When
Jews Are Christians," 44–45).

been growing significantly in size and–even in a Jewish country–there is no major city lacking a Messianic Jewish congregation."[13]

In the meantime, Jewish scholars are continuing to study the New Testament and the life of Jesus. The fifty contributors to the *Jewish Annotated New Testament* are perhaps the tip of the iceberg, and they have paved the way for an even bolder group of scholars. The historicity of the resurrection of Jesus will likely become a more vibrant issue of discussion for several reasons. First, the quantity of Jewish scholarship will almost certainly continue to grow, as will the specialized training in New Testament and related fields. This training will be comprehensive. The resurrection of Jesus is the central claim of the New Testament. There exists a healthy scholarly dialogue and the recent Jewish literature has only enhanced the study. From an academic point of view, there is no reason why any New Testament scholar (Jew or Gentile) should be unfamiliar with the particulars of this discussion. This will lead to more exhaustive and scholarly conclusions from those who specifically study the resurrection, and it may also curb the simplistic responses ("there must have been a hallucination") from those who make peripheral comments.

Second, there is a changing cultural climate. Secularism is steadily becoming more normative in Europe and the U. S. The Jewish study of Jesus has traditionally been done in an environment where Christianity, in one form or another, represented the dominant culture. This may have affected some of the conclusions or at least how these findings were publicized. Similarly, the new generation of scholars in Israel has grown up not knowing the "Christian" anti-Semitism that their parents and grandparents knew all too well. The upcoming scholarship will therefore need not be as polemical, which may yield new approaches to the resurrection as well. Third, the current New Testament scholarship by both Christians and Jews is interested in the Jewish context. The claim of the resurrection is about a Jewish man who lived in a Jewish place and influenced Jewish disciples. It is as much a discussion of Jewish history as it is of Christian origins. In the end, the resurrection of Jesus will perhaps be the pivotal issue in the ongoing Jewish study of Jesus in the twenty-first century. All things considered, the next generation or two of Jewish New Testament scholarship should be quite fascinating.

---

13. Shapiro, "Jesus for Jews, the Unique Problem of Messianic Judaism," 11.

BIBLIOGRAPHY

Alexander, Philip S. "Orality in Pharisaic-Rabbinic Judaism at the Turn of the Eras." In *Jesus and the Oral Gospel Tradition*, edited by Henry Wansborough, 159–84. Sheffield: Bloomsbury, 1991.

———. "Yeshu/Yeshua ben Yosef of Nazareth: Discerning the Jewish Face of Jesus." In *The Birth of Jesus: Biblical and Theological Reflections*, edited by George J. Brook, 9–21. Edinburgh: T. & T. Clark, 2001

Almog, Shmuel. *Anti-Semitism through the Ages.* Translated by Nathan H. Reiser. Oxford: Pergamon, 1988.

Alter, Michael J. *The Resurrection: A Critical Inquiry.* Bloomington, IL: Xlibris, 2015.

Ariel, Yaakov. "Christianity through Reform Eyes: Kaufman Kohler's Scholarship on Christianity." *JAJH* 89, no. 2 (2001) 181–91.

———. "A Different Kind of Dialogue? Messianic Judaism and Jewish-Christian Relations." *Cross Currents* 62, no. 30 (2012) 318–27.

———. *Evangelizing the Chosen People.* Chapel Hill: University of the North Carolina, 2000.

Asch, Sholem. *The Nazarene.* New York: Putnam's, 1939.

Aune, David E. *The New Testament in Its Literary Environment.* Philadelphia: Westminster, 1988.

Aus, Roger D. *The Death, Burial, and Resurrection of Jesus and the Death, Burial, and Translation of Moses in Judaic Tradition.* Lanham, MD: University Press of America, 2008.

Avery-Peck, Alan J. "The Galilean Charismatic and Rabbinic Piety: The Holy Man in Talmudic Literature." In *The Historical Jesus in Context*, edited by Amy Jill Levine et al., 149–65. Princeton: Princeton University, 2006.

Avery-Peck, Alan J., and Jacob Neusner, eds. *Judaism in Late Antiquity.* Vol. 3. Boston: Brill Academic, 2001.

Bacon, Benjamin W. "Jewish Interpretations of the New Testament." *AJT* 19, no. 2 (1915) 163–78.

Baeck, Leo. *Judaism and Christianity.* Philadelphia: Jewish Publication Society of America, 1958.

Baggett, David J., *Did the Resurrection Happen? A Conversation with Gary Habermas and Antony Flew.* Downers Grove, IL: IVP Academic, 2009.

Balthasar, Hans Urs von. *Martin Buber and Christianity.* London: Harvill, 1960.

Barkay, Gabriel. "The Garden Tomb: Was Jesus Buried Here?" *BAR* 12, no. 2 (1986) 40–57.

Baron, Salo W. *A Social and Religious History of the Jews*. Vol. 2. Philadelphia: Jewish Publication Society of America, 1952.

Barron, David. *Jews and Jesus: A Study of Dr. Klausner's "Jesus of Nazareth—His Time, His Life, and His Teaching."* Northwood, UK: Hebrew Christian Testimony to Israel, 1929.

Barth, Marcus. "What Can a Jew Believe about Jesus and Still Remain a Jew." *JES* 2, no. 3 (1965) 382–405.

Basser, Herbert W. *The Mind behind the Gospels: A Commentary to Matthew 1–14.* Boston: Academic Studies, 2009.

Batnitzky, Leora. "From Resurrection to Immortality: Theological and Political Implications in Modern Jewish Tthought." *HTR* 102, no. 3 (2009) 279–96.

———. "Jesus in Modern Jewish Thought." In *Jesus among the Jews: Representation and Thought*, edited by Neta Stahl, 159–70. London: Routledge, 2012.

Bauckhaum, Richard. *Jesus and the Eyewitnesses: The Gospels as Eyewitness Testimony.* Grand Rapids: Eerdmans, 2008.

———. *Jesus and the God of Israel: God Crucified and other Studies on the New Testament's Christology of Divine Identity.* Grand Rapids: Eerdmans, 2008.

———. *The Jewish World around the New Testament.* Grand Rapids: Baker Academic, 2010.

———. Review of *The Resurrection of Jesus: A Jewish Perspective*, by Pinchas Lapide. *Themelios* 11, no. 1 (1985) 28.

Baumgarten, A. I. "Jews, Pagans and Christians on the Empty Grave of Jesus." In *Proceedings of the 10th World Congress of Jewish Studies, Division B, v II*, edited by David Assaf, 37–44. Jerusalem: Magnus, 1990.

———. "Miracles and Halaka in Rabbinic Judaism." *JQR* 73, no. 3 (1983) 238–53.

Becker, Adam H., and Annette Yoshiko Reed, eds. *The Ways That Never Parted: Jews and Christians in Late Antiquity and the Early Middle Ages.* Tübingen: Mohr/ Siebeck, 2003.

Bellinger, William H., and William R. Farmer, eds. *Jesus and the Suffering Servant: Isaiah 53 and Christian Origins.* Harrisburg, PA: Trinity, 1998.

Ben-Chorin, Shalom. *Brother Jesus.* Atlanta: University of Georgia, 2001. Originally published as *Bruder Jesus: der Nazarener in jüdischer Sicht* in 1967.

———. "The Image of Jesus in Modern Judaism." *JES* 11 (1974) 401–30.

Berger, David. "Covenants, Messiahs and Religious Boundaries." *Tradition* 39, no. 2 (2005) 66–78.

———. *The Jewish-Christian Debate in the High Middle Ages: A Critical Edition of the Nizzahon Vetus.* Lanham, MD: Aronson, 1996.

———. "Jewish-Christian Relations: A Jewish Perspective." *JES* 20, no. 1 (1983) 5–32.

———. "Jews, Christians and 'The Passion.'" *Commentary* 112, no. 5 (2004) 23–31.

———. "On the Uses of History in Medieval Jewish Polemic against Christianity: The Quest for the Historical Jesus." In *Jewish history and Jewish Memory*, edited by Elisheva Carlbach et al., 25–39. Hanover, NH: Brandeis University, 1998.

———. *The Rebbe, the Messiah, and the Scandal of Orthodox Indifference.* London: Littman Library of Jewish Civilization, 2001.

———. "Religion, Nationalism, and Historiography: Yehezkel Kaufman's Account of Jesus and Early Christianity." In *Scholars and Scholarship: The Interaction between Judaism and other Cultures,* edited by Leo Landman, 149–68. New York: Scharf Publication Trust of the Yeshiva University Press, 1990.

Berger, David, and Michael Wyschogrod. *Jews and Jewish Christianity.* New York: KTAV, 1978.

Berlin, Adele, and Marc Zvi Brettler, eds. *The Jewish Study Bible.* Oxford: Oxford University Press, 2004.

Berlin, George L. *Defending the Faith: Nineteenth Century American Jewish Writers on Christianity and Jesus.* Albany: SUNY, 1989.

Berry, Donald L. "Buber's View of Jesus as Brother." *JES* 14, no. 2 (1977) 203–18.

Biale, David. "Counter-History and Jewish Polemics against Christianity: The "Sefer Toldot Yeshu" and the Sefer Zerubavel." *JSS* 6, no. 1 (1999) 130–45.

Bickerman, Elias J. "The Empty Tomb." In *Studies in Jewish and Christian History*, 712–25. Leiden: Brill, 2007.

Bird, Michael F., and J. G. Crossley. *How Did Christianity Begin? A Believer and Non-Believer Examine the Evidence.* London: SPCK, 2009.

Bird, Michael F., and Preston M. Sprinkle. "Jewish Interpretations of Paul in the Last Thirty Years." *CBR* 6, no. 3 (2008) 355–76.

Blidstein, Gerald J. "A Rabbinic Reaction to the Messianic Doctrine of the Scrolls." *JBL* 90, no. 3 (1971) 330–32.

Bock, Darrell L. "Faith and the Historical Jesus: Does a Confessional Position and Respect for the Jesus Tradition Preclude Serious Historical Engagement?" *JSHJ*, 9, no. 1 (2011) 3–25.

Bock, Darrell L., and Mitch Glaser. *The Gospel according to Isaiah 53: Encountering the Suffering Servant in Jewish and Christian Theology.* Grand Rapids: Kregel, 2012.

Bode, E. L. "Review of The Resurrection of Jesus: A Jewish Perspective." *BTB* 17, no. 3 (1987) 118.

Borowitz, Eugene. *Contemporary Christologies.* New York: Paulist, 1980.

———. "Jesus the Jew in Light of the Jewish-Christian dialogue." In *Proceedings of the Center for Jewish Christian Learning*, edited by A. E. Zannoni, 2:16–18. St. Paul: College of St Thomas, 1987.

———. *Liberal Judaism.* Cincinnati: UAHC, 1984.

———. *Renewing the Covenant: A Theology for the Postmodern Jew.* New York: JPS, 1991.

Boteach, Shmuley. *Kosher Jesus.* Jerusalem: Gefen, 2012.

Bowler, Maurice Gerald. *Claude Montefiore and Christianity.* Atlanta: Scholars, 1988.

Boyarin, Daniel. *Border Lines: The Partition of Judaeo Christianity.* Philadelphia: University of Pennsylvania, 2004.

———. *Dying for God: Martyrdom and the Making of Christianity and Judaism.* Stanford: Standford University, 1999.

———. *The Jewish Gospels.* New York: New, 2012.

Braaten, Carl E., and Robert W. Jenson, eds. *Jews and Christians.* Grand Rapids: Eerdmans, 2003.

Brand, Chad, ed. *Perspectives on Israel and the Church: 4 Views.* Nashville: B and H, 2015.

Bronner, Leila Leah. *Journey to Heaven: Exploring Jewish Views of the Afterlife.* Jerusalem: Urim, 2011.

———. "The Resurrection Motif in the Hebrew Bible: Allusion or Illusion?" *JBQ* 30, no. 3 (2012) 143–54.

Brown, Michael L. *Answering Jewish Objections to Jesus: Theological Objections.* Vol. 2. Grand Rapids: Baker, 2000.

—. *Answering Jewish Objections to Jesus: New Testament Objections.* Vol. 4. Grand Rapids: Baker, 2007.

—. *Answering Jewish Objections to Jesus: New Testament Objections.* Vol. 5. Grand Rapids: Baker, 2009.

—. "*Kipper* and Atonement in the Book of Isaiah." In *Ki Baruch Hu: Ancient Near Eastern, Biblical and Judaic Studies in Honor of Baruch A. Levine,* edited by Robert Chazan, William W. Hallo, and Lawrence Schiffman, 189–202. Winona Lake, IN: Eisenbrauns, 1999.

—. *Our Hands are Stained with Blood: The Tragic Story of "the Church" and the Jewish People.* Shippensburg, PA: Destiny Image, 1992.

Brumberg-Kraus, Jonathan D. "A Jewish Ideological Perspective on the Study of Christian Scripture." *JSS* 4, no. 1 (1997) 121–52.

—. "Jesus as Other People's Scripture." In *The Historical Jesus through Catholic and Jewish Eyes,* edited by Bryan F. LeBeau et al., 155–66. Bloomsbury: T. & T. Clark, 2000.

Bruteau, Beatrice. *Jesus through Jewish Eyes: Rabbis and Scholars Engage an Ancient Brother in a New Conversation.* Maryknoll, NY: Orbis, 2001.

Bryan, Christopher. *The Resurrection of the Messiah.* Oxford: Oxford University Press, 2011.

Buber, Martin. *Two Types of Faith.* New York: Macmillan, 1951.

Bultmann, Rudolph. *Jesus and the Word.* Translated by Louise P. Smith and Erminie H. Lantero. New York: Scribner and Sons, 1934.

Burridge, Richard A. *What are the Gospels?* 2nd ed. Grand Rapids: Eerdmans, 2004.

Bynum, C. W. *The Resurrection of the Body in Western Christianity 200–1336.* New York: Columbia University, 1995.

Carlback, Elisheva, and Jacob J. Schacter, eds. *New Perspectives on Jewish-Christian Relations.* Leiden: Brill, 2012.

Carrier, Richard, *On the Historicity of Jesus: Why We Might Have Reason to Doubt.* Sheffield, UK: Phoenix, 2014.

Carroll, James. *Constantine's Sword: The Church and the Jews—A History.* Boston: Houghton Mifflin, 2001.

Carson, D. A. *The Gospel According to John.* Grand Rapids: Eerdmans, 1990.

Carson, D. A., Peter T. Obrien, and Mark A. Seifrid, eds. *Justification and Variegated Nomism: The Paradoxes of Paul.* Grand Rapids: Baker Academic, 2004.

Carter, W. "Response." In *Anti-Judaism and the Gospels,* edited by William R. Farmer, 47–62. Harrisburg, PA: Trinity, 1999

Catchpole, David R. "The Role of the Historical Jesus in Jewish-Christian Dialogue." In *The Future of Jewish-Christian Dialogue,* edited by Dan Cohn-Sherbok, 183–216. Lewiston, NY: Mellen, 1999.

—. *The Trial of Jesus: A Study in the Gospels and Jewish Historiography from 1770 to the Present Day.* Leiden: Brill, 1971.

Chapman, David W. *Ancient Jewish and Christian Perceptions of Crucifixion.* Tübingen: Mohr/Siebeck, 2008.

Charlesworth, James H. *Jesus and Archaeology.* Grand Rapids: Eerdman's, 2006.

—. *Jesus' Jewishness: Exploring the place of Jesus within Early Judaism.* Philadelphia, American Interfaith Institute, 1991.

—. *Jews and Christians: Exploring the Past, Present, and Future.* New York: Crossroads, 1990.

———. *Resurrection: The Origin and Future of a Biblical Doctrine*. London: T. & T. Clark, 2008.

Cohen, Haim H. *The Trial and Death of Jesus*. New York: Harper & Row, 1971.

Cohen, Jeremy. *Christkillers: The Jews and the Passion from the Bible to the Big Screen*. New York: Oxford University Press, 2007.

———. "The Mystery of Israel's Salvation: Romans 11:25–26 in Patristic and Medieval Exegesis." *HTR* 98, no. 3 (2005), 247–81.

Cohen, Shaye J. D. *From the Maccabees to the Mishnah*. Louisville: Westminster Knox, 2006.

Cohn-Sherbok, Dan. *The Crucified Jew: Twenty Centuries of Christian anti-Semitism*. Grand Rapids: Eerdmans, 1997.

———. "The Resurrection of Jesus: A Jewish View." In *Resurrection Reconsidered*, edited by Gavin D'Costa, 184–200. Oxford: Oneworld, 1996.

Cohn-Sherbok, Dan, ed. *Divine Intervention and Miracles in Jewish Theology*. New York: Mellen, 1983.

Cook, Michael J. "Anti-Judaism in the New Testament." *USQR* 38, no. 2 (1983) 125–37.

———. "Evolving Jewish Views of Jesus." In *Jesus through Jewish Eyes: Rabbis and Scholars Engage an Ancient Brother in a New Conversation*, edited by Beatruce Bruteau, 3–24. Maryknoll, NY: Orbis, 2011.

———. "Interpreting "pro-Jewish" passages in Matthew." *HCUA* 54 (1983) 135–46.

———. "Jewish Reflections on Jesus: Some Abiding Trends." In *The Historical Jesus through Catholic and Jewish Eyes,* edited by Bryan F. LeBeau, 95–112. Harrisburg, PA: Trinity, 2000.

———. *Modern Jews Engage the New Testament: Enhancing Jewish Well-Being in a Christian Environment*. Woodstock, VT: Jewish Lights, 2008.

———. "Paul's Argument in Romans 9–11." *RandE* 103, no. 1 (2006) 91–111.

———. "Where Jewish Scholars on Jesus Go Awry: Last Supper, Sanhedrin, Blasphemy, Barabbas." *Shofar* 28, no. 3 (2012) 70–77.

Copan, Paul, and Craig A. Evans. *Who Was Jesus? A Jewish-Christian Dialogue*. Louisville: Westminster John Knox, 2001.

Copan, Paul, and Ronald K. Tacelli, eds. *Jesus' Resurrection: Fact or Figment? A Debate between William Lane Craig and Gerd Lüdemann*. Downers Grove, IL: IVP Academic, 2000.

Cornfield, Gaalyah. *The Historical Jesus: A Scholarly View of the Man and His World*, New York: Macmillan, 1982.

Court, J. M. "Review of *The Resurrection of Jesus: A Jewish perspective*." In *ET* 95, no. 10 (1984) 313–14.

Cox, Harvey G. "Rabbi Yeshua ben Joseph: Reflections on Jesus' Jewishness and the Interfaith Dialogue." In *Jesus' Jewishness: Exploring the Place of Jesus in Early Judaism*, edited by James Charlesworth, 27–62. New York: Crossroad, 1991.

Craig, William Lane. *Assessing the New Testament Evidence fior the Historicity of the Resurrection of Jesus*. Lewiston, NY: Mellen, 1989.

———. "The Guard at the Tomb." *NTS* 30, no. 2 (1984) 273–81.

———. "The Historicity of the Empty Tomb of Jesus." *NTS* 31, no. 1 (1985) 39–67.

Crossan, Jon Dominic. *The Historical Jesus: The Life of a Mediterranean Jewish Peasant*. San Francisco: Harper, 1991.

———. *Who Killed Jesus: Exposing the Roots of Anti-Semitism in the Gospel Story of the Death of Jesus*. San Francisco: Harper, 1996.

Cunningham, Philip, et al., eds. *Christ Jesus and the Jewish People Today*. Grand Rapids: Eerdmans, 2011.

Danby, Herbert. *The Jew and Christianity*. London: Sheldon, 1927.

Darby, M. *The Emergence of the Hebrew Christian Movement in Nineteenth-Century Britain*. Boston: Brill, 2010.

Daube, David. "Anointing at Bethany and Jesus' Trial." *ATR* 32, no. 3 (1950) 186–99.

————. *The New Testament and Rabbinic Judaism*. London: Athlone, 1956.

Davies, W. D. *Paul and Rabbinic Judaism*. Minneapolis: Fortress, 1980.

Davis, Stephen T., Daniel Kendall, and Gerald O'Collins, eds. *The Resurrection: An Interdisciplinary Symposium on the Resurrection of Jesus*. Oxford: Oxford University Press, 1999.

Deutsch, Yaacov. "The Second Life of the Life of Jesus: Christian Reception of Toledot Yeshu." In *Toledot Yeshu ("The Life Story of Jesus"): A Princeton Conference*, edited by Peter Schafer et al., 283–96. Tübingen: Mohr/Siebeck, 2011.

Dimont, Max. *Appointment in Jerusalem: A Search for the Historical Jesus*. New York: St. Martins, 1991.

————. *Jews, God and History*. New York: New American Library, 1962.

Donaldson, Terrance. *Jews and Anti-Judaism in the New Testament: Decision Points and Divergent Interpretations*. Waco, TX: Baylor University, 2010.

Driver, S. R., and A. Neubauer, eds. *The Fifty-Third Chapter of Isaiah according to the Jewish Interpreters*. New York: Ktav, 1969.

Dunn, James D. *The New Perspective on Paul*. Grand Rapids: Eerdmans, 2005.

Dunn, James D., ed. *Jews and Christians: The Parting of the Ways—A.D. 70 to 135*. Grand Rapids: Eerdmans, 1999.

Earman, John. *Hume's Abject Failure: The Argument Against Miracles*. Oxford: Oxford University Press, 2000.

Edersheim, Alfred. *The Life and Times of Jesus the Messiah*. Peabody, MA: Hendrickson, 1993.

Edgar, L. I. *A Jewish View of Jesus*. London: Jewish Religious Union for the Advancement of Liberal Judaism, 1940.

Ehrman, Bart D. *Did Jesus Exist?: The Historical Argument for Jesus of Nazareth*. New York: HarperOne, 2013.

————. *The New Testament: A Historical Introduction to the Early Christian Writings*. New York: Oxford University Press, 2008.

Eisenbaum, Pamela. "Following in the Footsteps of the Apostle Paul." In *Identity and the Politics of Scholarship in the Study of Religion*, edited by Jose Ignacio Cabezón and Sheila Greeve Davaney, 77–98 . London: Routledge, 2004.

————. *Paul Was Not a Christian: The Original Message of a Misunderstood Apostle*. New York: HarperOne, 2010.

————. "They Don't Make Jews Like Jesus Anymore." In *Moment Magazine*, 37, no. 2 (2012) 72.

Eisler, Robert. *The Messiahship of Jesus and John the Baptist*. London: Methuen, 1931.

Elgvin, Torleif. "Eschatology and Messianism in the Gabriel Inscription." In *JJMJS* 1 (2014) 5–25.

Elman, Yaakov, and Israel Gershoni. *Transmitting Jewish Traditions: Orality, Textuality, and Cultural Diffusion*. New Haven: Yale University, 2000.

Enelow, Hyman G. *A Jewish View of Jesus*. New York: Macmillan, 1920.

Evans, Craig A. *Fabricating Jesus*. Downers Grove, IL: IVP, 2006.

———. "Getting the Burial Traditions and Evidences Right." In *How God Became Jesus: The Real Origins of Belief in Jesus' Divine Nature—A Response to Bart D. Ehrman*, edited by Michael Bird et al., 71–93. Grand Rapids: Zondervan, 2014.

———. *Jesus and the Ossuaries: What Burial Practices Reveal about the Beginning of Christianity*. Waco, TX: Baylor University, 2003.

Evans, Craig A., and Donald A. Hagner, eds. *Anti-Semitism and Early Christianity: Issues of Polemic and Faith*. Minneapolis: Fortress, 1993.

Evans, Craig A., and N. T. Wright. *Jesus, the Final Days: What Really Happened*. Louisville: Westminster John Knox, 2009.

Eve, Eric. *The Jewish Context of Jesus' Miracles*. JSNTSup 231. New York: Sheffield Academic, 2002.

Falk, Harvey. *Jesus the Pharisee: A New Look at the Jewishness of Jesus*. New York: Paulist, 1985.

———. "Rabbi Jacob Emden's Views on Christianity." *JES* 19, no. 1 (1982) 105–11.

Fee, Gordon. *The First Epistle to the Corinthians*. Grand Rapids: Eerdmans, 1987.

Feher, Shoshanah. *Passing over Easter: Constructing the Boundaries of Messianic Judaism*. Walnut Creek, CA: Altamira, 1998P

Feinberg, C. L. "Pauline Theology Relative to the Death and Resurrection of Christ." *Bib Sac* 95, no. 379 (1938) 290–308.

Feiner, Shmuel. "The Contribution of Professor Salo W Barron to the Study of Ancient Jewish History: His Appraisal of Anti-Judaism and Proselytism." *AJS* 18, no. 1 (1993) 1–27.

———. *Haskalah and History, The Emergence of a Modern Jewish Historical Consciousness*. Liverpool: Littman Library of Jewish Civilization, 2004.

———. "Is the New Testament Anti-Semitic?" *Moment* 15, no. 6 (1990) 32–52.

Feldman, Louis. *Studies in Hellenistic Judaism*. Leiden: Brill, 1996.

Ferziger, Adam S. "From Demonic Deviant to Drowning Brother: Reform Judaism in the Eyes of American Orthodoxy." *JSS* 15, no. 3 (2009) 56–88.

Festinger, Leon, Henry W. Riecken, and Stanley Schachter. *When Prophecy Fails*. London: Pinter and Martin, 2008.

Flannery, Edward. *The Anguish of the Jews: Twenty-Three Centuries of Anti-Semitism*. New York: Macmillan, 1965.

Fleg, Edmund. *Jesus Told by the Wandering Jew*. New York: Dutton, 1935.

Flusser, D. "The Crucified One and the Jews." *Immanuel* 7 (1977) 25–37.

———. *Jesus*. Translated by R. Walls. New York: Herder, 1969.

———. *Jesus: Mit Selbstzeugnissen und Bilddokumenten*. 1968.

———. *Judaism and the Origins of Christianity*. Jerusalem: Magnes, 1988.

———. "A New Sensitivity in Judaism and the Christian Message." *HTR* 61, no. 2 (1968) 107–27.

Fonrobert, Charlotte E. "Jewish Christians, Judaizers, and Christian anti-Judaism." In *JANT*, edited by Amy-Jill Levine and Marc Zvi Brettler, 554–57. New York: Oxford University Press, 2011.

France, R. T. *The Gospel of Matthew*. Grand Rapids: Eerdmans, 2007.

Fredriksen, Paula. "The Birth of Christianity and the Origins of Christian Anti-Judaism." In *Jesus, Judaism and Christian Anti-Judaism*, edited by Paula Fredricksen and Adele Reinhartz, 8–30. London: Westminster John Knox, 2002.

———. *From Jesus to Christ*. New Haven: Yale University, 1988.

————. *Jesus of Nazareth, King of the Jews: A Jewish Life and the Emergence of Christianity.* New York: Knopf, 1999.

Fredriksen, Paula, ed. *On the Passion of Christ: Exploring the Issues Raised by the Controversial Movie.* Berkeley: University of California Press, 2006.

————. "What You See Is What You Get: Context and Content in Current Research on the Historical Jesus." *Theology Today* 52, no. 1 (1995) 75–97.

Fredriksen, Paula, and Adele Reinhartz, eds. *Jesus, Judaism and Christian Anti-Judaism.* London: Westminster John Knox, 2002.

Freudmann, Lillian. *Anti-Semitism in the New Testament.* Lanham, MD: University Press of America, 1993.

Friedman, R. E., and S. D. Overton. "Death and Afterlife: The Biblical Silence." In *Judaism in late antiquity,* edited by A. J. Avery-Peck and J. Neusner, 3:35–60. Boston: Brill Academic, 2001.

Fruchtenbaum, Arnold. *Israelogy: The Missing Link in Systematic Theology.* San Antonio, Ariel Ministries, 1994.

Frymer-Kensky, T., et al., eds. *Christianity in Jewish Terms.* Boulder, CO: Westview, 2002.

Gager, John G. "Scholarship as Moral Vision: David Flusser on Jesus, Paul, and the Birth of Christianity." *JQR* 95, no. 1 (2005) 60–73.

Galambush, Julie. *The Reluctant Parting: How the New Testament's Jewish Writers Created a Christian Book.* New York: HarperOne, 2006.

Galarneau, Joy Elizabeth. "A Feminist Interpretation of Pinchas Lapide's Jewish Theology of Christianity as a Model for Christian Self-Understanding." PhD diss., Fordham University, 2009.

Gale, Aaron M. "Matthew Introduction and Annotations." In *JANT*, edited by Amy-Jill Levine and Marc Zvi Brettler, 1–54. New York: Oxford University Press, 2011.

Galvin, J. P. "A Recent Jewish View of the Resurrection." *Expository Times* 91 (1980) 277–79.

Garber, Zev. *Mel Gibson's Passion: The Film, the Controversy, and Its Implications.* West Lafayette, IN: Purdue University Press, 2006.

Garber, Zev, ed. *The Jewish Jesus: Revelation, Reflection, Reclamation.* West Lafayette, IN: Purdue University Press, 2011.

————. *Teaching the Historical Jesus.* London: Routledge, 2014.

Gathercole, Simon. *Where Is Boasting?: Early Jewish Soteriology and Paul's Response in Romans 1–5.* Grand Rapids: Eerdman's, 2002.

Geller, M. J. "Jesus' Theurgic Powers: Parallels in the Talmud and Incantation Bowls." *JJS* 28, no. 2 (1977) 141–55.

Gigniliat, Marc S. *A Brief History of Old Testament Criticism: From Benedict Spinoza to Brevard Childs.* Grand Rapids, Zondervan, 2012.

Gilbert, Gary. "Acts of the Apostles, Introduction and Annotations." In *JANT*, edited by Amy-Jill Levine and Marc Zvi Brettler, 197–252. Oxford, Oxford University Press, 2011.

Gillman, Neil. *The Death of Death: Resurrection and Immortality in Jewish Thought.* Woodstock, VT: Jewish Lights, 1997.

Ginsberg, L. "The Religion of the Jews at the Time of Jesus." *HUCA* 1 (1924) 307–21.

Girhardson, Birger. *Memory and Manuscript, Oral Tradition and Written Transmission in Rabbinic Judaism and Early Christianity, with Tradition and Transmission in Early Christianity.* Grand Rapids: Eerdmans, 1998.

Goldberg, Michael. *Jews and Christians: Getting our Stories Straight.* Nashville: Abingdon, 1985.

Golden, Steven H. "A Jewish Perspective of Jesus." In *BTB* 34, no. 2 (2004) 54–68.

Goldin, Hyman. *The Case of the Nazarene Reopened.* New York: Exposition, 1948.

Goldin, Judah. "On Honi the Circle-Maker: A Demanding Prayer." In *HTR* 56, no. 3 (1963) 233–37.

Goldmeier, H. "Changing Views of American Jews." *Religious Education* 71, no. 1 (1976) 57–67.

Goldstein, M. *Jesus in the Jewish Tradition,* New York: Macmillan, 1950.

Gompertz, Rolf. *My Jewish Brother Jesus.* Shawnee Mission, KS: Intercollegiate, 1977.

Goodman, Martin. *Rome and Jerusalem, the Clash of Ancient Civilizations.* London: Penguin, 2007.

Goodman, Martin, and Philip Alexander, eds. *Rabbinic Texts and the History of Late-Roman Palestine.* Oxford: Oxford University Press, 2010.

Goodman, Paul. *The Synagogue and the Church: Being a Contribution to the Apologetics of Judaism.* London: Routledge and Sons, 1908.

Goodstein, Laurie. "Poll Shows Major Shift in Identity of U.S. Jews." *New York Times,* October 1, 2013.

Goshen-Gottstein, Alon. "Judaism and Incarnational Theologies: Mapping out the Parameters of Dialogue." *JES* 39, nos. 3–4 (2002) 219–47.

Graetz, Heinrich. *History of the Jews.* Vol. 2. Philadelphia: JPS, 1974.

Grayzel, Solomon. *A History of the Jews from the Babylonian Exile to the End of World War II.* Philadelphia: JPS, 1947.

Greenberg, Irving. "Anti-Semitism in 'The Passion.'" *Commonwealth* 131, no. 9 (2004) 10–13.

———. *For the Sake of Heaven and Earth: The New Encounter between Judaism and Christianity.* Philadelphia: JPS, 2004.

Greenstone, J. H. *The Messiah Idea in Jewish History.* Philadelphia: JPS, 1906.

Gregerman, Adam. "Kosher Jesus, It's 'Kosher' to Accept Real Jesus?" *Forward,* February 9, 2012.

Grelot, Pierre. "The Resurrection of Jesus: Its Biblical and Jewish Background." In *Resurrection and Modern Biblical Thought,* edited by Paul de Surgy, 1–29. New York: Corpus, 1970.

Grunewald, Ithamar, Shaul Shaked, and Gedaliahu Strousma, eds. *Messiah and Christos: Studies in the Origins of Christianity, Presented to David Flusser on the Occasion of his Seventy-Fifth Birthday.* Tübingen: Mohr, 1992.

Gundry, Robert H. "The Essential Physicality of Jesus' Resurrection according to the New Testament." In *Jesus of Nazareth Lord and Christ,* edited by Joel B. Green and Max Turner, 204–19. Grand Rapids: Eerdmans, 1994.

———. *Soma in Biblical Theology: With Emphasis on Pauline Anthropology.* Cambridge: Cambridge University, 1976.

Gurtner, Daniel M. *This World and the World to Come: Soteriology in Early Judaism.* London: Bloomsbury, 2013.

Guttman, Alexander. "The Significance of Miracles for Talmudic Judaism." *HUCA* 20 (1947) 363–406.

Habermas, Gary R. "Experiences of the Risen Jesus: The Foundational Historical Issue in the Early Proclamation of the Resurrection." *AJOT* 45, no. 3 (2006) 288–97.

————. "Jesus' Resurrection and Contemporary Criticism: An Apologetic." *CTR* 4 (1989) 159–74.

————. "Jesus' Resurrection and Contemporary Criticism: An Apologetic (Part II)." *CTR* 4 (1990) 373–85.

————. "The Late Twentieth-Century Resurgence of Naturalistic Responses to Jesus' Resurrection." *TJ* 22 (2001) 179–96.

————. "Resurrection Research from 1975 to the Present: What Are Critical Scholars Saying?" *JSHJ* 2 (2005) 135–53.

Habermas, Gary, and M. Licona. *The Case for the Resurrection of Jesus*. Grand Rapids: Kregel, 2004.

Hagner, Donald. *The Jewish Reclamation of Jesus*. Grand Rapids: Zondervan, 1984.

————. "Paul in Modern Jewish Thought." In *Pauline Studies: Essays Presented to Professor F. F. Bruce on His 70th Birthday*, edited by Donald A. Hagner, 143–65. Grand Rapids: Eerdmans, 1980.

HaLevi, Yehuda. *The Kuzari*. Translated by H. Hirschfeld. New York: Schocken, 1964.

Harris-Shapiro, Carol. *Messianic Judaism: A Rabbi's Journey through Religious Change in America*. Boston: Beacon, 1999.

Harvey, Richard. "Passing over the Plot? The Life and Work of Hugh Schonfield (1901–1988)." *Mishkan* 37 (2002) 35–48.

Harvey, Warren Zev. "Harry Austryn Wolfson on the Jews' Reclamation of Jesus." In *Jesus among the Jews: Representation and Thought*, edited by Neta Stahl, 136–52. New York: Routledge, 2012.

————. "Spinoza on Biblical Miracles." *JHI* 74, no. 4 (2013) 659–75.

Hedrick, Charles W. "Paul's Conversion/Call: A Comparative Analysis of the Three Reports in Acts." *JBL* 100, no. 3 (1981) 415–32.

Heilman, Samuel, and Menachem Friedman. *The Rebbe: The Life and Afterlife of Menachem Mendel Schneerson*. Princeton: Princeton University, 2010.

Hengel, Martin. *Crucifixion: In the Ancient World and the Folly of the Message of the Cross*. Minneapolis: Fortress, 1977.

————. *The Son of God: The Origin of Christology and the History of Jewish-Hellenistic Religion*. Translated by J. Bowden. London: SCM, 1976.

Heschel, Susannah. *Abraham Geiger and the Jewish Jesus*. Chicago: University of Chicago, 1998.

————. *The Aryan Jesus: Christian Theologians and the Bible in Nazi Germany*. Princeton: Princeton University, 2008.

————. "Jesus in Modern Jewish thought." In *JANT*, edited by Amy Jill Levine and Marc Zvi Brettler, 581–82. Oxford: Oxford University Press, 2011.

Hieke, Thomas, and Thomas Nicklaus, eds. *The Day of Atonement: Its Interpretation in Early Jewish and Christian Traditions*. Leiden: Brill, 2011.

Himmelfarb, Martha. "Afterlife and Resurrection." In *JANT*, edited by Amy Jill Levine and Marc Zvi Brettler, 549–51. Oxford: Oxford University Press, 2011.

————. "The Messiah Son of Joseph in Ancient Judaism." In *Envisioning Judaism Studies in Honor of Peter Schäfer on the Occasion of his Seventieth Birthday*, edited by Ra'anan S. Boustan et al., 771–90. Tübingen: Mohr/Siebeck, 2013.

Hirsch, E. G. *My Religion, and the Crucifixion Viewed from a Jewish Standpoint*. New York: Arno, 1892.

Hoffman, Matthew. *From Rebel to Rabbi: Reclaiming Jesus and the Making of Modern Jewish Culture*. Stanford, CA: Stanford University 2007.

———. "The Renewed Quest for the Jewish Jesus." *Tikkun* 18, no. 2 (2003) 77–79.

Holmoka, Walter. *Jesus Reclaimed: Jewish Perspectives on the Nazarene*. New York: Berghahn, 2015.

———. "Leo Baeck and Christianity." *European Judaism* 40, no. 1 (2007) 129–35.

Horbury, William. *Jews and Christians in Contact and Controversy*. Edinburgh: T. & T. Clark, 1998.

———. "Review of The Resurrection of Jesus: A Jewish Perspective." *Theology* 88 (1985) 306–8.

———. "Tertullian and the Jews in Light of *De Spectaculis*." *JTS* 23 (1972) 455–59.

———. "The Trial of Jesus in Jewish Tradition." In *The Trial of Jesus*, edited by E. Bammel, 103–21. Naperville, IL: Allenson, 1970.

Horowitz, Elliott. "Isaiah's Suffering Servant and the Jews: From the Nineteenth Century to the Ninth." In *New Perspectives on Jewish-Christian Relations: In Honor of David Berger*, edited by Elisheva Carlebach and J. J. Schachter, 419–36. Leiden: Brill, 2012.

Hume, David. "Of Miracles." In *An Enquiry into Human Understanding*, edited by Tom L. Beauchamp, 169–86. Oxford: Clarendon, 2000.

Hunterberg, M. *The Crucified Jew*. New York: Bloch, 1920.

Hurtado, Larry. *Lord Jesus Christ: Devotion to Jesus in Earliest Christianity*. Grand Rapids: Eerdmans, 2005.

Ilan, Tal, "It's Magic: Jewish Women in the Jesus Movement." In *The Beginnings of Christianity: A Collection of Articles*, edited by Jack Pastor and M. Mor, 161–72. Jerusaelm: Yad Ben-Zvi, 2005.

Isaacs, Ronald H. *Miracles: A Jewish Perspective*. Northvale, NJ: Aronson, 1997.

Jacob, Walter. *Christianity through Jewish Eyes*. Cincinnati: Hebrew Union College, 1974.

Jacobs, Joseph. *As Others Saw Him: A Retrospect A.D. 54*. London: Heinemann, 1895.

Jacobs, Steven Leonard. "'Can We Talk?' The Jewish Jesus in Dialogue with Jews and Christians." *Shofar* 28, no. 3 (2010) 135–48.

———. "Two Takes on Christianity: Furthering the Dialogue." *JES* 47, no. 4 (2012) 508–24.

Jaffee, Martin S. *Torah in the Mouth: Writing and Oral Tradition in Palestinian Judaism 200 BCE–400 CE*. Oxford: Oxford University Press, 2001.

Jocz, Jacob. *The Jewish People and Jesus Christ after Auschwitz*. Grand Rapids: Baker, 1981.

———. *The Jewish People and Jesus Christ: A Study in the Controversy between Church and Synagogue*. London: SPCK, 1954.

Johnson, David. *Hume, Holiness and Miracles*. Ithaca, NY: Cornell University, 1999.

Kabak, A. A. *The Narrow Path: The Messiah of Nazareth*. Translated by J. L. Meltzer. Tel Aviv: Institute for the Translation of Hebrew Literature, 1968. Originally published in Hebrew in 1934.

Kac, Arthur. *The Messiahship of Jesus: Are Jews Changing Their Attitude toward Jesus?* Grand Rapids: Baker, 1986.

Kaplan, Aryeh. *The Real Messiah? A Jewish Response to Missionaries*. New York: Mesorah, 1976.

Kasher, Hannah. "Biblical Miracles and the Universality of Natural Laws: Maimonides' Three Modes of Interpretation." *JJTP* 8, no. 1 (1999) 25–53.

Katz, Steven. "Christology: A Jewish View." *SJT* 24, no. 2 (1971) 184–200.

Kaufmann, Yehezkel. *Christianity and Judaism: Two Covenants*. Jerusalem: Magnus, 1988.

Keener, Craig S. *The Historical Jesus of the Gospels*. Grand Rapids: Eerdmans, 2009.

———. *Miracles: The Credibility of the New Testament Accounts*. Grand Rapids: Baker Academic, 2011.

Kellner, Menachem. "How Ought a Jew View Christian Beliefs about Redemption?" In Tikva *Christianity in Jewish Terms*, edited by Frymer-Kensky, Novak, Ochs, Fox Samuel and Signer, 239–53. Boulder: Westview, 2002.

Kendall, R. T., and D. Rosen. *The Christian and the Pharisee*. Nashville: Faithwords, 2007.

Kessler, Edward. *An English Jew*. Edgware, UK: Mitchell, 2002.

———. *An Introduction to Jewish-Christian Relations*. Cambridge: Cambridge University, 2010.

———. "Jesus from a Jewish Perspective." In *Jesus in History, Thought and Culture: An Encyclopedia*, edited by J. Houlen, 479–83. Oxford: ABC-CLIO.

———. "Jewish Scholarly Studies of Jesus." In *Jesus in History, Thought and Culture: An Encyclopedia*, edited by J. Houlden, 483–87. Oxford: ABC-CLIO, 2003.

Kirschner, Robert S. "Maimonides' Fiction of Resurrection." *HCUA* 52 (1981) 163–93.

Klausner, Joseph. *From Jesus to Paul*. Translated by W. F. Stinespring. New York: Macmillan, 1943. Originally published in 1922.

———. *Jesus of Nazareth: His Life, Times, and Teaching*. Translated by H. Danby. London: Allen and Unwin, 1927.

———. ישו הנצרי : זמנו, חייו ותורתו. Jerusalem: 1922.

Klenicki, Leon, ed. *Toward a Theological Encounter: Jewish Understandings of Christianity*. New York: Paulist, 1991.

Klinghoffer, David. *Why the Jews Rejected Jesus: The Turning Point in Western Civilization*. New York: Doubleday, 2005.

Knohl, Irving. *The Messiah before Jesus: The Suffering Servant of the Dead Sea Scrolls*. Translated by D. Maisel. Berkeley: University of California, 2000.

———. *The Messiahs and Resurrection in the Gabriel Revelation*. London: Continuum, 2009.

Kogan, Michael S. *Opening the Covenant: A Jewish Theology of Christianity*. Oxford: Oxford University Press, 2007.

Kohanski, Alexander S. "Martin Buber's Approach to Jesus." *Princeton Seminary Bulletin* 67, no. 1 (1975) 103–15.

Kohler, Kaufmann. *The Origins of the Synagogue and the Church*. New York: Macmillan, 1929.

———. "Saul of Tarsus." In *Jewish Encyclopedia*, edited by Isidore Singer, 11:79–87. New York: Funk and Wagnalls, 1901–1906.

Komarnitsky, Kris. *Doubting Jesus' Resurrection: What Happened in the Black Box?* Draper, UT: Stone Arrow, 2014.

Korn, Eugene B., and John T. Pawlikowski, eds. *Two Faiths, One Covenant? Jewish and Christian Identity in the Presence of the Other*. London: Sheed and Ward, 2004.

Krauss, Samuel. *Das Leben Jesu nach Judischen Quellen*. Berlin: Calvary, 1902.

Kraut, B. "A Liberal Jew Looks at Christianity." *Tradition*, 21, no. 4 (1985) 80–86.

Kreisel, Howard T. "Miracles in Medieval Jewish Philosophy." *JQR* 75, no. 2 (1984) 99–133.

Krell, M. *Intersecting Pathways: Modern Jewish Theologians in Conversation with Christianity.* Oxford: Oxford University Press, 2003.

Kummel, Werner G. "Review of *The Resurrection of Jesus: A Jewish Perspective.*" *Theologische Rundschau* 51, no. 1 (1986) 92–97.

Küng, Hans, and Pinchas Lapide. *Brother or Lord: A Jew and a Christian Talk Together about Jesus.* Glasgow: Collins Sons, 1977.

————. "Jesus a Bond or a Barrier." *JES* 14, NO. 3 (1977) 466–83.

Lachs, Samuel T. *Rabbinic Commentary on the New Testament: The Gospels of Matthew, Mark and Luke.* Hoboken, NJ: Ktav, 1987.

Landman, Leo. *Scholars and Scholarship: The Interaction between Judaism and Other Cultures,* New York: Scharf Publication Trust of the Yeshiva University Press, 1990.

Langerman, Y. Tsvi. "Maimonides and Miracles: The Growth of (dis)belief." *Jewish History* 18, nos. 2–3 (2004) 157–72.

Langton, Daniel. *The Apostle Paul in the Jewish Imagination: A Study in Modern Jewish-Christian Relations.* Cambridge: Cambridge University, 2010.

————. "Claude Montefiore and Christianity: Did the Founder of Anglo-Liberal Judaism Lean Too Far?" *JJS* 50, no. 1 (1999) 98–119.

————. *Claude Montefiore: His Life and Thought.* Portland, OR: Mitchell, 2002.

————. "Paul in Jewish Thought." In *JANT*, edited by Amy-Jill Levine and Marc Zvi Brettler, 585–87. Oxford: Oxford University Press, 2011.

Lapide, Pinchas. *Auferstehung: e. jud. Glaubenseriebnis.* Stuttgart: Calwer, 1978.

————. *Israelis, Jews and Jesus.* Translated by P. Heinegg. Garden City, NY: Doubleday, 1979.

————. *The Resurrection of Jesus: A Jewish Perspective.* London: SPCK, 1983.

Lapide, Pinchas, and Peter Stuhlmacher. *Paul: Rabbi and Apostle.* Minneapolis: Augsburg, 1984.

Lasker, Daniel J., et al. *The Polemic of Nestor the Priest: Quissat muj adalat al-usquf and sefer Nestor ha Komer.* Jerusalem: Ben-Zvi Institute for the Study of Jewish Communities in the East, 1996.

LeBeau, Bryan F., Leonard Greenspoon, and Dennis Hamm, eds. *The Historical Jesus through Catholic and Jewish Eyes.* Harrisburg, PA: Trinity, 2000.

Leiberman, Chaim. *The Christianity of Sholem Asch.* Originally published in Yiddish by Abraham Burstein. New York: Philosophical Library, 1953.

Lerner, Michael. "Jesus the Jew." *Tikkun* 19, no. 3 (2004) 33–37.

Levenson, Jon D. *The Death and Resurrection of the Beloved Son: The Transformation of Child Sacrifice in Judaism and Christianity.* New Haven: Yale University, 1995.

————. *Resurrection and the Restoration of Israel: The Ultimate Victory of the God of life.* New Haven: Yale University, 2008.

————. "The Sacred Executioner." *Commentary* 94, no. 4 (1992) 56–60.

Levine, Amy-Jill. "Anti-Judaism and the Gospel of Matthew." In *Anti-Judaism and the Gospels,* edited by William R. Farmer, 9–36. Harrisburg, PA: Trinity, 1999.

————. "Christian Faith and the Study of the Historical Jesus: A Response to Bock, Keener, Webb." *JSHJ* 9, no. 1 (2011) 96–106.

————. "Luke, Introduction and Annotations." In *JANT*, edited by Amy-Jill Levine and Marc Zvi Brettler, 96–151. Oxford: Oxford University Press, 2011.

————. "Matthew and Anti-Judaism." *CTM* 34, no. 6 (2007) 409–16.

————. "Mathew, Mark and Luke: Good News or Bad?" In *Jesus, Judaism and Christian anti-Judaism*, Paula Fredriksen Adele and Reinhartz, 77–98. London: Westminster John Knox, 2002.

————. *The Misunderstood Jew: The Church and the Scandal of the Jewish Jesus.* New York: HarperOne, 2007.

————. "Review of *Brother Jesus: The Nazarene through Jewish eyes.*" *JAAR* 73, no. 1 (2005) 222–24.

————. "Review of The Mystery of Romans: The Jewish Context of Paul's Letter." *JQR* 89, nos. 1–2 (1998) 222–24.

————. "Review of Paul and Hellenism." *JQR* 86, nos. 1– 2 (1995) 230–32.

————. *The Social and Ethnic Dimension of Matthean Salvation History.* Lewiston, NY: Mellen, 1988.

Levine, Amy-Jill, D. C. Allison, and J. D. Crossan, eds. *The Historical Jesus in Context,* Princeton: Princeton University, 2006.

Levine, Amy-Jill, and Marc Brettler, eds. *Jewish Annotated New Testament.* Oxford: Oxford University Press, 2011.

Licona, Michael. *The Resurrection of Jesus: A New Historiographical Approach.* Downers Grove, IL: IVP Academic, 2010.

————. *Why Are There Differences in the Gospels? What We Can Learn from Ancient Biography.* Oxford: Oxford University Press, 2016.

Lindeskog, G. *Die Jesus frage im neuzeitlichen Judentum.* Uppsala: Almquist and Wiksells, 1938.

Liver, J. "The Doctrine of the Two Messiahs in Sectarian Literature in the Time of the Second Commonwealth." *HTR* 52, no. 3 (1959) 149–86.

Lockshin, M. "Jesus in Medieval Jewish Tradition." In *JANT*, edited by Amy-Jill Levine and Marc Zvi Brettler, 581–82, Oxford: Oxford University Press, 2011.

Lüdemann, Gerd. *What Really Happened to Jesus: A Historical Approach to the Resurrection.* Louisville: Westminster John Knox , 1996.

Maccoby, Hyam. *Judas Iscariot and the Myth of Jewish Evil.* London: Halban, 1992.

————. *The Mythmaker: Paul and the Invention of Christianity.* London: Weidenfeld and Nicholson, 1986.

————. *Paul and Hellenism.* Philadelphia: Trinity, 1991.

————. *Revolution in Judaea: Jesus and the Jewish Resistance.* New York: Taplinger 1973.

Mach, Michael. "Jesus' Miracles in Context." In *The Beginnings of Christianity*, edited by Jack Pastor and Menachem Mor, 173–201. Jerusalem: Yad ben-Zvi, 2005.

Madigan, Kevin J., and Jon D. Levenson. *Resurrection: The Power of God for Christians and Jews.* New Haven: Yale University Press, 2009.

Magid, Shaul. *Hassidism Incarnate: Hassidism, Christianity, and the Construction of Modern Judais.* Redwood City, CA: Stanford University Press, 2014.

————. "The New Jewish Reclamation of Jesus in Late Twentieth-Century America: Realigning and Rethinking Jesus the Jew." In *The Jewish Jesus: Revelation, Reflection, Reclamation*, edited by Zev Garber, 358–82. West Lafayette, IN: Purdue University Press, 2011.

Magness, Jodi. "Ossuaries and the Burials of Jesus and James." *JBL* 124, no. 1 (2005) 121–54.

Maller, Allen S. "Isaiah's Suffering Servant: A New View." *JBQ* 37, no. 4 (2009) 243–49.

Manek, J., "The Apostle Paul and the Empty Tomb." *Novum Testamentum* 2, nos. 3–4 (1958) 276–80.

Matt, Hershel J. "How Shall a Believing Jew View Christianity." *Judaism* 24, no. 4 (1975) 391–405.

McMichael, Steven J. "The Resurrection of Jesus and Human Beings in Medieval Christian and Jewish Theology and Polemical Literature." *Studies in Christian-Jewish Relations* 4 (2009) 1–18.

Melamed, Yitzak. ""Christus Secundum Spiritum": Spinoza, Jesus and the Infinite Intellect." In *Jesus among the Jews: Representation and thought*, edited by Neta Stahl, 140–49. London: Routledge, 2012.

Mendels, Doron. *Identity, Religion and Historiography, Studies in Hellenistic History.* Sheffield: Sheffield Academic, 1998.

Mendelssohn, Moses, and M. Gottlieb, ed. *Writings on Judaism, Christianity and the Bible*. Waltham, MA: Brandeis University, 2011.

Meyers, Eric M. "The Jesus Tomb Controversy." *Near Eastern Archaeology* 69, nos. 3–4 (2006) 116–18.

Mishkin, David. "Did He Or Didn't He? Jewish Views of the Resurrection of Jesus." *Issues: A Messianic Jewish Perspective* 11, no. 6 (1997) 1–6.

———. "The Emerging Jewish Views of the Messiahship of Jesus and Their Bearing on the Question of His Resurrection." *HTS Teologiese Studies*, 71, no. 1 (2015) Art #2881.

———. "The Resurrection of Jesus in Contemporary Jewish Scholarship." *Mishkan* 68 (2011) 50–63.

———. *The Wisdom of Alfred Edersheim*. Eugene, OR: Wipf and Stock, 2008.

Mitchell, David C. "A Dying and Rising Josephite Messiah in 4Q372." *JSP* 18, no. 3 (2009) 181–205.

———. "Messiah ben Joseph: A Sacrificial Atonement for Israel." *RRJ* 10 (2007) 77–94.

———. "Rabbi Dosa and the Rabbis Differ: Messiah ben Joseph in the Babylonian Talmud." *RRJ* 8 (2005) 77–90.

Mittleman, A. J. "Christianity in the Mirror of Jewish Thought." *First Things* 25 (1992) 14–21.

———. "Modern Jewish Views of Jesus: A Search for Self." In *Breaking Down the Wall between Americans and East Germans: Jews and Christians through Dialogue*, edited by J. Fischel and S. M. Ortmann, 161–76. Lanham, MD: University Press of America, 1987.

Moffic, Evan. *What Every Christian Needs to Know about the Jewishness of Jesus.* Nashville: Abington, 2015.

Montefiore, Claude G. *Judaism and St Paul: Two Essays*. London: Goshen, 1914.

———. *Rabbinic Literature and Gospel Teaching*. New York: Ktav, 1970.

———. *The Synoptic Gospels*. London: Macmillan, 1909.

Moore, Daniel F. *Jesus, an Emerging Jewish Mosaic*. London: T. & T. Clark, 2008.

Nadler, Steven. *A Book Forged in Hell: Spinoza's Scandalous Treatise and the Birth of the Secular Age*. Princeton University Press, Princeton, 2011.

Nanos, Mark *The Mystery of Romans*. Minneapolis: Fortres, 1996.

———. "Paul and Judaism." In *JANT*, edited by Amy-Jill Levine and Marc Zvi Brettler, 551–54. Oxford: Oxford University Press, 2011.

———. "Romans, Introduction and Annotations." In *JANT*, edited by Amy-Jill Levine and Marc Zvi Brettler, 253–86. Oxford: Oxford University Press, 2011.

Neff, David. "Jesus through Jewish Eyes: Why Jewish New Testament Professor Amy-Jill Levine Thinks Jews Should Kknow More about Jesus, and Christians More about First-Century Judaism." *CT* 56, no. 4 (2012) 52–54.

Neusner, Jacob. "The Absoluteness of Christianity and the Uniqueness of Judaism: Why Salvation Is Not of the Jews." *Interpretation* 43, no. 1 (1989) 18–31.

———. Foreword to *Memory and Manuscript, Oral Tradition and Written Transmission in Rabbinic Judaism and Early Christianity, with Tradition and Transmission in Early Christianity*, by Birger Gerhardsson. Grand Rapids: Eerdmans, 1988.

———. *The Incarnation of God*. Philadelphia: Fortress, 1988.

———. *A Rabbi Talks with Jesus*. New York: Doubleday, 1993.

Neusner, J., and B. Chilton. *Jewish and Christian Doctrines: The Classics Compared*. London: Routledge, 2000.

Newman, Carey, James R. Davila, and Gladys S. Lewis, eds. *The Jewish Roots of Christological Monotheism: Papers from the St. Andrews Conference on the Historical Origins of the Worship of Jesus*. Boston: Brill, 1999.

Newman, Hillel I. "The Death of Jesus in the Toldot Yeshu Literature." *JTS* 50, no. 1 (1999) 59–79.

Newman, L. E. *Repentance: The Meaning and Practice of Teshuva*. Woodstock, VT: Jewish Lights, 2010.

Notley, R. Steven, Marc Turnage, and Brian Becker, eds. *Jesus' Last Week: Jerusalem Studies in the Synoptic Gospels*. Vol. 1. Leiden: Brill Academic, 2006.

Novak, David. *Jewish-Christian Dialogue: A Jewish Justification*. Oxford: Oxford University Press, 1989.

———. "The Quest for the Jewish Jesus." *MJ* 8, no. 2 (1988) 119–38.

———. "When Jews Are Christians." *First Things* 17 (1991) 42–46.

Pannenberg, Wolfhart. "History and the Reality of the Resurrection." In *Resurrection Reconsidered*, edited by Gavin D'Costa, 62–72. Oxford: Oneworld, 1996.

Pastor, Jack, and Menachem Mor, eds. *The Beginnings of Christianity*. Jerusalem: Yad ben-Zvi, 2005

Patai, Rafael, ed. *Encyclopedia of Zionism and Israel*. New York: McGraw-Hill, 1971.

———. *The Messiah Texts*. Detroit: Wayne State University, 1979.

Pawlikowski, John T. "Review of *The Mythmaker: Paul and the Invention of Christianity*." *Christian Century* 103, no. 35 (1986) 1041.

Pickup, Martin. "The Emergence of the Suffering Messiah in Rabbinic Literature." *Approaches to Ancient Judaism* 11 (1997) 143–62.

Petuchowski, Jacob Joseph. "'Immortality—Yes, Resurrection—No!' 19th Century Judaism Struggles with a Traditional Belief." *Proceedings of the American Academy for Jewish Research* 50 (1983) 133–47.

Peuch, Emile. "Jesus and Resurrection Faith in Light of Jewish Texts." In *Jesus and Archaelogy*, edited by James H. Charlesworth, 639–59. Grand Rapids: Eerdmans, 2006.

Price, Robert M., and Jeffrey J. Lowder, eds. *The Empty Tomb: Jesus beyond the Grave*. Amherst, NH: Prometheus, 2005.

Pritz, Ray. *Nazarene Jewish Christianity*. Jerusalem: Magnes, 1992.

Radowsky, Alvin. "Miracles." In *Encounter; Essays on Torah and Modern Life*, edited by H. C. Shimmel and A. Carwell, 42–74. Jerusalem: Feldheim, 1989.

Raphael, Simcha Paul. *Jewish Views of the Afterlife*. Northvale, NJ: Aronson, 2009.

Redman, Barbara J. "One God: Toward a Rapprochement of Orthodox Judaism and Christianity." *JES* 31, nos. 3–4 (1994) 307–22.

Re'emi, S. P. "Review of the Resurrection of Jesus: A Jewish Perspective." *SJT* 38, no. 3 (1985) 419–20.

Reinhartz, Adele. *Befriending the Beloved Disciple*. New York: Bloomsbury Academic, 2002.

———. "The Gospel of John: How the 'Jews' Became Part of the Plot." In *Jesus, Judaism and Christian anti-Judaism*, edited by Paula Fredriksen and Adele Reinhartz, 99–116. London: Westminster John Knox, 2002.

———. "John, Introduction and Annotations." In *JANT*, edited by Amy-Jill Levine and Marc Zvi Brettler, 152–96. Oxford, Oxford University Press, 2011.

———. "Judaism and the Gospel of John." *Interpretation* 63, no. 4 (2009) 382–93.

———. "The New Testament and Anti-Judaism: A Literary-Critical Approach." *JES* 25, no. 4 (1988) 534–37.

———. "A Nice Jewish Girl Reads the Gospel of John." *Semeia* 77 (1997) 177–93.

———. "Reflections on Gibson's 'The Passion of Christ.'" *AJS* (2004) 12–13.

Rembaum, Joel E. "The Development of a Jewish Exegetical Tradition Regarding Isaiah 53." *HTR* 75, no. 3 (1982) 289–311.

Reuther, Rosemary Radford. *Faith and Fratricide*. New York: Seabury, 1974.

Rivkin, Ellis. "A Jewish View of the New Testament." In *Evangelicals and Jews in an Age of Pluralism*, edited by M. H. Tanenbaum, M. R. Wilson, and J. A. Rudin, 85–104. Grand Rapids: Baker, 1984.

———. "The Meaning of Messiah in Jewish Thought." In *Evangelicals and Jews in Conversation, on Scripture, Theology, and History*, edited by M. H. Tanenbaum, M. R. Wilson, and J. A. Rudin, 54–75. Grand Rapids: Baker, 1978.

———. "Review of *The Mythmaker: Paul and the Invention of Christianity*." *Judaism* 38, no. 2 (1989) 225–34.

———. *What Killed Jesus?* Nashville: Abingdon, 1984.

Rosenthal, G. S. *The Many Faces of Judaism: Orthodox, Conservative, Reconstructionist and Reform*. New York: Behrman House, 1978.

Rosenzweig, Franz. *The Star of Redemption*. Translated by W. W. Hallo. 1921. Repr., New York: Rinehart and Winston, 1971.

Rosman, Moshe. *How Jewish Is Jewish History?* Liverpool: Littman Library of Jewish Civilization, 2008.

Rosner, Fred, ed. and trans. *Moses Maimonides' Treatise on Resurrection*. New York: Aaronson, 1997.

Rosner, Jennifer. "Messianic Jews and Jewish-Christian Relations." In *Introduction to Messianic Judaism, Its Ecclesial Context and Biblical Foundations*, edited by David J. Rudolph and Joel Willits, 145–58. Grand Rapids: Zondervan, 2013.

Roth, Cecil. "Atonement." In *Encyclopedia Judaica*, edited by Cecil Roth, 3:830–31. Jerusalem: Keter, 1971.

———. *History of the Jews*. New York: Shocken, 1961.

———. "Toledot Yeshua." In *Encyclopedia Judaica*, edited by Cecil Roth, 15:1207–8. Jerusalem: Keter, 1971.

Rotschild, Fritz, ed. *Jewish Perspectives on Christianity*. New York: Crossroad, 1990.

Rottenberg, Isaac C. "Messianic Jews: A Troubling Presence." *First Things* 28 (1992) 26–32.

Rubenstein, Richard. *After Auschwitz: Radical Theology and Contemporary Judaism.* Indianapolis: Bobbs-Merrill, 1966.

———. *My Brother Paul.* New York: Harper & Row, 1972.

Rudolph, David J. *A Jew to the Jews: Jewish Countours of Pauline Flexibility in 1 Corinthians 9:19-23.* Eugene, OR: Pickwick, 2016.

———. "Messianic Jews and Christian Theology: Restoring an Historical Voice to the Contemporary Discussion." *Pro Ecclesia* 14, no. 1 (2005) 58–84.

Rydelnik, Michael A. "The Jewish People and Salvation." *Bib Sac* 165, no. 660 (2008) 447–62.

———. "Was Paul Anti-Semitic? Revisiting 1 Thessalonians 2:14–16." *Bib sac* 165, no. 657 (2008) 58–67.

Ryder, William Henry. "The Recent Literature upon the Resurrection of Christ." *HTR* 11, no. 1 (1909) 1–27.

Sachar, Abraham Leon. *A History of the Jews.* New York: Knopf, 1930.

Sadan, T. "Jesus of Nazareth in Zionist Thought." PhD diss., Hebrew University, 2006.

Salvadore, Joseph. *Jesus-Christ et Sa Doctrine: Histoire de la Naissance de l'Eglise, de Son Organisation et de ses Progres Pendant le Premier Siecle.* Paris: Guyot et Scribe, 1838.

Salvoni, Fausto. "Modern Studies on the Resurrection of Jesus." *Restoration Quarterly* 5, no. 2 (1961) 89–99.

Sanders, E. P. *Paul and Palestinian Judaism.* London: SCM, 1977.

Sandmel, David Fox. "Jews, Christians, and Gibson's *The Passion of the Christ.*" *Judaism* 7 (2006) 12–20.

———. "Joseph Klausner, Israel, and Jesus." *Currents* 31, no. 6 (2004) 456–64.

Sandmel, Samuel. *Anti-Semitism in the New Testament?* Philadelphia: Fortress 1978.

———. *The Genius of Paul.* New York: Shocken, 1958.

———. *A Jewish Understanding of the New Testament.* Cincinnati: Hebrew Union College, 1956.

———. *Judaism and Christian Beginnings.* New York: Oxford University Press, 1978.

———. "Parallelomania." *JBL* 81, no. 1 (1962) 1–13.

———. *We Jews and Jesus.* New York: Oxford University Press, 1965.

Saperstein, Marc. "Jewish Images of Jesus through the Ages." In *Proceedings of the Center for Jewish Christian Learning,* edited by M. C. Athens, 10:23–29. St. Paul: University of St. Thomas, 1995.

Sarachek, Joseph. *The Doctrine of the Messiah in Medieval Jewish Literature.* New York: Jewish Theological Seminary of America, 1932.

Schafer, Peter. "Introduction." In *Toledot Yeshu ("The Life Story of Jesus"): A Princeton Conference,* edited by Peter Schafer et al., 1–12. Tübingen: Mohr/Siebeck, 2011.

———. *Jesus in the Talmud.* Princeton: Princeton University 2009.

———. *The Jewish Jesus: How Judaism and Christianity Shaped Each Other.* Princeton: Princeton University, 2012.

Schafer, Peter, Michael Mearson, and Yaacov Deutsch, eds. *Toledot Yeshu ("The Life Story of Jesus"): A Princeton Conference.* Tübingen: Mohr/Siebeck, 2011.

———. "The Jew Who Would Be God." *New Republic* 243, no. 9 (2012) 36–39.

Schiffman, Lawrence H. "The Concept of Messiah in Second Temple and Rabbinic Literature." *RandE* 84, no. 2 (1987) 235–46.

———. *From Text to Tradition: A History of Second Temple and Rabbinic Judaism.* Hoboken, NJ: KTAV, 1991.

Schoeps, Hans Joachim. *The Jewish-Christian Argument: A History of Theologies in Conflict*. Translated by D. E. Green. New York: Holt, Reinhart and Winston, 1963.

Schonfield, H. *The Passover Plot*. London: Hutchinson, 1965.

Schremer, Adiel. *Brothers Estranged: Heresy, Christianity, and Jewish Identity in Late Antiquity*. Oxford: Oxford University Press, 2010.

Schrieber, M. "The Real 'Suffering Servant': Decoding a Controversial Passage in the Bible." *JBQ* 37, no. 1 (2009) 35–44.

Schwartz, Daniel R. *Reading the First Century: On Reading Josephus and Studying Jewish History of the First Century*. Tübingen: Mohr/Siebeck, 2013.

———. *Studies in the Jewish Background to Christianity*. Tübingen: Mohr/Siebeck, 1992.

Schwartz, G. D. "Is There a Jewish Reclamation of Jesus." *JES* 24, no. 1 (1987) 104–9.

Schweitzer, Albert. *The Quest for the Historical Jesus*. London: A. and C. Black, 1926.

Segal, Alan F. "How I Stopped Worrying about Mel Gibson and Learned to Love the Historical Jesus: A Review of Mel Gibson's *The Passion of Christ*." *JSHS* 2 (2004) 190–208.

———. "Jesus in the Eyes of One Jewish scholar." In *The Historical Jesus through Catholic and Jewish Eyes*, edited by Bryan F. LeBeau, 147–54. Harrisburg, PA: Trinity, 2000.

———. *Life after Death*. New York: Random House, 2004.

———. "Life and Death: The Social Sources." In *The Resurrection: An Interdisciplinary Symposium on the Resurrection of Jesus*, edited by Steven Davis, Daniel Kendall, and Gerald O'Collins, 57–92. Oxford: Oxford University Press, 1997.

———. *Paul the Convert: The Apostolate and Apostleship of Saul the Pharisee*. New Haven: Yale University 1990.

———. "Paul's Religious Experience in the Eyes of Jewish Scholars." In *Israel's God and Rebekah's Children: Essays in Honor of Larry W. Hurtado and Alan F. Segal*, edited by D. B. Capes et al., 321–44. Waco, TX: Baylor University Press, 2007.

———. "Paul's Thinking about Resurrection in Its Jewish Context." *NTS* 44, no. 3 (1998) 400–419.

———. *Rebecca's Children: Judaism and Christianity in the Roman World*. Cambridge, MA: Harvard University, 1986.

———. "The Resurrection: Faith or History." In *The Resurrection of Jesus, John Dominic Crossan and N.T. Wright in Dialogue*, edited by R. B. Stewart, 121–38. Minneapolis: Fortress, 2006.

———. "Review of *Paul and Hellenism*." *USQR*, 45, nos. 1–2 (1991) 142–46.

———. "The Risen Christ and the Angelic Mediator Figure in Light of Qumran." In *Jesus and the Dead Sea Scrolls*, edited by James H. Charlesworth, 302–28. New York: Doubleday. 1992.

Segal, Eliezer. "'The Few Contained the Many': Rabbinic Perspectives on the Miraculous and the Impossible." *JJS* 34, no. 2 (2003) 273–82.

Seid, J. *God-Optional Judaism: Alternatives for Cultural Jews Who Love Their History, Heritage, and Community*. New York: Citadel, 2001.

Setzer, Claudia. "Excellent Women: Female Witnesses to the Resurrection." *JBL* 116, no. 2 (1997) 259–72.

———. "1 Peter, Introduction and Annotations." In *JANT*, edited by Amy-Jill Levine and Marc Zvi Brettler, 436–42. Oxford: Oxford University Press, 2011.

———. "The Historical Jesus." *Tikkun* 4, no. 10 (1995) 73–77.

———. "Jewish Responses to Believers in Jesus." In *JANT*, edited by Amy-Jill Levine and Marc Zvi Brettler, 577–80. Oxford: Oxford University Press, 2011.

———. *Jewish Responses to Early Christianity*. Minneapolis: Fortress, 1994.

———. *Resurrection of the Body in Early Judaism and Christianity*. Boston: Brill Academic, 2004.

———. "Resurrection of the Dead as Symbol and Strategy." *JAAR* (2001) 65–102.

———. "'You Invent a Christ!' Christological Claims as Points of Jewish-Christian Dispute." *USQR* 44, nos. 3–4 (1991) 315–38.

Shapiro, Fydra. "Jesus for Jews, the Unique Problem of Messianic Judaism." *JRS* 14 (2012) 1–14.

Sheridan, Sybil. "Jesus from a Jewish Perspective." In *Abraham's Children: Jews, Christians and Muslims in Conversation*, edited by N. Solomon, R. Harries, and T. Winter, 87–98. London: T. & T. Clark, 2005.

Sherwin, B. "Jews and the World to Come." *First Things* 1, no. 64 (2006) 13–16.

———. "'Who Do You Say That I Am?' (Mark 8:29): A New Jewish View of Jesus." *JES* 31, nos. 3–4 (1994) 255–67.

Shinar, Avigdor. אותו האיש—יהודים מספרים על ישו. Jerusalem: Sephre Hemed, 1999.

Shular, P. L. "Response to 'Anti-Judaism and the Gospel of Matthew.'" In *Anti-Judaism and the Gospels*, edited by William R. Farmer, 37–46. Harrisburg, PA: Trinity, 1999.

Sigal, Gerald. *The Jew and the Christian Missionary: A Jewish Response to Missionary Christianity*. New York, Ktav, 1981.

———. *The Resurrection Fantasy: Reinventing Jesus*. Bloomington, IN: Trinity, 2012.

Sigal, Philip. "Review of *The Resurrection of Jesus: A Jewish Perspective*." *Reformed Journal* 35, no. 4 (1985) 25–28.

Silva, Moises. "The Pharisees in Modern Jewish Scholarship." *WTJ* 42, no. 2 (1980) 395–405.

Silver, A. H. *A History of Messianic Speculation in Israel: From the First to the Seventeenth Centuries*. New York: Macmillan, 1927.

Simon, M. "Gittin: Translation into English with Notes, Glossary and Indices." In *The Soncino Talmud*, edited by I. Epstein, 1–139. Oxford: Oxford University Press, 1937.

Singer, Tovia. *Let's Get Biblical*. Monsey, NY: Outreach Judaism, 2001.

Skarsaunne, Oskar. *Jewish Believers in Jesus: The Early Centuries*. Grand Rapids: Baker Academic, 2007.

Smith, S. D. "The Effect of the Holocaust on Jewish-Christian Relations." In *Challenges in Jewish-Christian Relations*, edited by J. K. Aitken and E. Kessler, 137–52. New York: Paulist, 2006.

Sommer, Benjamin D. *The Bodies of God and the World of Ancient Israel*. Cambridge: Cambridge University, 2009.

Soulen, R. K. *The God of Israel and Christian Theology*. Minneapolis: Fortress, 1996.

Sperling, S. David. "Jewish Perspectives on Jesus." In *Jesus Then and Now: Images of Jesus in History and Christology*, edited by M. Meyer and C. Hughes, 251–59. Harrisburg, PA: Trinity, 2001.

Spinoza, Benedict. *On the Improvement of the Understanding / The Ethics / Correspondence*. Translated by R. H. M. Elwes. Mineola, NY: Dover, 1955.

Stahl, Neta. *Jesus among the Jews: Representation and Thought*. London: Routledge, 2012.

———. *Other and Brother: Jesus in the 20th- Century Jewish Literary Landscape.* Oxford: Oxford University Press, 2012.

———. "Zionism and the Literary Representation of Jesus." *MJS* 11, no. 1 (2012) 1–23.

———. צלם יהודי : ייצוגיו של ישו בספרות העברית של המאה ה 20. Tel Aviv: Resling, 2008.

Stanton, G. "Early Objections to the Resurrection of Jesus." In *The Gospels and Jesus*, by G. Stanton, 148–64. Oxford: Oxford University Press, 2002.

Stein, Robert H. *Mark, Baker Exegetical Commentary on the New Testament.* Grand Rapids: Baker Academic, 2008.

Steinsaltz, Adin. *Talmud Bavli (Babylonian Talmud).* Hebrew ed. Volume Gittin, 244. Jerusalem: Israel Institute for Talmudic Publications, 2000.

Stendahl, K. "The Apostle Paul and the Introspective Conscience of the West." *HTR* 56 (1963) 199–215.

———. *Paul among Jews and Gentiles.* Philadelphia: Fortress, 1976.

———. "Review of *The Resurrection of Jesus: A Jewish Perspective.*" *Book Newsletter of the Augsburg Publishing House* (1984) 508.

Stuhlmacher, Peter, and Bernd Janowski, eds. *The Suffering Servant: Isaiah 53 in Jewish and Christian Sources.* Grand Rapids: Eerdmans, 2004.

Swinburn, R. *The Resurrection of God Incarnate.* Oxford: Oxford University Press, 2003.

Talmon, Shemaryahu. "Oral Traditions and Written Transmissions, or the Heard and Seen World in Judaism of the Second Temple Period." In *Jesus and the Oral Gospel Tradition*, edited by Henry Wansbrough, 121–58. Sheffield: JSOT, 1991.

Taylor, A. E. *David Hume and the Miraculous.* Cambridge: Cambridge University, 1927.

Telushkin, Joseph. *Jewish Literacy: The Most Important Things to Know about the Jewish Religion, Its People, and Its History.* New York: Morrow, 1991.

Trattner, E. R. *As a Jew Sees Jesus.* New York: Scribner's Sons, 1931.

Trepp, L. "Divine Intervention and Miracles in Jewish Thought." In *Divine Intervention and Miracles in Jewish Theology*, edited by Dan Cohn-Sherbok, 131–68. Lewiston, NY: Mellen, 1996.

Twelftree, Graham. *Jesus the Miracle Worker.* Downers Grove, IL: Intervarsity, 1999.

Verhay, A. "Review of *The Resurrection of Jesus: A Jewish Perspective.*" *Reformed Review* 38, no. 1 (1984) 88–89.

Vermes, Geza. *Jesus the Jew: A Historian's Reading of the Gospel.* London: Collins, 1973.

———. "Redemption and Genesis xxii: The Binding of Isaac and the Sacrifice of Jesus." In *Scripture and Tradition in Judaism*, by Geza Vermes, 193–227. Leiden: Brill, 1961.

———. *The Resurrection of Jesus: History and Myth.* London: Penguin, 2008.

Visotzky, Burton L. "Jesus in Rabbinic Tradition." In *JANT*, edited by Amy-Jill Levine and Marc Zvi Brettler, 580–81. Oxford: Oxford University Press, 2011.

Vlach, Michael. *Has the Church Replaced Israel? A Theological Evaluation.* Nashville: B and H Academic, 2010.

Votaw, Clyde W. "The Modern Jewish View of Jesus." *BW* 26, no. 2 (1905) 101–19.

Walker, Thomas. *Jewish Views of Jesus.* New York: Macmillan, 1931.

Wansbrough, H. "Jesus and Israel: One Covenant or Two?" *JJS* 48, no. 1 (1997) 151–54.

Weaver, Walter P. "The Jewish Quest for Jesus." In *The Historical Jesus of the Twentieth Century*, 230–50. Harrisburg, PA: Trinity, 1999.

Wegner, Judith Romney. *Chattel or Person? The Status of Women in the Mishnah.* Oxford: Oxford University Press, 1988.

Weiss-Rosmarin, Trude. *Judaism and Christianity: The Differences*. New York: Jewish Book Club. 1943.

Weiss-Rosmarin, Trude, ed. *Jewish Expressions on Jesus*. New York: KTAV, 1977.

Wenham, David. *Paul: Follower of Jesus or Founder of Christianity?* Grand Rapids: Eerdmans, 1995.

Wenham, John W. *Easter Enigma: Are the Resurrection Accounts in Conflict?* Cambridge: Cambridge University, 1993.

———. "Review of *The Resurrection of Jesus: A Jewish perspective.*" *EQ* 57 (1985) 371–72.

Wine, Sherwin. *Judaism beyond God: A Radically New Way to be Jewish*. New York: KTAV, 1985.

Wink, Walter. "Easter: What Happened to Jesus?" *Tikkun* 23, no. 2 (2008) 46–47.

Wilder, Amos N. "Paul through Jewish Eyes." *JBR*, 12, no. 3 (1944) 181–87.

Wills, Lawrence M. "The Depiction of the Jews in Acts." *JBL* 110, no. 4 (1991) 631–54.

———. "Mark, Introduction and Annotations." In *JANT*, edited by Amy-Jill Levine and Marc Zvi Brettler, 55–95. Oxford, Oxford University Press, 2011.

———. *The Quest of the Historical Gospel: Mark, John and the Origins of the Gospel Genre*. London: Routledge, 1997.

Wise, Isaac M. *The Martyrdom of Jesus of Nazareth: A Historical-Critical Treatise on the Last Chapters of the Gospel*. Cincinnati: General, 1874.

Witherington, Ben, III. *The Jesus Quest: The Third Search for the Jew of Nazareth*. Downers Grove, IL: IVP Academic, 1997.

Wolf, Arnold Jacob, "Jesus and the Jews." *Judaism* 42, no. 3 (1993) 368–74.

———. "Jesus as an Historical Jew." *Judaism* 46, no. 3 (1997) 375–80.

Wolfson, Elliot R. "Judaism and Incarnation: The Imaginal Body of God." In *Christianity in Jewish Terms*, edited by Tikva Frymer-Kensky et al., 239–53. Boulder, CO: Westview, 2002.

Wright, N. T. *The Resurrection of the Son of God*. Minneapolis: Fortress, 2003.

Wyschogrod, M. *The Body of Faith*. New York: Seabury, 1983.

———. "Christology: The Immovable Object." *Religion and Intellectual Life* 3, no. 4 (1986) 77–80.

———. "Incarnation." *Pro Ecclesia* 2, no. 2 (1993) 2–27.

———. "A Jewish Perspective on Incarnation." *MT* 12, no. 2 (1996) 195–209.

———. "A Letter to Cardinal Lustiger." In *Abraham's Promise: Judaism and Jewish Christian Relations*, edited by R. Kendall Soulen, 202–10. Grand Rapids: Eerdmans, 2004.

———. "Resurrection." *Pro Ecclesia* 1, no. 1 (1992) 104–12.

———. "Sin and Atonement in Judaism." In *Abraham's Promise: Judaism and Jewish Christian Relations*, edited by R. Kendall Soulen, 53–74. Grand Rapids: Eerdmans, 2004.

Yuter, Alan J. "Is Reform Judaism a Movement, a Sect or a Heresy?" *Tradition* 24, no. 3 (1989) 87–98.

Yuval, Israel. *Two Nations in Your Womb*. Berkeley: University of California, 2006.

Zakovich, Yair. *The Concept of the Miracle in the Bible*. Translated by. T. Yuval. Tel Aviv: MOD, 1990.

Zannoni, Arthur E. *Jews and Christians Speak of Jesus*. Minneapolis: Fortress, 1994.

Zass, Peter. "Colossians, Introduction and Annotations." In *JANT*, edited by Amy-Jill Levine and Marc Zvi Brettler, 362–71. New York: Oxford University Press, 2011.

Zeitlin, Irving M. *Jesus and the Judaism of His Time*. Cambridge: Poly, 1968.
Zeitlin, Solomon. *Who Crucified Jesus?* New York: Harper, 1942.

NAME INDEX

SUBJECT INDEX

49587913R00151

Made in the USA
Middletown, DE
20 October 2017